Moments of Disruption

Moments of Disruption

Levinas, Sartre, and the Question of Transcendence

KRIS SEALEY

Cover image: "Rupture of Selfhood" by Frankie Frieri

Published by State University of New York Press, Albany

© 2013 State University of New York

All rights reserved

Printed in the United States of America

No part of this book may be used or reproduced in any manner whatsoever without written permission. No part of this book may be stored in a retrieval system or transmitted in any form or by any means including electronic, electrostatic, magnetic tape, mechanical, photocopying, recording, or otherwise without the prior permission in writing of the publisher.

For information, contact State University of New York Press, Albany, NY
www.sunypress.edu

Production by Eileen Nizer
Marketing by Fran Keneston

Library of Congress Cataloging-in-Publication Data

Sealey, Kris, 1978–
   Moments of disruption : Levinas, Sartre, and the question of transcendence / Kris Sealey.
      pages cm
   Includes bibliographical references and index.
   Summary: "Ethical and political implications of Levinas' and Sartre's accounts of human existence"—Provided by publisher.
   ISBN 978-1-4384-4865-7 (alk. paper)
   ISBN 978-1-4384-4864-0 (pbk. : alk. paper)
   1. Lévinas, Emmanuel.   2. Sartre, Jean-Paul, 1905–1980.   3. Transcendence (Philosophy)   I. Title.

B2430.L484S44 2013
194—dc23
                                                      2013000131

10 9 8 7 6 5 4 3 2 1

*In loving memory of my father, Curtis Sealey,
the first to teach me the value of a sound argument
And for little Isaiah, my rock and my light*

Contents

Acknowledgments — ix

Introduction — 1

Chapter 1
The Role of Being in Sartre's Model of
Transcendence-as-Intentionality — 15

Chapter 2
Positionality in Levinas's Transcendence-as-Excendence — 43

Chapter 3
Levinasian Positionality in Sartre's Account of Nausea — 73

Chapter 4
Levinasian Positionality Implicit Sartre's Affective Experiences — 95

Chapter 5
Levinas and Sartre on the Question of the Other — 117

Concluding Remarks — 151

Notes — 155

Bibliography — 201

Index — 205

Acknowledgments

An earlier version of chapter 4, section II, of this work appeared in the *Journal of the British Society for Phenomenology* 41, no. 3 (2010), under the title "Finding Levinasian Passivity in Sartre's Descriptions of Shame." I am grateful to both the journal and to Jackson Publishing and Distribution for their permission to include this work. A version of chapter 2 also appeared in *Levinas Studies, An Annual Review* 5 (2010), under the title, "Levinas' Early Account of Transcendence: Locating Alterity in the *Il y a*." I would like to thank Duquesne University Press for allowing me to incorporate this into my book. An alternate version of section I of chapter 3 of this work also appeared in *Research in Phenomenology* 40, no. 3 (2010), under the title "The Primacy of Disruption in Levinas' Account of Transcendence." My thanks go out to Brill for allowing me to use this work here. For the cover art of this book, I acknowledge Mr. Frankie Frieri. His tremendous talent and unwavering patience materialized the imagery that captures this book's title. I am grateful that our paths happened to cross at the precise moment they did.

My dissertation research at The University of Memphis provided the groundwork for this book. As such, I owe much gratitude to the members of my dissertation committee: Robert Bernasconi, Bill E. Lawson, Mary Beth Mader, and Tom Nenon all provided the careful guidance and honest criticism that made that work (and ultimately, this book) possible.

This project began as a twenty-five minute conference presentation at the 2003 meeting of the North American Sartre Society, at Purdue University. Those arduous twenty-five minutes, as well as the following nine years it took for that paper to grow into the book before you, would have ended quite differently was it not for the unequivocal support, mentorship, and tough love of Robert Bernasconi. He has been with me during the entire journey of this book, as an interlocutor, mentor, and friend.

Quite arguably, I would not have pursued a degree in philosophy without his quiet "intervention," and I owe much of my growth as a scholar to his presence in my life. Words cannot express my gratitude for his time, patience, and careful analysis of numerous drafts of these chapters.

Thanks are also due to Roy Martinez, who, on explaining what "SPEP" (Society for Phenomenology and Existentialist Philosophy) meant, convinced me to at least *think* about pursuing philosophy as an undergraduate at Spelman College. The thought of sending him a copy on completion of this book (signed, like the signed copy of his *Kierkegaard and the Art of Irony* he gave me some thirteen years ago) thrilled me to no end. I was deeply saddened to know about Dr. Martinez's passing in 2009. The memory of his encouragement and mentoring, during my intellectual search at Spelman College, often gave me strength to continue writing the chapters of this book.

During the last six years as an assistant professor at Fairfield University, I received tremendous support in writing this book. The support from the College of Arts and Sciences, as well as the Department of Philosophy, made it possible for me to conduct much of the research that went into this project. Our administrative assistants, Charlene Wallace and Joan Huvane, were tremendously helpful throughout. I'm also grateful to the current Chair of our department, Steven Bayne, for his support and guidance. I am particularly indebted to Dennis Keenan, whose invaluable feedback on drafts of my work opened up the trajectory of this project in ways I could never have anticipated. Our many conversations about the role of impersonal existence in Emmanuel Levinas's early work has shaped my own reading of Levinas's work. This is abundantly clear in the following chapters. I thank him for this insight, and for the hand of genuine friendship that he and his wife, Liz, have extended to my family and me. I am also thankful for Fairfield University's Robbin Crabtree, Sara Brill, Joy Gordon, Jocelyn Boryczka, Gwen Alphonso, Marcie Patton, Sonya Huber, Anna Lawrence, and Emily Orlando. Their superhuman intelligence and academic productivity continues to elevate the bar of scholarly excellence.

Many professional organizations and institutions have made the completion of this project possible. I am grateful for the financial support of the Department of Philosophy and the Rock Ethics Institute at Penn State University. Their Anna Julia Cooper Writing Fellowship provided me with the resources (and sanctity) needed to complete the last and most formative chapter of this work. During my week at Penn State, I received feedback from a caring and critical audience of professors and graduate students. In particular, I am grateful to Vincent Colapietro, Shannon

Sullivan, Nancy Tuana, and Michael Paradiso-Michau. Graduate students like Axelle Karera and Ayesha Abdullah took time out of there insanely busy schedules to share their thoughts on my research, and for this I am extremely grateful. The North American Sartre Society, the North American Levinas Society, and the Collegium of Black Women Philosophers also provided the stage that ultimately shaped his project into its final form. Over the years, elements of this book were presented at various meetings of all three conferences, and I have benefited from the engagement with scholars in these organizations. I am especially grateful to Drew Dalton for his advice and camaraderie during the 2008 North American Levinas Society meeting at Seattle University. John Drabinski's unwavering support has also been nothing short of lifesaving during the process of writing this book. I am also thankful for women like Kathryn Gines, Donna-Dale Marcano, Anika Simpson, Kristie Dotson, Rozena Maart, and Nathifa Greene, who all give me inspiration during our time together every April at the Collegium. Quite recently, I've also been fortunate enough to know Linda Martin Alcoff. As a friend, mentor, and source of support, she has enriched my life in many ways.

Without a doubt, an endeavor such has this would not be a reality without the love and support of my family, both near and far. From thousands of miles away, my mother Deborah never stopped believing in me and this project, particularly during those moments when I thought it impossible to finish. My grandparents, Linda and Irwin, have poured their hearts and souls into my growth as a person and a scholar, and for that I will always be grateful. My brothers, Kyle and Levi, have always been near, despite the section of the Atlantic that separates us. Closer to the place I've come to call home, I owe a tremendous debt to Linda Wooley, Stacy, and Gerry, the people I am fortunate enough to call family. Together with Justin and David, they supported me through the most tumultuous times of this project.

Most important of all, I thank my husband, David Terence Wooley Jr. He has been my first reader, and rescuer in times of crisis. I owe every page of this book to the human being that he is.

Introduction

This book postpones the discussion of Sartre's and Levinas's conceptions of the Other until its last chapter. Nevertheless, a large part of its motivation lies in the fact that the name of Jean-Paul Sartre conjures the proclamation that "hell is other people," while Emmanuel Levinas is that name which reminds us that, in the end we are held "hostage" by the Other. Enough scholars have analyzed these positions, making clear how each harkens to those intellectual traditions in which Sartre and Levinas are situated, respectively. Nevertheless, the curious relation between these two claims has always struck me as loaded with implications that far exceed the explanation pertaining to the difference between the existentialist and poststructuralist camps. Can the recognition of my being hostage to the Other also underscore the sense of hell brought on in that concrete moment of Sartrean intersubjectivity? Why would the trauma imbedded in the Levinasian claim not also be the torture implied in Sartre's?

My project began in pursuit of these and other such questions, and ended up with "transcendence," or rather, the unfolding of the relation between formal structures of transcendence and more concrete phenomenological analyses. Not only in the case of their phenomenologies of the Other, but in several other lived moments of disruption and "limit experiences," Sartre's and Levinas's descriptive analyses read as nearly indistinguishable from each other. Said otherwise, when the focus is on their faithfulness to the phenomenon, the similarities revealed truly explain how someone (like myself) can be equally Sartrean and Levinasian in her philosophical commitments. Nevertheless, according to the standard interpretation in recent French Continental philosophy, the positions that these thinkers occupy could not be more diametrically opposed. Such interpretations hold that the hell of intersubjectivity, portrayed so poignantly in Sartre's *No Exit* makes no accommodations for the radical call to responsibility that underlies my being held hostage by face of the

Other. The rupture of Roquentin's world, made avidly alive in *Nausea*, is to be understood as something other than Roquentin encountering the Levinasian *il y a*. And last, the shame of my being-for-the-Other, described in the pages of *Being and Nothingness*, is not quite evidence for the structural priority of passivity over spontaneity, which informs Levinas's conception of identity in *Existence and Existents*.

Though these accounts hold some legitimacy, it is important to remember that they are informed by the notions of transcendence with which Sartre and Levinas, respectively, begin. Despite Roquentin's ordeal, transcendence remains exhausted by the movement of intentionality. This is Sartre's starting point, and it is sustained throughout the entirety of his work. As such, the experience of nausea does not reveal the rustling anonymity of the *il y a*, because *that* account would find ground in an alternative formalization of transcendence as "excendence." In other words, transcendence would have to be what Levinas claims it to be, namely, that radical exiting of being, or the disruption of the intentionality that illuminates being with meaning and sense. Herein lies the most fundamental difference between Levinas and Sartre, a difference without which (for instance) the hell of Sartre's intersubjectivity could arguably indicate the hostage situation of Levinas's obsessive responsibility for the Other.

It is a consequence of these and other such observations that this book brings Sartre and Levinas into precisely *this* conversation—a conversation that begins with "transcendence." On careful juxtaposition of certain key tropes (selfhood, spontaneity, passivity, and temporality, to name a few), it demonstrates that the question of transcendence is the fundamental question around which French Continental philosophy ought to be bringing these two intellectuals. However, as it currently stands, the relevant scholarship has not yet done so. There is but a handful of expositions that recognizes the value in bringing Sartre and Levinas into a single scholarship, and they have used questions of Jewish identity, ethics, and to a lesser degree, politics to guide their analyses. To be clear, these are important moments of intersection, the pursuit of which has contributed much to philosophy. Nevertheless, in understanding the relationship between Sartre and Levinas without, at the outset, making central their respective accounts of transcendence, the takeaways are cursory at best, and misguided at worst.

As this book demonstrates, this is because the vast difference between Sartre's and Levinas's formal accounts of transcendence stands at odds with (concrete) phenomenological accounts that, in both thinkers, describe the fundamental place of disruption in human existence. When the question of transcendence guides one's reading of these Sartrean and Levinasian phenomenologies, there is a depth of engagement that not only enriches our understanding of their individual work, but ultimately brings their ideas to bear in ways that neither of them could, in isolation. To this end, I offer my analysis as a corrective to philosophy's tendency to place, and then study Sartre and Levinas in the existentialist and post-structuralist camps, respectively. I call for a reading of their work that is explicitly informed by their proposed formal accounts of transcendence (how each determines transcendence at the structural level of analysis). In positioning them as such, the following threefold discovery develops. The reader will find that, first, both thinkers approach the relationship between human freedom and responsibility from surprisingly similar conceptions of identity-as-disrupted. Second, Sartre and Levinas ground this picture of disruption in concrete descriptions that are indistinguishable from each other. This becomes clear when their phenomenologies are juxtaposed in the manner carried out in the chapters that follow. Third, and perhaps most notably, this similarity is *in spite* of their strikingly different accounts of transcendence. This book shows that when Sartre's concrete analyses are placed alongside Levinas's, they not only reveal a "subject in disruption" similar to Levinas's, but they also exist in tension with a formal account of transcendence (the account in Sartre) that prioritizes freedom at the expense of passivity. Said otherwise, this book argues that Sartre and Levinas are more alike, in their acknowledgment of certain lived experiences of disruption, than the difference between the Sartrean and Levinasian accounts of transcendence would let on.

In making clear that these varying formal accounts of transcendence stand alongside markedly similar descriptive analyses of the priority of disruption, this work offers questions in need of pursuit by both Sartrean and Levinasian scholarship. How is it that Sartre's formal account is one of a consciousness that is exhausted through and through by a movement of intentionality (such that transcendence, on this account *is* intentionality), while the lived experience of this consciousness (in moments of shame, for instance) mirrors the vulnerability, dissonance, and disruptiveness found in the Levinasian self? Asked otherwise, what might be the real difference between Levinas's transcendence-as-excendence (the structure of which grounds his notion of identity-in-disruption) and Sartre's entire phenomenological enterprise? To this end, this analysis urges scholars of Sartre's work to be equally as committed to understanding Levinas. Likewise, its call is to the Levinasian scholar to be similarly immersed in the work of Jean-Paul Sartre.

However, involved in this project are stakes that extend much further than this somewhat specialized corner of philosophical thought. I have made a case for this new possibility of Sartre and Levinas working together, to perhaps symbiotically fill voids that are a consequence of their formal commitments. My analysis is predominantly theoretical, and as such, does not explicitly offer a sociopolitical or ethical analysis. Nonetheless, the following chapters do lay the foundation for a novel way to articulate an ethos that is equally and squarely grounded in "humanity as free" *and* "humanity as vulnerable." Sartre's work can be used (and *has* been used) to advocate the former only when studied in isolation from Levinas's. In a similar vein, one reads Levinas's work to advocate the latter only insofar as this reading happens in isolation from Sartre. But in bringing them together, this ethos comes to the fore, which can then be used to reconceptualize the ways in which we think about the political in relation to the ethical. Politically, my analysis facilitates a questioning of both the presuppositions and scope of a social contract theory that grounds political formations solely on (free) contract-making. In other words, we can ask again the question of the kinds of identities (the "who" of these identities) involved in the lived experiences of community and solidarity. It also mandates that we think through the place and possibility of sacrifice (which is to say, a way of being and choosing that is more than the pursuit of self-preservation) in the political. To put this in more summative terms, the much larger stake of this comparative analysis is the very blurring of the line that determines politics and ethics to be mutually exclusive. The hell that is other people, signifying the restriction that my freedom encounters in the Other, might reveal a disruption in the face of the Other that is not an *affront* to transcendence, but rather the *promise* of transcendence. If we bracket an understanding of transcendence that is solely in terms of intentionality, this disruption rings with the kind of primordial indebtedness that would not only explain my "being for the Other," but also the actual condition for the possibility of political existence.

The Argument's Trajectory

My bringing Jean-Paul Sartre and Emmanuel Levinas together identifies a strategy they both employ, which is a grounding of philosophical claims on descriptive analyses of concrete experience. In this regard, both appreciate that which most unifies the pluralities of phenomenological endeavors, which is to redirect philosophy's attention to the "things themselves," or the phenomenon. In his appraisal of such redirection, Sartre describes consciousness as a "series of bursts . . . which throw us . . . into the dry dust of the world, on to the plain earth, amidst things."[1] The ontology he presents in *Being and Nothingness* originates from this descriptive ground, as is the case in Levinas's earlier work that determine the structures of human existence from the kinds of experiences to which we are privy.[2]

Hence, despite the many points of divergence between their work, Sartre and Levinas are in dialogue. The formal structures that each determine to be constitutive of the human condition are legitimized by the concrete experiences whose possibility they condition. The focus of this study is limited to their formal accounts of transcendence, since it is on this issue that Sartre's and Levinas's departure is the most striking. My discussion of several of his phenomenological descriptions establishes that when it comes to his conception of transcendence, Sartre, despite himself, betrays the loyalty of the "formal" to the "concrete." He outlines a transcendence in his earlier work, *The Transcendence of the Ego*,[3] and later develops it in *Being and Nothingness*,[4] to leave out what is of most significance in his phenomenological descriptions of affectivity, embodiment and nausea (to name a few). Instead of accounting for the vulnerability conveyed in such moments, Sartre interprets these concrete experiences from a conceptual space that is outlined in advance by his understanding of transcendence. I show that this space ultimately disappoints, since it consists of an ontology in which concrete experience is given in terms of a consciousness that has ecstatically surpassed itself toward the world. On this account, consciousness relates to objects across a distance of nonimplication, and is structurally empty of all being. In this regard, all experience is given in terms of freedom, or at least, the freedom of possibility.

Sartre's conception of transcendence is very much an appropriation of Husserl's model of intentionality, which holds that consciousness is nothing other than a reflection of objects of experience. In this sense, transcendence-as-intentionality already nullifies any (Cartesian) distinctions between "subjective" and "objective" regions of being.[5] Nevertheless, the ambiguity that he captures in the descriptions on which I focus portray a blurring of "subject" and "object" poles of experience in a different sense. For instance, in the experience of being-seen by the Other, one finds that subjects are no longer able to project ecstatically beyond themselves (into the world). Such a subject is a personalization in being, without yet laying claim to autonomous subjectivity. In a similar sense, Sartre's descriptions of shame before the Other is clearly placed beyond his formal categories of reflective and prereflective experience.[6] As such, shame would already be outside of the parameters that determine an intentional surpassing of being toward the world.

To this end, I claim that Sartre's model of an ecstatic transcendence, or "transcendence as intentionality," leaves out that level of human experience depicted by his own phenomenological descriptions. This phenomenology points to an alternative encounter with Being that grounds a vulnerability at the heart of subjective life. In this sense, I identify Sartre's descriptions to be doing something very similar to Levinas's, which is a calling into question of the assumption that subjectivity is equivalent to absolute and unchecked spontaneity. In Levinas's descriptive work, he refrains from referring to these moments of affectivity as "experiences" in the strict sense, insofar as they trouble the possibility of the kind of self-sufficient subject to which an experience can belong. He conceives of "subject" as a personalization in being, so even in its affective encounter with existence, it is still (or already) an interiority in its own right. But this inner life is not, exhaustively, in terms of a movement of "consciousness" toward the "world." To say this otherwise, Levinas finds, in his descriptions of affectivity, the "evidence" that supports a conception of subjectivity as primordially rooted in being, severely implicated in and exposed to existence. For him, transcendence-as-intentionality, which would be a radical surpassing of this positionality or rootedness, pertains to only an *aspect* of the human condition. As such, it does not yet explain the possibility of those moments that are precisely effects of this primordial positioning.

So though the descriptions in Levinas's *and* Sartre's work portray an ambiguous relationship with being, it is Levinas who formulates an account of transcendence that captures the human condition beyond the structures of intentionality. In both *Existence and Existents* and *On Escape*,[7] where he traces the meaning of fatigue, insomnia, and shame (to name a few), Levinas's concrete investigations determine the more formal structures to which these moments point. In this vein, he develops his conception of transcendence, against which I posit Sartre's transcendence-as-intentionality, as an "excendence" from being. The term *excendence* opposes Levinas's reading of Western philosophy's understanding of transcendence as a journey toward a better, more infinite, or less confined mode of being. Its structure is such that the subject's desire to surpass Being is not a desire to overcome finitude, but rather to *exit* Being in an absolute sense. Transcendence-as-excendence points to a desire for what is completely otherwise than Being, and not merely for an alternative modality of being. According to Levinas, what qualifies as the accomplishment of this radical exit is quite aporetic, since it is in finding oneself at the *end* of one's powers to take leave of Being that transcendence-as-excendence is concretized. In other words, the movement happens in an absolute moment of vulnerability and subjection. It is only from the vantage point of modernity's conception of transcendence that this signifies as a failure. But for Levinas, this signifies an opening up onto that which is radically otherwise.

He determines the human condition to be such that we can never surpass ourselves, or our position in Being, precisely because we are fundamentally riveted to that position. However, it is in *failing* to exit ourselves in this way that excendence is concretized, taking us to the hither side of being, where moments of affectivity and sacrifice resist the categories of both being and nonbeing. Levinas rewrites the narrative of a triumphant subject to emphasize passivity as the locus through which escape occurs. In his later work (particularly by the time of the publication of *Totality and Infinity*[8] in 1969), he drops the term *excendence* altogether, and uses *transcendence* as though it captured this renegotiated movement. However, I stress throughout this book that Levinas's understanding of transcendence stands against the model employed by a philosophy like Sartre's, precisely because it conceptualizes this desire for a radical exiting of all ontological categories. It is for this reason that I systematically refer to Levinas's model as "transcendence-as-excendence."

Transcendence, on Sartrean terms, is an ecstatic escape from "self." His account holds that consciousness, as a negation of being, has thus surpassed being completely. So even though Sartre recognizes an inevitable connectedness between consciousness and being, this connection amounts to a relation of negativity. Hence, he understands consciousness as a complete escape from being, and captures this escape in his conception of transcendence. The critique he lays against Husserl, in *The Transcendence of the Ego*, begins with this radical sense of spontaneity. Because consciousness is always a "bursting forth," dispelling all pretensions to interiority, Sartre reads Husserl's transcendental ego as both gratuitous and nonreflective of conscious life. Insofar as we experience the world, we have already escaped being (and our being) completely. Any positing of a transcendental "ego" pole would compromise this radical spontaneity that, for Sartre, conditions the appearing of a "world."

For Levinas, the concrete meaning of transcendence lies in the interruption of this movement of intentionality. It is concretized when subjects encounter themselves as disrupted by radical alterity that is beyond the "world" whose appearance is conditioned by a Sartrean transcendence. The notion of disruption opens up another, though related, intersection between Levinas and Sartre. Both identify, at the foundation of their analysis, a noncoincidence between the subject and the subject's "self." Sartre's is a discovery through his analysis of acts of reflection, whereby consciousness creates an ego-pole on which it then reflects explicitly. This ego pole, or the consciousness-reflected-on, is never equivalent to reflecting-consciousness, because consciousness is necessarily noncoincident with itself, relating to itself across a distance of nothingness. For Sartre, this is the price to be paid for intentionality, and ultimately, for radical freedom. Consciousness must perpetually escape from itself, and remain empty of all being. This lack of coincidence is portrayed as a locus of anguish, since it brings to the forefront the unremitting responsibility that accompanies a pure and unadulterated freedom.

Levinas finds a similar noncoincidence or "ipseity" at the heart of his conception of identity. And like Sartre, he identifies, in this lack of coincidence, the conditions for a crisis. However, unlike Sartre's determination, Levinas identifies this noncoincidence to be *prior* to spontaneity, and not the grounds that condition spontaneity. Despite the fact that the subject does not map onto her "self," she still remains completely riveted to that self (a self that, for Levinas, captures a rootedness in being). In this vein, his understanding of noncoincidence does the work of calling radical freedom into question, since the subject continues to be riveted to a base despite her intentional relation with being. This is the kind of structure that generates my desire for the "otherwise than being." The more severe my rivetedness to myself is, or the more pervasive and overwhelming the presence of being is, the more urgent my desire for an exit becomes. I can never abnegate the obligation to be myself, or to occupy precisely this position in being. But in the face of this inevitability, my desire to take leave already indicates a certain rejection of this inevitability. In this regard, Levinas finds transcendence-as-excendence to be already accomplished in the very *desire* for that which is otherwise. "Getting out" is accomplished when I encounter that to which I am forever bound (namely, myself or my position in being) as a source of unsettling disruption. It is in this sense that identity, for Levinas, is structured in terms of disruption and "fraying." Its fundamental encounter with being is across a vulnerability and radical passivity that is prior to the movement of intentionality.

Texts that bring Sartre and Levinas together often do so around the theme of ethics, or more specifically, the Other.[9] The last chapter of this book explores this intersection in a unique way. Like the comparisons in preceding chapters, I find poignant similarities in Sartre's and Levinas's descriptions of what it means for two subjects to encounter each other. However, unlike these preceding analyses, I locate, in the Sartrean account of authenticity, a formal account of intersubjectivity that clearly calls into question a radically free consciousness. To be sure, Sartre's model of transcendence-as-intentionality is sustained throughout the entire trajectory of his career. In this regard, *Being and Nothingness,* in 1945, is no different from the incomplete work in *Notebooks for an Ethics,* published posthumously in 1992. But even though his ethics continues the narrative of freedom as that which is "most original" to the structure of consciousness, he also establishes that, in choosing authenticity as my fundamental project, I am obligated to take the Other's condition into consideration. In this vein, I argue that this choice of authenticity resonates with Levinas's conception of substitution in ways one would not expect, given the ontology of radical freedom to which Sartre subscribes. Substitution marks Levinas's turn to a lexicon of ethical obsession that articulates the radical disruption of subjective freedom. What he describes in his earlier work as a disrupted identity that encounters being passively is given in the account of substitution as an extreme responsibility for the Other. I am disrupted and "open" insofar as my being is always already called to take the place of the Other's suffering. In *Otherwise than Being or Beyond Essence,* Levinas explains that it is only in this ethical language that one finds resources adequate enough to convey the sense in which subjectivity is constituted by its own disruption. For my purposes in this project, I understand disruption in general to describe Levinas's conception of subjectivity as an openness onto radical alterity. In this sense, the subject's substitution for the Other is already concretized in the liability of every act of spontaneity to be called into question, even if those acts do not directly pertain to the Other.

My work in chapter 5 recognizes the important differences between this Levinasian conception and Sartre's account of authenticity. At the same time, I argue for a reading of authenticity that takes seriously the responsibility of free agents to act on behalf of the disenfranchised fringes of their society. The potential for tension between this and Sartre's more individualistic transcendence-as-intentionality is clear, insofar as the priority these respectively give to uncontested freedom can be diametrically opposed. Nonetheless, the claim running throughout my work significantly weakens this opposition. At the formal level of Sartre's ontology is his account of consciousness as a spontaneous locus of freedom, whose relation with being is strictly across the movement of intentionality. However, "behind" this account are descriptions of experiences that indicate another kind of relation to being. Subjects find themselves burdened by the weight of existence, which is an obligation that is given over instead of freely chosen. While Levinas reads this phenomenology as an indication of the personal existent as vulnerable or indebted, it is only in Sartre's more political formulation of authenticity that he takes up at least a modulation of this indebtedness. Transcendence-as-intentionality's conceptual space cannot account for this aspect of the human condition. Nonetheless, it is reasonable to project, from Sartre's concrete phenomenology of a subject-in-disruption, the idea of freedom being limited by the call to act on behalf of the Other.

Overview

Chapter 1 begins with Sartre's account of transcendence in his 1936–1937 essay, *The Transcendence of the Ego*. There, he critiques Husserl for forcing our concrete experience into formal structures of consciousness that are in no way validated concretely (the very complaint I level against Sartre). He shows that Husserl's transcendental ego is not only gratuitous when it comes to accounting for the phenomenon, but most importantly, it cannot be supported by the phenomenon. This critique clearly outlines the foundation of Sartre's notion of transcendence, in which consciousness relates to being negatively and ecstatically. This means that, instead of a transcendental feature of consciousness, the ego would be a transcendent object *for* consciousness, similar to other objects of experience. To say this differently, a necessary consequence of consciousness relating to being strictly through a movement of intentionality is its pure emptiness of being. This early understanding of transcendence-as-intentionality informs the phenomenological ontology that Sartre develops in *Being and Nothingness*, where our everyday experiences are read in terms of this formal structure of transcendence.

I follow this with an analysis of Levinas's transcendence-as-excendence in chapter 2. In *Existence and Existents* and *On Escape*, Levinas uncovers a primordial "positioning" of the subject in existence, which indicates a rivetedness to being, or to "being oneself." On Sartre's account of transcendence, the possibility of experience is grounded in consciousness' projection beyond the "self." However, according to Levinas, the bond between "subject" and "self" is never completely broken; it is simply loosened, only to recoil again. There is always a return to self, which he identifies as most signifying in experiences like shame, nausea, fatigue, and insomnia. The model of transcendence that he uses to account for these experiences maintains this rivetedness to self. Hence, it reflects a relation with being that is otherwise than an escape from being. This notion of transcendence-as-excendence fails to get us out of being (or rather, out of our position in being), but it is an exit in its own right. To transcend in excendence means that I am "with myself," on all sides, no matter where I turn. But at the same time, I encounter this fullness of my being with repulsion. Levinas uses the subject's revolt against her being to ground a noncoincidence between the subject and this position (or between the subject and herself), which, for him, realizes the escape captured in excendence. Hence, he articulates an account of subjectivity such that we are riveted to ourselves, but can never be completely one with that to which we are riveted. Transcendence-as-excendence is the only genuine exiting, given this structure of identity. The Other occupies a large part of Levinas's project but I address this role of alterity only in chapter 5. I read his work very much like he reads it—as primarily on transcendence and *not* ethics. To be sure, ethics will provide the language needed to articulate the radical exiting of positioned subjects who are in relations of noncoincidence with themselves. But at the same time, this ethical language describes a subject as fundamentally exposed to, or disrupted by radical alterity. I understand transcendence-as-excendence to be grounded on this disruption of totalities, the most pertinent of which is the intentional network of meanings that constitute subjectivity. In any event, I argue that Levinas is better positioned to explain the possibilities of certain experiences (identified by himself and Sartre alike), given his account of transcendence-as-excendence.

Chapter 3 continues to emphasize "disruption" as that which is at the core of Levinas's account of transcendence. In this sense, I read the Face as more fundamentally describing a radical rupturing of the subject, than it does an actual encounter with another person. Alongside this I argue that Sartre's descriptions of the experience of nausea, coming from the novel, *Nausea*,[10] portray a remarkably similar disruption of intentionality. In this regard, one would expect a more Levinasian account of identity (and ultimately transcendence) to follow from the concrete descriptions in this novel. Sartre describes the possibility of an encounter with being such that it is no longer in terms of the "subject" and "object" of experience. Given its resonance with Levinas's account in *Existence and Existents* of a "subject" burdened by the weight of existence, I read this phenomenology of nausea as a rupture of Sartre's narrative of consciousness as a pure surpassing of being. Nevertheless, Sartre continues to find, in his descriptions, an absolutely free consciousness called to a responsibility to constitute the world according to its free projects. Said otherwise, the breakdown of all signification, which he describes, ultimately points back to consciousness' freedom to create a world *for itself*.[11]

The fourth chapter continues to pursue my claim that several of Sartre's concrete descriptions point in the direction of a Levinasian account of identity and transcendence. Sartre's notion of facticity captures those moments of nonfreedom found at the level of concrete experience, whereby consciousness undergoes the "givens," or facts of being, instead of actively constituting meaning through its projects. He includes in his conception of facticity, the phenomenon of acquiring a being-for-others (as one consciousness feels itself being looked-at), the experience of one's embodiment in moments of shame, as well as the brute fact of existence as it shows up in moments of vertigo and nausea. I argue that, at the formal level, facticity retains a primacy of freedom that is not reflected in the concrete experiences Sartre intends facticity to explain. I present his account of the body, particularly the case of "pain-consciousness," and his account of shame, to show traces of a level of Levinasian passivity (or pure affectivity). This significantly calls into question his formal account of consciousness as strictly a pure nothingness of being, and replaces it with an account of consciousness that is more primordially positioned in being.

My last chapter focuses on Sartre's and Levinas's accounts of alterity, again identifying similarities at their descriptive levels of analyses. I identify, in Sartre's account of authenticity, grounds for a rigorous sense of responsibility toward the Other, much like in Levinas's conception of substitution. To be sure, these conceptions of responsibility differ in very important ways, the explanation of which rest on two distinct accounts of identity—Levinasian and Sartrean. However, I argue that Sartre's conception of absolute responsibility is superior to Levinas's when it comes to the question of taking *action* on behalf of the Other. His is an account that explicitly considers the challenges of acting within the parameters of political life, while Levinas seems to regard the political as the totality ruptured by the obsession of substitution. In the end, though both conceptions of responsibility are radical, it is on their own terms, and within the contexts of the projects out of which they arise, that I read them. At the same time, my work in chapters 1 through 4 prepare for the possibility of using Sartre's own concrete descriptions to call into question his formal account (of radical freedom). It is in this vein that I find his position on authenticity to be one that gives a robust ethical obligation toward the Other that can, indeed, act as a limitation on his formal account of radical freedom.

CHAPTER 1

The Role of Being in Sartre's Model of Transcendence-as-Intentionality

In *Being and Nothingness*, Sartre develops Husserl's notion of intentionality into what can be read as an 'existentialist phenomenology.'[1] The Sartrean commitment lies in using this phenomenological method to account for our concrete, and ultimately politicized, mode of being in the world. In this sense, his reading of Husserl, in *The Transcendence of the Ego*, formulates the position that the existence of consciousness is absolute, while at the same time, very much immersed in the world of which it is a reflection. To this end, Sartre works to distance his exposition from Husserl's *epoché*, claiming that it is both unfounded by, and unnecessary for the deployment of Husserl's phenomenological method. More importantly, he finds the *epoché* to be that moment of Husserl's corpus in which he undermines what is of most value in his claim concerning the structure of intentionality.[2]

Hence, *The Transcendence of the Ego* works to establish that the ego is an object in the world, and that it is "for consciousness" much like everything else that makes an appearance. This replaces the Husserlian claim that the ego remains as that transcendental pole *of* consciousness, after the objectivity of the world "falls away" through the phenomenological reduction. This is what Husserl uses to establish the absolute existence of consciousness. Sartre recognizes that the existence of consciousness is absolute in his own phenomenological account. Nevertheless, he is wary of legitimizing this absolute existence by means of the *epoché*, and develops alternative mechanisms through which to validate the claim that consciousness alone can appear to itself. It can be argued that Sartre's claim is an overreading of the implications of Husserl's *epoché* insofar as it regards the bracketing of the existence of an external world as not sufficiently recognizing the effects of a transphenomenal being.[3] *The Transcendence of the Ego* and *Being and Nothingness* both rest on the premise that the reduction fails to explain why the world experienced is precisely *this* world, and not otherwise. To be sure, this is not a necessarily justified critique of a method that only seeks to suspend all judgments concerning the existence of the external world (or to regard such judgments as hypothetical) for the sake of establishing the intentional structure of consciousness. Nonetheless, the shape of Sartre's existential phenomenology is very much indebted to this way of understanding Husserl.[4] For this reason, the work in this chapter, and in those that follow, assumes a certain legitimacy to Sartre's appropriation of Husserl, but only for the sake of appreciating those Sartrean positions on the freedom and transcendence of consciousness.

For better or for worse, it is clear that Sartre's renunciation of the phenomenological reduction comes from a thorough commitment to questions of politics and ethics. With good reason, his earlier work in *Being and Nothingness* is read as the most anarchical and individualist moment in his career.[5] At the same time, the "realist" nature of the phenomenology of *Being and Nothingness* clearly signals Sartre's concerns for the sense in which humans suffer, and the inevitable root of that suffering resting *in* the world.[6] In *The Transcendence of the Ego*, Sartre explains, "Unfortunately, as long as the I remains a structure of absolute consciousness, one will still be able to reproach phenomenology for being an escapist doctrine, for again, pulling a part of man out of the world and in that way, turning our attention from real problems."[7] *The Transcendence of the Ego* undeniably provides the groundwork on which Sartre established the lengthier account of consciousness in *Being and Nothingness*. Hence, by the time of the publication of this later text (in 1945), it was already the case that Sartre's motivation was based in those social-political structures out of which suffering in the world acquired signification.

To this end, *Being and Nothingness* presents an account of being, which would explain the patterns of concrete existence. The work's ontology explains the sense in which consciousness is radically empty of being (possessing an "ontological freedom"[8]), alongside its encountering a resisting "reality" from the world. The notion of facticity is used to capture this resistance, and grounds those aspects of our experience that show up as though they are "given" to us, immutable and "to be dealt" with. As it is employed by Sartre, facticity does not undermine the ontological freedom of consciousness, since it is undeniably the case that consciousness is structurally apart from being (in-itself being). In the words of David Detmer, consciousness ". . . can separate itself from all that is external to it, and from whatever might attempt to ensnare or enslave it, and in so doing, disentangle itself from the chain of causal determinacy."[9] So even though facticity is a structure of experience that pertains to certain "brute givens." it is still the case that experience is also structured as an intentionality.[10] Consciousness is always a consciousness of something (other than itself), which is to say that consciousness is exhausted by its relationality to the object of its experience. But this also means that consciousness is always *not* the object of its experience. In a general sense, intentionality implies that consciousness is radically empty of all (inert, or in-itself) being. It is in this sense that Detmer describes consciousness as "disentangled from the chain of cause determination." There are certain patterns of existing that consciousness faces, but precisely because such patterns are related to across intentionality, consciousness "faces" them, and is already *not* what it would have been under their determinative influence.

The work of this chapter traces the implications of Sartre's conception of facticity, and argues that his account prioritizes the transcendence of consciousness.[11] In my analysis, I deploy Sartre's conception of intentionality interchangeably with his understanding of transcendence. This is insofar as intentionality, on Sartre's account, necessarily positions consciousness in a relation to some object that is precisely not-consciousness. In this regard, "Sartre wants consciousness to [be able to] reach an object that is truly outside of it."[12] The object must be transcendent to consciousness, and the very relation to that object presupposes a self-surpassing on the part of consciousness. Hence, my exposition reads, in the structure of intentionality, an implied escape (or surpassing). To the extent that intentionality is sustained throughout the effects of facticity, so too do I determine the transcendence of consciousness to be sustained. In other words, I argue that the Sartrean consciousness of *Being and Nothingness* is a complete escape from being, despite the factical component of experience. I recognize that Sartre's later work (around the period marked by the *Critique of Dialectical Reasoning*) emphasizes certain forms of (real) social and political oppression, and such emphasis undermines the plausibility that consciousness is a radical transcendence of being. However, I hold that the narrative of absolute transcendence, established in *Being and Nothingness*, is carried over in these more socioeconomic accounts of experience, in which Sartre recognizes that freedom can be compromised by social, economic, and political factors. As such, there is a prioritizing of the value of freedom in these later expositions, which, for this reason, positions them in a continuity with the work of *Being and Nothingness*.

I. The Implications of the Intentional Structure of Consciousness

In his essay on the theory of intentionality, Sartre confirms his appreciation of Husserl's phenomenology. He identifies the method as one that would allow us to move away from the "digestive philosophies" of idealism and realism, precisely because it recognizes the world as both "external to consciousness," but also as relative to consciousness insofar as the latter is inevitably immersed in the world.[13] "Consciousness and world are given in one stroke,"[14] which, for Sartre, means that "everything is finally on the outside, everything, including consciousness itself." In this regard, the Husserlian account of intentionality positions consciousness as a radically empty field of spontaneity (and not as some container of ideal objects that point to their external correlates). At the same time, "world" is that which is transcendent to consciousness, making it necessary for consciousness to go "beyond itself" in order to relate to "world." In this reading of Husserl, Sartre determines that without "world" remaining transcendent, consciousness is no longer the field of radical spontaneity on which Husserl builds his phenomenological method.

To be sure, Husserl adopts a form of idealism by 1913, from which Sartre distances himself in *The Transcendence of the Ego*. Though it is not an explicit treatise on transcendence, this 1937 text sets up the groundwork for Sartre's formal model of transcendence-as-intentionality.[15] In large part, the essay lays out a critique of Husserl's phenomenological method as an idealism that compromises the truth of the theory of intentionality, which is that all consciousness is "consciousness of" that which is other than consciousness.[16] As a corrective, Sartre develops the idea of the ego as a transcendent object *for* consciousness, and not a transcendental (and unifying) pole *of* conscious experience. This view is mirrored in his essay on intentionality, where he reinforces the position that consciousness is but a reflection of objects of experiences. He agrees with Husserl's claim that both "consciousness" and "world" are equally fundamental, separate in abstraction only. However, he also determines that, included in this conception of intentionality, is "this necessity for consciousness to exist as consciousness of something other than itself."[17] In this regard, experience is always already the experience of a consciousness that has transcended those objects of experience. As a movement of intentionality, consciousness is "out there," *in* the phenomenon. "[It] is the nature of consciousness to intend objects, that is, to point away from itself and out toward the things with which it is concerned."[18]

It is on this foundation that Sartre formulates his phenomenological ontology of experience. The being of consciousness is radically otherwise than the being of the objects of experience. Consciousness is purely an activity of relating to things, and unlike "things," has no inside (consciousness is nonsubstantial). The ontology of *Being and Nothingness* shows that, though an experience of objects presupposes an inevitable intentional (surpassing) movement of consciousness, the actual being of those phenomena does *not* fall away at the level of concrete experience. As such, this being would have phenomenological implications that ought to be taken into account. Hence, Sartre's ontology is meant to ground a phenomenological analysis of experience in a field of "in-itself" being. To be sure, in-itself being does not become part of that experience. Sartre recognizes that by the time we make the claim that consciousness is having an experience, we are already at the level of "world," and thus no longer at the level of being in-itself. To this end, David Detmer's question is a pertinent one: "How can a book [like *Being and Nothingness*] that takes a phenomenological approach deal with ontology, the study of being? After all, phenomenology is concerned with phenomena—that is, with what appears to consciousness—and precisely not (at least in its more orthodox versions) with what really exists."[19] Nonetheless, Sartre proposes the ontological question insofar he recognizes being in-itself as that (contingent) foundation on which consciousness (and "world") upsurges into existence.[20] This is the most notably the reason for Sartre's rejection of the phenomenological reduction. He holds that it renders phenomenology unable to account for the effects of the "in-itself" or transphenomenal being that grounds intentional experience.

Husserl's Position, According to Sartre

Husserl claims that, unlike what we find in Kant, the principle that lies behind any series of appearances of an object is shaped by what that object actually is. That is to say, the meaning (or the truth) of the object is not distinct from the way that object appears to consciousness. In this sense, epistemological as well as ontological questions are addressed in terms of the object *as it is given over* to consciousness. However, in starting with the appearance of objects (with the phenomena), one is ultimately led to the question of that *to which* the phenomena appears. In other words, an appearance necessarily presupposes something (or someone) that receives the appearance. For this reason, Husserl's (and by extension, Sartre's) phenomenology is an elucidation of those principles of consciousness that shape the phenomenon of the world.

For Husserl, these principles of consciousness represent that point of absolute certainty, from which systems of knowledge must begin. Put differently, it is from the intentionality of consciousness that the sciences receive their metaphysical grounding. Husserl establishes this in what he refers to as a leaving behind of the natural attitude. As a phenomenologist, one brackets all assumptions concerning the values one ascribes to an actually-existing external reality, and in so doing, no longer takes for granted the independently objective existence of objects of experience. Subsequent to this phenomenological reduction, consciousness remains as that (alone) which possesses absolute existence. In the words of Aron Gurwitsch, "What remains after the phenomenological reduction has been affectuated is . . . the field of noeses with their noematic correlates."[21]

Despite his renunciation of Husserl's exercise of bracketing, Sartre also conceptualizes the existence of consciousness as the absolute starting point from which phenomenology (and the sciences) attains its certitude. As phenomena, objects in the world depend, for their appearing,[22] on the absolute existence of consciousness. It is *for* consciousness that they appear.[23] On the other hand, consciousness is the only being that can appear to itself, and in this sense, the only being whose existence is self-grounded. Michael Sukale writes, "[something] is a relative existent when it is an object *for* something. The *world* for example is a relative existent because it is an object for consciousness. Consciousness however is not relative because it is not *for* anything. . . ."[24] For this reason, Sartre identifies consciousness as the phenomenon whose existence is absolute. Its existence is independent of its appearing to anything (even to itself).[25]

"Indeed," Sartre tells us, "the existence of consciousness is an absolute existence because consciousness is consciousness of itself."[26] In other words, the necessity with which all consciousness is simultaneously self-consciousness, is evidence for its absolute existence. Consciousness is a "special phenomenon," since there is always self-consciousness simultaneous to consciousness of a transcendent phenomenon. To recall, implied in the structure of intentionality is that appearances for consciousness are transcendent; they are "other than" or "not" the consciousness for which they make an appearance. This means that consciousness cannot be, for itself, its own phenomenon, insofar as it would have already surpassed that appearance. Nevertheless, there is a sense in which a kind of "self-consciousness" necessarily accompanies every experience, since, for Sartre, there is no consciousness that is not also *self*-consciousness.

It is important to understand that this does not compromise the intentional structure of consciousness, the implication of which is that appearances for consciousness must be transcendent to consciousness. An account of an everyday experience might be of use here. In our present experience, certain objects appear to us (computer screens, keyboards, the windows to our left, and so on). Sartre tells us (in both *The Transcendence of the Ego* and *Being and Nothingness*) that I am conscious of these objects only because I am conscious of myself as being conscious of them. Put differently, I have an awareness of myself *in the form of* an awareness of these objects that comprise my present experience. This is not to say that I appear to myself the way an object of experience appears to me. In other words, "consciousness is not for itself its own object."[27] All this means is that I must necessarily be self-conscious in the mode of "myself qua having this experience" in order for the experience to even be possible. Hence, consciousness is aware of itself through its awareness of the objects of experience, establishing that self-consciousness is a product of there being consciousness of an object. Phyllis Kenevan affirms that this is essential to a movement of intentionality: "This condition expresses the structure of consciousness as *intentional*. [Consciousness] posits an object other than itself. It is also, as consciousness, *self*-consciousness. [This] self-consciousness is always a *non-positional* consciousness; that is, it cannot posit itself as object."[28] It is in this sense that consciousness is necessarily self-consciousness at the same time its being is intentional through and through. It is as "a prereflective (or nonpositional) taste" that I am aware of myself while objects of experience appear for me.[29]

Sartre's Critique of Husserl[30]

Sartre's critique of Husserl is founded on this understanding of the structure of consciousness. As absolute, the being of consciousness cannot depend on that which is outside of consciousness. No other phenomenon has this ability to appear to itself, and subsequently legitimize its being on its own. For Sartre, a transcendental pole behind experience places this in jeopardy. I discuss this in more detail shortly, in what I name Sartre's "detrimental" critique of Husserl. Appearing to itself in this way, consciousness depends on nothing outside of itself for its "being there." Phyllis Sutton summarizes Sartre's quarrel with Husserl as follows, establishing what I call Sartre's "gratuitous" critique of the *epoché*. "[Sartre] denies Husserl's claim that the transcendental ego, qua subject of consciousness, is presented to intuition. [Second], Sartre's strategy against Husserl . . . is to claim that the transcendental ego is unnecessary for its traditional function of unifying consciousness."[31] For Husserl, a pure ego remains standing after employing the phenomenological reduction, which he then takes to mean that it constitutes the being of consciousness. Was this the case, experience would then have the equivalent of "object" and "subject" poles. "To the strictly phenomenological observation [or reduction] the intentional act appears thus as a ray directed toward the object and issuing from a *center or a source of radiancy* [emphasis added]."[32] However, insofar as this transcendental pole does not make an appearance (either explicitly or implicitly), Sartre finds it unverifiable from the vantage point of the very phenomenological method to which Husserl's analysis subscribes. Furthermore, he finds it superfluous insofar as experience is given as unified and belonging to consciousness without positioning a pure ego "behind" conscious acts. As a consequence, much of Sartre's phenomenological ontology rests on his naming of this "polarized" (or egocentric) conception of experience as unnecessary for the phenomenologist's method of inquiry.[33]

Sartre describes the self-consciousness accompanying all experience as nonpositional.[34] Hence, despite the fact that such self-consciousness will not necessarily amount to self-knowing, it must always be the case that consciousness appears to itself. Without this (appearing to itself), the very relation of intentionality becomes compromised. "It is . . . part and parcel of the intentionality of consciousness that it be consciousness of an object other than itself. Intentionality is a *relation* to an object, and so it must be *between* something and something else. In order for consciousness to be consciousness of an object other than itself there must be some sort of awareness of self in opposition to awareness of the object."[35] Sartre locates such awareness of self at the nonpositional level.

Hence, nonpositional self-consciousness preserves the structure of intentionality insofar as it is a prerequisite for consciousness's transcending movement beyond itself. It is also supportive of the claim that consciousness exists absolutely, depending on nothing outside of itself for its being (as an appearing). In other words, consciousness is *both* nonpositionality self-aware *and* conscious of that which is "by nature outside of [consciousness]."[36] Roland Breeur's description is quite apt in this regard.

"The lung is not intentionally involved with the air," but an act of perception rests on this intentional relation to that which is perceived. I may not possesses knowledge of "myself as perceiving an object," in the sense that I can very well be oblivious to my engagement with the object. Nevertheless, "the act of perception is . . . conscious of itself."[37]

Sartre uses this distinction between positional and nonpositional consciousness to then establish that to which I eluded earlier on, and what I call his "detrimental" critique of the transcendental ego. The model of transcendence that he develops in *Being and Nothingness* rests on this critical reading of the transcendental ego, as well as the account of intentionality from which Sartre launches his critique.[38] He demonstrates that, in positing the ego as an aspect of the transcendental nature of consciousness, or as belonging to the conditions for the possibility of experience, it can no longer be said consciousness possesses an absolute existence. In other words, Husserl's transcendental ego destroys both the intentional and absolute features of consciousness. "[However] formal, however abstract one may suppose it to be, the *I*, with its personality, would be a sort of center of opacity, [and] if one introduces this opacity . . . consciousness is no longer a spontaneity."[39] Said differently, an ego that stands behind acts of consciousness is ultimately outside of the scope of experience. It is not an appearance *for* consciousness, precisely because it represents the conditions which make possible the appearance of objects in general. This would imply that there exists an aspect of conscious life of which there is no immediate self-awareness. Consciousness is no longer self-consciousness through and through, which means that it cannot be the absolute existence from which phenomenology must start. Hence, for Sartre, the transcendental ego introduces into consciousness a type of existence that is broken off from appearing to consciousness.[40]

Sartre's critique of the phenomenological reduction is heavily shaped by his commitment to this idea of an absolute consciousness that is strictly a movement of intentionality. He understands, in the theory of intentionality, the determination that all consciousness is consciousness of an object that is not-consciousness, which establishes that "consciousness" and "world" are separate in abstraction only. A world of objects is no longer separated off from consciousness, since the latter is exhaustively an (intentional and self-aware) engagement with that world. If the ego is not an appearance (dependent on the absolute existence of consciousness), but is, instead, a structure of consciousness, existing independently of its appearing, "we would then [again] be in the presence of a monad."[41] There would be introduced into consciousness an aspect that is not implicated in the world via intentionality, hence potentially re-creating the problem of how two distinct beings are able to relate. So while the theory of intentionality implicates consciousness in the world wholly and completely, the ego, as transcendental, cuts it off into a private and inaccessible monad.[42]

Sartre's Position: Consciousness is an Impersonal Field of Spontaneity

Sartre takes the ego "out" of consciousness, and places it on the side of objects of experience, as an object *for* consciousness. Not only does this position place consciousness back into the world, as completely a reflection of "world," but it is also one that is, according to Sartre, more phenomenologically sound than Husserl's egological position. Sartre presents evidence to show that, at the most immediate level of experience (the prereflective level), there is no ego that either inhabits or accompanies acts of consciousness. Put otherwise, it is only through a subsequent *reflective* act that we "discover" our ego as the "subject" of our intentional experience.[43] However, this is only because a reflective act of consciousness can spontaneously *create, for itself,* an ego on which to reflect. "The consciousness which says *I Think* is precisely not the consciousness which thinks."[44] Hence, every time we apprehend an ego (*our* ego), it is already "not us," or not of consciousness.

One of phenomenology's founding premises—that we ought not to affirm more (or less) than concrete experience would allow—grounds Sartre's argument for the transcendent nature of the ego. "[The] *I* of the *I Think* is an object grasped with neither apodictic nor adequate evidence," he tells us. "The evidence is not apodictic, since by saying *I* we affirm far more than we know. It is not adequate, for the *I* is presented as an opaque reality whose content would have to be unfolded."[45] At the most concrete level, there is no 'I.' This does not mean that Husserl's ego does not exist; it only means that it is a transcendent object for reflective consciousness, and not a transcendental structure of prereflective consciousness. To be sure, the ego differs from all other objects of experience, insofar as it is apprehended as the *source of origin* of conscious acts. In other words, consciousness creates the ego as though *it* were created *by* the ego. But insofar as the ego is necessarily transcendent (a necessity that "saves" the intentional and absolute structure of consciousness), Sartre points out that it is but a "pseudo-spontaneity." "The ego is a *virtual* [emphasis mine] locus of unity, and consciousness constitutes it in a *direction contrary to* that actually taken by the production."[46] The personal aspect of consciousness (that aspect apprehended when we take on a reflective attitude toward ourselves) is subsequent to a more prior *impersonal* consciousness—impersonal precisely because *all* objects of experience, including the object "representative" of the "self," lies outside.[47]

From this analysis, one begins to see the radical sense in which Sartre determines consciousness to be spontaneous. More importantly, according to Sartre, Husserl's theory of intentionality *requires* that consciousness be spontaneous in this radical sense. Sartre's portrayal of the freedom of consciousness is not only nonegological, but it presupposes that consciousness is *never* identical with itself. The formal model of transcendence that is developed in *Being and Nothingness* is founded on this noncoincidence. The ego is not constitutive of the structure of consciousness, precisely because this structure is exhaustively, "an absolute escape from." Though consciousness spontaneously constructs the ego, as a structure that might "hold it in place," it is that very spontaneity which ultimately threatens the ego's existence, from all sides.[48] "[Man] has the impression of ceaselessly escaping from himself, of overflowing himself, of being surprised by riches which are always unexpected."[49]

II. The Role of Being in Sartre's Theory of Consciousness

Thus far, I have presented what Sartre identifies to be the consequences of Husserl's theory of intentionality, the most specific of which is Sartre's nonegological (or impersonal) conception of consciousness. At this stage in my analysis, I determine the ways in which this account (and critique) of Husserl determines what *Being and Nothingness* develops as the relationship between consciousness and being. For Sartre, consciousness "is" only as a reflection of all that is (all of being). In its reflecting of being, there has already been an ordering or arrangement of being such that, through consciousness, there is a reflection of "world."[50] An egological account destroys the lucidity required for this process of reflection, which is why the ego must be, for Sartre, on the "outside." His ontological framework functions to support his understanding of these notions of transcendence and intentionality.[51]

To be sure, a predifferentiated being (what is "not-yet-world") is never a phenomenon for consciousness, and in this regard, being is *transphenomenal*. The idea of a transphenomenal being plays a decisive role in the realism of Sartre's project, insofar as the world, though posited by consciousness, also exists independently of consciousness. In other words, objects are truly transcendent to consciousness insofar as they rest on the foundation of a transphenomenal being. To be sure, the qualities of these objects ultimately refer to the active constituting of consciousness. Said otherwise, the very possibility of there being "objects" with meanings and interconnections is a consequence of consciousness-as-intentionality, and not a consequence of being itself.[52] But transphenomenal being does account for the sense in which these objects are given over as independent of consciousness.

I am interested in tracing the implications of this "givenness" of the world for Sartre's conception of facticity (or, more precisely, for his conception of the relationship between facticity and transcendence). I argue that, despite Sartre's somewhat inconsistent rendition of its implications, facticity does not undermine the formal (or structural) transcendence of consciousness. This is primarily because the "brute" (or factical) aspects of experience will always show up as already meaningful for consciousness, which is to say that its formal spontaneity persists, uncompromised. In this regard, my work is in conversation with the analyses of scholars like Thomas Anderson and Thomas Martin, who both grapple with what might have been Sartre's position on the implications of consciousness's facticity. Martin writes of two "distinct" readings of Sartrean facticity, one of which understands "human reality" as "simply pure, unconditioned freedom as transcendence."[53] He identifies a second possible reading that would understand "human reality as transcendence *and* facticity, or, more precisely, that freedom is always situated such that transcendence and facticity are inseparable . . ."[54] Although Thomas Anderson also recognizes the unitary "facticity-transcendence" dyad, his interpretation of this "inseparability" means that, for Sartre, "[no] matter what its facticity or situation, freedom always nihilates, denies, detaches itself from it by intending nonexisting ends."[55] In other words, on Anderson's account, Martin's first reading of Sartre very much collapses into the second (and what, according to Martin, is an alternative) reading. According to Martin, if transcendence and facticity come hand-in-hand, it is also the case that facticity "limits" the workings of freedom, even though this limitation is not a determination.[56] From Anderson's reading, this is ultimately evidence for an understanding of Sartrean freedom as "absolute and without limit.," since it is always the case that those limiting obstacles/resistances acquire their "coefficients of adversity" from the transcendence of consciousness.[57]

Though these distinctions are useful for a reading of Sartre, their significance does not quite pertain to my juxtaposing Sartre's work alongside Levinas's. This will become clear as my claims are further developed. However, suffice it to say that I am in agreement with Anderson's position that a Sartrean phenomenological analysis illustrates a total freedom of consciousness. Nevertheless, I additionally argue that the concrete descriptions employed are always in tension with the formal structures (of radical spontaneity) that Sartre intends them to illustrate. This is not to say (along with Detmer) that *Being and Nothingness* gives an absolute freedom in an ontological sense and a more limited freedom in the practical sense. My reading of Sartre alongside Levinas will reveal that, even for the more practical account of freedom, Sartre's formal structures would have it that freedom is always more fundamental, and exhaustively accounts for "human reality." Hence, any and all "limitation" that one identifies at this practical level will ultimately support the premise of "ontologically absolute freedom." My work argues that, to the extent that they resonate with the work found in Levinas, Sartre's concrete descriptions potentially reveal entirely alternative formal structures.

In his essay on the history of existentialism, Jean Wahl explains that Sartre's phenomenology borrows heavily from Heidegger. Like Heidegger, "Sartre has 'the ontological concern,' the need to study the idea of Being . . ."[58] From his essay on the imagination, we already see Sartre's endeavors to "fix" phenomenology's failure to address this idea of being. "Now phenomenological descriptions [done upon performing the reduction] can discover, for instance, that the very structure of transcendental consciousness implies that consciousness is constitutive *of a world*. But it is evident that they will not teach us that consciousness must be constitutive *of* such a world that is exactly the one where we are, with its earth, its animals, its men and the story of these men. We are here in the presence of a primary and irreducible fact which presents itself as a contingent and irrational specification of the noematic essence of the *world*."[59] As has already been shown, Sartre's position is critical of the phenomenological reduction insofar as it is gratuitous and detrimental to the phenomenological method. Now, we also see that, for Sartre, Husserl's bracketing leaves unaccounted for the givenness or resistance that consciousness encounters in its (free) constituting activity. As such, the reduction fails to give an account of the precise relation between existence (or rather, that mode of existence of consciousness) and the Being that "lies behind" existence.

Husserl's reduction does make clear that the meaning of phenomena that constitute our experience is to be found in their manner of being intended by consciousness. So, for instance, the meaning of a rose would depend on that act of consciousness, of which it is a noematic correlate. If one apprehends the rose as pleasing, its meaning is "rose as pleasing." Conversely, it could mean "rose to be avoided," were one *not* to apprehend it as pleasing (in the case of some adverse allergy to rose pollen, for example). The reduction establishes the absolute existence of consciousness, by showing that the phenomenon of the world depends, for its being, on a transcendental constituting field that is itself independent of the being of the world. However, in *The Psychology of Imagination*, Sartre tells us that this exercise leaves out the fact that "the matter" of these noema cannot be accounted for solely in the acts of consciousness. To put this differently, there is a noetic difference between an imagined-rose and a perceived-rose. The latter appears as an object existing "out there" in the world, while the former does not. According to Sartre, it is impossible for consciousness to "cause" an imagined-rose to appear as a perceived-rose, precisely because the *matter* of these two *noemas* is different. In this sense, the phenomenological reduction does not "give Being its due."[60] In Thomas Busch's discussion of the influence of the phenomenological reduction on Sartre's novel, *Nausea*, he points out that Husserl himself makes similar concessions. "[In] his discussion of the 'nullifying of the world,' [Husserl] said with regard to actual experience patterns, 'we cannot extract such patterns purely from the essence of perception in general.'"[61] Hence, it seems as though Husserl recognized what Sartre points out as a shortcoming of the reduction, which might indicate that he understood his objectives as simply varying from Sartre's. Nonetheless, insofar as Sartre *does* address it, he finds it necessary to augment the "noematic essence of the world" (completely derived from acts of consciousness) with an account of the underlying "matter" (which *cannot* be derived from acts of consciousness) on which these noema rest.

Transphenomenal Being

In this vein, his ontology presents two categories (or modes) of being—that mode which is consciousness (or being-for-itself) and the mode which is nonconscious (or being-in-itself).[62] The objects that make an appearance (to, or for, consciousness) all exist in the mode of being-in-itself, which is to say that they "are what they are." This is in contrast to the manner of the being of consciousness. Sartre's "human reality" is for itself, and as such, escapes the confines of identity. This would then assure that the mode of being of consciousness is exhausted by its being in relation to something other than itself. For Sartre, it would also assure that consciousness is always radically free, insofar as it is always free from the restrictions of identity.[63] To reiterate, both modes of being rest on a single "transphenomenal being" that will account for the matter of both consciousness and "world," though remaining beyond the phenomena of which existence is comprised. In other words, transphenomenal being supports the two "ways of being" that Sartre identifies, while never making an appearance *for* consciousness. This is not to compromise the absolute existence of consciousness, or its radical spontaneity. Within Sartre's ontology, consciousness is maintained as that absolute point of certainty for the phenomenological enterprise. In this sense, its existence (or appearing) is not relative to something other than itself. So though Sartre will place consciousness in a necessary and nihilating relation to transphenomenal being, consciousness continues to bear an absolute existence that is independent of the phenomenon.[64]

To reiterate, consciousness is always consciousness *of* something. Transphenomenal being ensures this independent (or rather, transcendent) nature of objects of experience insofar as it presides as the "materiality" of the phenomenon itself. This means that consciousness must move *out* of a region of interiority, "confronted with a concrete and full presence which *is not* consciousness,"[65] in order for there to be an appearance for consciousness. For Sartre, an adequate account of how this takes place necessarily opens onto the question of being—that which is other than consciousness, and on which the phenomena of experience rest. In so doing, "we have left pure appearance [pure phenomenological description] and have arrived at full being."[66] Hence, underlying all phenomena for consciousness, there is this fully "present" being. It is only in this sense that these phenomena are truly transcendent, and that a (freely transcending) movement of intentionality can be accounted for. Being-in-itself does not make an appearance as such, so its pure presence is in a strictly non-phenomenological sense. This does not mean that phenomena hide some "noumenal reality" behind its existence-as-appearing. In other words, Sartre is not re-creating the "double relativity of Kant's *Erscheinung*."[67] Consciousness "touches" transphenomenal being most immediately, insofar as, through the movement of intentionality, it appears (which is to say that its appearance is already "with meaning") *in the form of* the phenomena that comprise experience. Hence, transphenomenal being reveals itself directly as a meaningful world that is *there* for consciousness.[68]

Subsequently, without this field of transphenomenal being, consciousness never engages in a transcendence, or moves outside of itself. In other words, without this grounding of the world of appearances, there is nothing that avoids an idealist conception of what it means to have an experience. So transphenomenal being supports the movement of a spontaneous intentionality, forcing consciousness outside itself in an experience of an object. But it is only through the intentionality of consciousness that being-in-itself is a "world." So even though Being, as "what-it-is," stands independently, its *meaning* is relative to the being of consciousness.

According to Sartre, it is ultimately from this idea of being that we obtain the full implications of Husserl's theory of intentionality. In grounding objects of experience on an underlying transphenomenal being, Sartre truly emphasizes the sense in which the intentional movement places consciousness "out there" in a world that will contain certain "coefficients of adversity." As consciousness surpasses toward the transcendent phenomenon, in a movement of intentionality, it also encounters those "given" aspects of being, and of *its* being.[69] As the "matter" of phenomena, transphenomenal being is given over to consciousness (or rather, consciousness finds itself faced with it) in a nonconstitutive relationship.[70] Sartre captures this factical aspect of consciousness in the claim that consciousness is always a *situated* movement of intentionality, transcending toward objects of experience within the confines of facticity. In other words, concrete freedom is always a situated freedom.[71] However, the fundamental relation that Sartre identifies between consciousness and transphenomenal being is such that these conceptions of facticity and "being in situation" do not undermine the radical freedom of consciousness. Though transphenomenal being seems to indicate an aspect of the human condition that resembles a fullness of being, it ultimately functions as a *support* for the freedom of consciousness.[72] This becomes clear is a more thorough understanding of the relationship between consciousness and being, particularly insofar as this relationship is founded on negativity.

III. Intentionality Rests on a Negative Relation to Being

Since being-in-itself appears, as a phenomenon, through the being of consciousness, Sartre determines that both (being-in-itself and consciousness) are distinct in abstraction only. "[The] concept of being has this peculiarity of being divided into two regions without communication, [and] we must nevertheless explain how these two regions can be placed under the same heading."[73] The being of the phenomenon (transphenomenal being) and the being of consciousness are one and the same, existing "without communication" only insofar as they both represent distinct modalities of this one being.

The intentionality of consciousness rests on this necessary "communication" or relationship. As a movement of intentionality, consciousness transcends toward that which it "is not"—the transcendent object whose manner of being is "being-in-itself." However, this does not mean that Sartre proposes two distinct *beings*. There is being, inseparably one, but determined through two phenomenologically distinct yet relating modes.[74] The *mode* of the being of consciousness "is not" the *mode* of the being of the in-itself. It is across this fundamental negation that being-in-itself and being-for-itself relate. More importantly, through transcendence *as* negation, Sartre reinforces the absolute freedom of consciousness. "[Being-for-itself] is free because consciousness, as a negating activity, introduces nothingness into the world . . . The nothingness with which consciousness encases its objects . . . separates being-for-itself from the world of cause and effect, thus removing being-for-itself from determination and giving it radical freedom."[75] In this sense, the freedom of consciousness is despite the underlying condition of (transphenomenal) being. Furthermore, it is *because* Sartre construes this relation with being as one of negativity that he can also determine consciousness to be, exhaustively, a movement of intentionality.[76]

Consciousness is the Source of the 'Not' in Being

From Sartre's critique of Husserl in *The Transcendence of the Ego*, consciousness is always "consciousness of that which is not consciousness." It must be a lucid reflection of all of being. For this reason, Sartre places the ego *outside* of consciousness, and into the world. In a similar sense, Sartre places *all* of being outside of consciousness—consciousness *is* only as a radical negation of being's fullness. In order for consciousness to exist as strictly a revealing intuition of that which is not-consciousness, all of being must necessarily reside on the *outside*.

Sartre cites, as the phenomenological "evidence" for this, those interrogative acts that permeate our human experience. When consciousness formulates a question, there is introduced, into the fullness of being-in-itself, the "lack" across which being reveals itself as an *absence*. "In every question we stand before a being which we are questioning . . . [and the] permanent possibility of non-being, outside of and within, conditions our questions about being."[77] In other words, the act of questioning is always accompanied by the possibility that the response (to that question) might be in the negative. This means that this act must originate in a creative freedom, through which being can appear as "what it is *not*," despite its fullness and density. The condition for this possibility lies in consciousness's ability to introduce "a certain negative element . . . into the world."[78] It is in this sense that Sartre conceives of the being of consciousness as the "not" of transphenomenal being (the "not" of this plenitude). Through negation, consciousness surpasses this ontological density, to represent that mode through which there can be creative spontaneity.

One of Sartre's examples describes a person entering a crowded room, expecting to find her acquaintance there. As her eyes peruse each face in the crowd, and until she encounters her acquaintance, these faces, in their positivity, appear for her as what they "are not." The realization that her friend is nowhere to be found is, simultaneously, an introduction of the quality of a lack into the fullness of the room. It shows up as a room that "lacks" her friend. This negative meaning cannot originate from being itself, since being simply "is what it is," or pure fullness. As such, it must come from that original negation (that original "germ of nothingness") at the heart of being, which is consciousness. This relation of negativity allows Sartre to secure a real intentional movement of consciousness. Said otherwise, the "communication" between being-in-itself and being-for-itself is one that grounds the radical freedom, spontaneity, and transcendence of consciousness.

In the end, Sartre's is not an account guilty of reproducing an idealism, since consciousness is always conscious of that which is "not consciousness." It is also not the case that consciousness and phenomena are two distinct *beings* in need of reuniting, since the being on which the phenomena rest is the same being on which consciousness rests.[79] This relation of negation grounds the intentional structure of consciousness, insofar as the latter (nonbeing) is a "consciousness of" all of being (revealed immediately in the phenomenon of "world").

IV. Sartre's Model of Transcendence: The Movement of a Radically Free Consciousness

In his discussion of the role of negation in *Being and Nothingness*, Peter Caws points out that "[it] is Sartre's merit to have seen that negation does not belong in the objective world . . ."[80] This reference to an "objective world" is used in a very imprecise sense, since, for Sartre, "objectivity" is already a part of a revelation of the meaning of being. It is already a noematic correlate to acts of consciousness, and as such, populated with negativities. We might understand Caws's statement to mean that it is *through consciousness* and not by virtue of the brute "matter" of the world, that there is negation. Hence, Caws merits Sartre for identifying consciousness as the proper source of the "nots" that constitute everyday experience.[81]

This negative formulation of existence has its foundation in *The Transcendence of the Ego*, where Sartre says, "[The] spontaneity [that is consciousness] *goes toward* the I, rejoins the I, lets the I be glimpsed beneath its limpid density, but it itself is given above all as *individuated and impersonal* spontaneity."[82] This is yet another instance in which the transcendent nature of the ego is used to underscore the *ecstatic* nature of consciousness. Consciousness is a spontaneity, which perpetually moves toward not only the "I object," but toward *all* objects of experience. Sartre determines that it is through this ecstatic movement that consciousness takes on a separate (distinct) existence, which is to say that individuation occurs (despite the "I" being an object *for* consciousness) through these ekstases.[83] Phyllis Kenevan points out that consciousness is "shattered in its very being" by these movements. "[Consciousness] is a split process of present intention, past retentions, and future protensions . . . it is [also] split into pre-reflective and reflective consciousness, and it is non-positional *self*-consciousness of a positional consciousness of something *other* than itself."[84] Consciousness is its past, but in the mode of no longer being it. It is its future, but in the mode of not-yet being it. The present is similarly constituted across instants to which consciousness relates through these past and future *ekstases*. From Sartre's analysis, there is no instantaneous present when consciousness "is what it is," precisely because it relates to both itself and to being ecstatically.[85] Likewise, in the case of positional self-reflection, consciousness is no longer the self it apprehends in certain *self*-reflective acts. One might say that it *is* this self, but in the mode of no longer being it.

These ekstases emphasize that consciousness has, for its being, the being of that which it is not. It *makes* itself not-be the objects of experience as well as the self on which it reflects, by a perpetual surpassing or transcendence. Hence, in order to understand the sense in which consciousness exists as a nothingness of being, one must come to terms with this negating, transcending (intentional) activity of consciousness that, for Sartre, exhausts consciousness's mode of being.

The Free Creativity of Consciousness

In making itself not-be (its "self," its past or its future), consciousness rejects, or withdraws from all of being.[86] Transcending negation "is presumably a means of detaching human beings from the causal nexus of events,"[87] and this is included in Sartre's sense of radical freedom.[88] Its intentional structure requires that it must make itself "not be" that of which there is consciousness (or "not be" all of the revelation of being). Of this relationship between transcendence and negation, Thomas Martin writes, "[In] being conscious of X, consciousness is *not* X. In this way, consciousness *transcends* its object."[89] To be sure, there is a difference to be noted between what it means for consciousness to "transcend its object," on the one hand, and for consciousness to "transcend being," on the other. This is insofar as Sartre's conception of an object of experience is what makes an appearance for consciousness (is already a phenomenon), and whose existence is apprehended as independent of the existence of consciousness. "Being" (in the pure and undifferentiated sense) is not part of the phenomenal world, which is to say that it precisely does *not* make an appearance. Both consciousness and its object of experience represent two modes or ways of being, which places both in an ontological relation with this transphenomenal being. Nevertheless, Sartre's *phenomenological* account of consciousness holds that this relation is one of negativity. For the purpose of this work (which is to bring Sartre and Levinas into dialogue across conceptions of transcendence and freedom), it suffices to determine that being-for-itself (as a mode of transphenomenal being) is exhaustively a negation, or emptiness of being. On the contrary, being-in-itself is phenomenologically accounted for as a *fullness* of being. To this end, I understand Sartre's analysis as one in which the intentionality of consciousness also implies that consciousness is a total movement of transcendence of being, distancing itself from the full positivity of being.

It is in this vein that Sartre writes, "[This] nothingness [the nothingness of consciousness] is not anything except human reality apprehending itself as excluded from being and perpetually beyond being."[90] The existence of consciousness (its existing as nonbeing) signifies the "beyond being" that is at the end of a journey of transcendence.[91] He offers this model of transcendence (as negation) as that which provides the conditions for the possibility of experience. Hence, the phenomenological account in *Being and Nothingness* sustains the claim that experiences in general (and the ones Sartre describes in particular) are concretizations of this formal model of transcendence. Put otherwise, transcendence-as-intentionality holds the formal conditions for the possibility of experience.[92] In a typical experience, consciousness makes itself "not be" the particular object that appears, by carrying out a (negating) surpassing movement. The distance thus set up, between itself and the phenomena, conditions the possibility of experience. Throughout *Being and Noth-*

ingness, Sartre's analysis of concrete experience underscores this formal structure, and as such, his position is that the experience of the world is conditioned by this conception of transcendence. "This *nothing* is human reality itself as the radical negation [the radical transcendence of being] by means of which the world [of which there is experience] is revealed."[93] Because consciousness has always already gone beyond being (already negated being), objects are able to show up for us as such.[94] What follows are two such cases in which, according to Sartre, this formal structure of surpassing is concretized.

The Waiter in Bad Faith

Sartre's description of the waiter in bad faith is particularly pertinent, because it reiterates the thesis in *The Transcendence of the Ego*, which is that consciousness, as a radical spontaneity, perpetually surpasses the "self" it freely creates *for* itself. "[From] within, the waiter in the café cannot be immediately a café waiter in the sense that this inkwell is an inkwell . . . as if, from the very fact that [he sustains] this role in existence [he does] not transcend it from every side."[95] Sartre identifies the waiter's exaggerated movements and all-too-eager mannerisms as evidence of his efforts to convince himself that his being is exhausted by this waiter-identity. But this is accomplished only in bad faith, a self-deception through which consciousness exists as though it were trapped within the fullness of being. The actual mode of existence of consciousness means that this is a failed endeavor. David Detmer's discussion of bad faith clearly establishes that the "vagueness and ambiguity" of our human condition establish the ideal breeding grounds for such projects of (or in) bad faith. He reminds us that, according to Sartre, consciousness "is what it is not, and is not what it is." "[This] ambiguity facilitates a kind of self-deception in which I can play up either the sense in which I am my facticities, or the sense in which I transcend and am not them."[96] Neither option is a complete truth, but in so doing, neither is a complete lie. The waiter already exists at a distance from his waiter-identity, since it is an object *for* him (on which he sometimes explicitly contemplates at times, or at other times, implicitly uses as the motivation for his fundamental project). He *is* this identity in the mode of "not being it," which is to say that there is a sense in which he has already transcended "himself" from all sides.[97] Robert Bernasconi writes that, curiously enough, it is through his exaggerated motions (employed precisely in an attempt to *realize* his "waiter-ness") that the waiter has surpassed his being a waiter. This harkens to the "slippery ambiguity" between transcendence and facticity, which David Detmer describes. The movements of the waiter go over and beyond the call of whatever duty a French waiter might have, and as such, "[he] succeeds in rejecting the attempt to reduce him to nothing more than being a waiter."[98]

Sartre's concrete descriptions of examples of bad faith work to buttress his claim that consciousness is an absolute freedom. It is only as free (in this sense) that consciousness can engage in bad faith.[99] The waiter is a nothingness of being who, *as* a nothingness of being, attempts to put on the fullness of being. Ultimately, any attempt to coincide with ourselves ends in failure, but it is a failure whose possibility rests on the condition of the freedom of consciousness, or a failure that *indicates* precisely how free we are. The condition on which the waiter freely creates himself is that he already escapes what he makes of himself. To use another one of Sartre's examples of bad faith, "If I make myself sad, it is because I am not sad—the being of the sadness escapes me by and in the very act by which I affect myself with it."[100] Again, this underscores the radical sense of Sartre's conception of freedom. Consciousness must make of itself what it must be; "making sustains [its] being, [because] it is never sustained by being."[101]

The ideas espoused in *The Transcendence of the Ego* are fully developed here, in these descriptions of bad faith. "[Consciousness] determines its existence at each instant, without our being able to conceive anything *before* it. Thus each instant of our conscious life reveals to us a creation *ex nihilo*. Not a new *arrangement*, but a new existence."[102] Sartre uses this need for radically new birth as evidence of an unbounded freedom. In the chapters that follow, this will be a noteworthy point of contact with the Levinasian analysis of existence, insofar as the latter also presents a phenomenology of "the instant" in terms of radical birth. However, unlike what we see in Sartre, Levinas uses this to ground his conception of the human condition as one burdened by the *obligation* to exist, or to take up one's existence with effort. I show that, despite what can be regarded as vastly differently interpretative analyses, these moments in Sartre and Levinas are similar in many respects.

The Experience of Anguish

Of this free creativity, Sartre writes, "There is something distressing for each of us, to catch in the act this tireless creation of existence of which *we* [our ego] are not the creators. At this level man has the impression of ceaselessly escaping from himself, of overflowing himself, of being surprised by riches which are always unexpected."[103] Here, Sartre describes the experience of anguish, whereby consciousness apprehends itself as radically free.[104] In the mode of bad faith, consciousness is always aware (at least prereflectively) that its mode of existence is a self-deception. In other words, the waiter is aware that his existence has no objective value (or value independent of what comes out of his own constituting activity). As such, *he* is the one who freely decides this to be a justified mode of existence.[105] In this sense, anguish always exists as a possibility that percolates under acts of bad faith. In other words, the individual can, at any moment, apprehend himself as the sole author of his being, with his freedom being the only and most ultimate source of justification.

A significant construction of consciousness's creativity is the world's network of value. An object is of value insofar as I freely take on a worldview, in which this object has a place. Sartre's account of bad faith is like Husserl's "natural attitude," since consciousness understands value to be an objective "given," independent of its constitutive powers. Anguish would signal the "falling away" of such attitudes, in order to apprehend value as meaningful solely within the parameters of a fundamental project. In a similar sense, the waiter, in a possible experience of anguish, apprehends all those objective features of his existence—"the obligation of getting up at five o'clock, of sweeping the floor of the shop before the restaurant opens, of starting the coffee pot going"—as valuable only within his *chosen* fundamental project of being (or "playing at being") a waiter.

On Sartre's account of transcendence-as-intentionality, the experience of anguish reveals our absolute freedom. We freely create ourselves (by surpassing being toward that which we must become), and as such, we are always free to take on an entirely different fundamental project. Sartre's descriptions of vertigo, both in *The Transcendence and the Ego* and in *Being and Nothingness*, is a clear portrayal of this. The individual undergoes vertigo when, on reflecting on the extent to which he is free, he realizes that *nothing* makes the route contrary to the one he chooses less legitimate, or less possible, than the one he aims to realize. So even though we might apprehend certain life-paths as "fearful" or "to be avoided," a pursuit of them always remains *our* option. "A fear felt in a situation when one is close to a precipice on a narrow mountain path concerns the possibility of an accident; falling off the cliff (being pushed over, slipping on a loose stone)."[106] All precautions are taken to avoid this tragedy by choosing the path of caution as we move along the cliff. Yet, in the midst of realizing that choice (by perhaps looking avidly for loose rocks on the ground, so as to avoid them), we can encounter our freedom to realize yet another possibility of actually *hurling* ourselves over the precipice. There is nothing (save "ourselves") standing between our current project and this (opposing) project of suicide. Reflectively apprehending one's freedom in this way constitutes an experience of anguish. "Such anguish would concern one's own possibility of *deliberately* [emphasis mine] throwing oneself over the precipice."[107] Both choices are equally "legitimate," in the sense that their standards of legitimacy are but free constructions. This is why Sartre, in *The Transcendence of the Ego*, describes the experience of freedom as the experience of escaping oneself, "from all sides."[108] Freedom has no limits, in the sense that it is limited by itself only.[109] This radical sense of freedom implies that, unlike the being of the phenomenon, consciousness depends on itself alone for its existence.

VI. Facticity in Consciousness's Relation to Being

To reiterate, Sartre understands Husserl's *epoché* to be dismissive of the real contributions of the brute fact of being to an experience of the world.[110] So alongside his account of radical freedom and the absolute existence of consciousness, there is a full recognition of the effects of pure being. To be sure, the absolute existence of consciousness is affirmed when the "objectivity" of the world falls away. But Sartre also recognizes the sense in which this free creative activity is explicitly informed by the brute fact of being. Consciousness is a free and negating transcendence of being, but its experience is also coupled with an inevitable facticity.[111] This means that consciousness encounters the being that underlies the phenomena of experience while, at the same time, existing as a free and transcending negation of being. In this sense, he argues that both transcendence and facticity are equally fundamental to the structure of consciousness, equally contributing to the immediate truth of experience.

In this vein, Sartre writes, "much more than he appears 'to make himself,' man seems 'to be made' by climate and the earth, race and class, language, the history of the collectivity of which he is a part, heredity, the individual circumstances of his childhood, acquired habits, the great and small events of his life."[112] Concrete experience is indeed shaped by these factors, insofar as we cannot choose that they be other than what they are. As a result, such "givens" are often encountered as obstacles we face in realizing our fundamental projects. According to Sartre, this is because, at the foundation of the nothingness of being-for-itself is the fullness of being-in-itself, which means that, by its very upsurge into existence, consciousness is "hemmed in by being" from all sides. In this sense, we always find ourselves having to negotiate certain features of our existence—the "thereness" of our body (or rather, *that* we are embodied), social place, past experiences, and our environment (to name a few).

These "givens" show up for consciousness as certain "resistances," but, according to Sartre, this resistance is already evidence of a nihilating (free) activity. "[This] residue [of pure being] is far from being originally a limit for freedom; in fact, it is thanks to this residue—that is, to the brute in-itself as such—that freedom arises as freedom."[113] In other words, freedom is concretized as the freedom to encounter and transcend obstacles, in pursuit of a given end. Hence, Sartre's formalized account of a consciousness that is "hemmed in by being" does not mean that it is *determined* by being.[114] Nothing other than consciousness itself determines consciousness. This brute presence of being, which is at the foundation of consciousness, only means that (concretely) freedom is always engaged. "Outside of this engagement the notions of freedom, of determination, of necessity lose all meaning."[115]

In demonstration, I return to the waiter in bad faith. Sartre describes this individual as "playing at being a waiter in a café,"[116] and this is suggested by his exaggerated gestures, as he attempts to coincide completely with his waiter-identity. However, along with this, Sartre also points out that "there is no doubt that [the individual is] in a sense a café waiter—otherwise [he] could just as well call [himself] a diplomat or a reporter."[117] Though the café waiter is always more free than the in-itself identity to which his antics reduce him, it is not the case that the waiter can make of himself something other than a waiter while he carries out his duties. "My Manhattan is not served to me by someone who is masquerading as a waiter. The waiter plays at being a waiter, as opposed to imitating waiters for his amusement, because he or she *is* [emphasis mine] a waiter."[118] The waiter encounters real (socioeconomic) resistances that prevent him from instantaneously switching fundamental projects and thus, professions. At the same time, he is in bad faith, because he acts as though these limitations were not ultimately illuminated by an end that he (freely) posits. To be sure, any attempt on his part to realize the being of a diplomat or reporter (at the instant in which he is a waiter) would fail. However, Sartre points out, "success is not important to freedom."[119] For this reason, Sartre's conception of facticity, in which resonates the obstacles that we encounter as a result of the fullness of transphenomenal being, does not make us less than absolutely free. Freedom means that consciousness can posit for itself an end, void of all external determination, and without any pregiven necessity. This way of positing ends (or goals) attests to a "nihilation of being" or to freedom. An engaged consciousness already indicates an escape from being, precisely because Sartre's account of engagement does not preclude, but rather reinforces, a free projection of ends.

The only necessity imposed on consciousness is the necessity to be free. In other words, consciousness *must* freely posit ends for itself and surpasses being as a result, since it is not free *not* to be free. "[The] fact of not being able not to be free is the *facticity* of freedom."[120] In this sense, consciousness exists contingently, possessing a freedom it has not chosen. So though there is no reason for my being (other than what I freely create), I must exist or project ecstatically beyond being. Sartre identifies this (contingent) existence as part of consciousness's *facticity*, insofar as freedom is an *obligation* to be free, without reprieve. Freedom is not chosen, but is rather the burden that consciousness must bear. In this sense, facticity and contingency point to a similar feature of consciousness, which is why Sartre refers to them as "really one." They both refer to the transphenomenal being that is the foundation of consciousness, but without consciousness being able to own this foundation.

This is captured Sartre's conception of "situation." "We shall use the term *situation* for the contingency of freedom in the plenum of being of the world inasmuch as this datum, which is there only *in order not to constrain* freedom, is revealed to this freedom only as already *illuminated* by the end which freedom chooses."[121] As situated, consciousness finds itself having to create itself on a foundation it does not own. Its situation is not a free creation (in the strict sense); rather, consciousness is given over to it. There is also a similar conception in Levinas's account of identity, such that subjective life rests on a foundation in existence that can never be incorporated by the freedom of that subjective life. This will be important in my later discussions that bring both thinkers together, but suffice it to say that, unlike Sartre, Levinas does not use this "un-chosen foundation of existence" to support a formal account of radical transcendence from being. For Sartre, insofar as one's situation appears as either against or in the favor of one's projects, the "plenum of being" is already revealed as meaningful, indicating that it has already been surpassed by consciousness. One might read his account of "situation" as indicating consciousness's "positionality" (a term with significant implications in the Levinasian account of the human condition) or rootedness in being. Nonetheless, "being in situation" ultimately emphasizes the exact way in which consciousness, on Sartre's account, has always already transcended that position.

Insofar as a situation is an obstacle to a free project, consciousness has made itself "not be" the obstacle before it. It relates to it across intentionality, and in this sense, the obstacle shows up as the correlate of a (free) act. "There is freedom only in situation, and there is a situation only through a freedom."[122] It is for this reason that it is difficult (if not impossible) to determine where freedom ends and situation begins.[123] Nonetheless, it is clear that the being that surrounds consciousness does not impede, but rather supports the latter's free transcendence. Being is always encountered as meaningful, even though that meaning might be of the order of a certain resistance to the realization of a goal. Even in such instances, consciousness has already escaped its clutches.

I have demonstrated that, for Sartre, the relation between consciousness and being is one of an ecstatic transcendence. Consciousness exists as a negation of being. It dispels all being from it, and in this sense, has surpassed the fullness and determination of being's plenitude. The accounts of facticity, engagement, and "being in situation" lend further support to this. On Sartre's reading, intentionality requires that consciousness negatively transcend being, and as a consequence, he locates the conditions of experience in this formal account of a freely transcending consciousness. In the next chapter, I show that Levinas's model of transcendence is also explicitly shaped by what he determines to be our primary relation with being. However, instead of understanding this relation as one of intentionality, he finds that the human existent is in a more primordial *non*constituting relation with being (or, in more Levinasian, terms, anonymous existence). Out of this analysis will develop a conception of identity varying greatly from Sartre's.

CHAPTER 2

Positionality in Levinas's Transcendence-as-Excendence

In this chapter I establish that Levinas advocates for a model of transcendence that is built on the existent's positionality in (or rivetedness to) Being, to the degree that this structure is necessitated by the subject's concrete experiences.[1] These experiences are, in turn, possible given what he identifies as the structure of human identity (or selfhood).[2] Although Levinas finds, in these experiences, moments when phenomenology's thematization is ruptured, it is ultimately out of the phenomenological method that he conceptualizes transcendence as an *excendence* from being.[3] Said otherwise, the legitimacy of his investigation rests in the priority he gives to the concrete over the formal. By this chapter's end, I show that, for Levinas, it is our rivetedness to Being that makes possible this movement of excendence.[4] His conception of positionality, which captures this rivetedness, shows that, to a large extent, transcendence is concretized in the ways in which we experience embodiment. Positionality introduces a level to the structure of human subjectivity, whereby the subject is a "lived" passivity, despite his or her projections of intentionality through which meaning is created. Levinas's account establishes that it is precisely when that position (or our experience of it) is at its most intense, and *not* in an abnegation from that position, that transcendence-as-excendence takes place.

In being positioned, I am burdened by an obligation that I neither choose nor give meaning to, since the event of positionality categorically remains outside of a constituted "world." In many ways, this Levinasian conception of positionality echoes much of what Sartre describes in facticity. To recall from the last chapter, those factical aspects of consciousness represents a (negating) foundation in being, of which consciousness is *not* the creator. In this regard, Sartrean facticity conveys a transcending movement of consciousness that is always "in situation," or anchored in being. However, Levinas's conception of positionality describes an encounter with being that is more accurately likened to rivetedness than to an anchoring. His phenomenological descriptions, which I discuss in the following sections, account for being as "an oppressive weight that we cannot shake off."[5]

I argue for a resonance between these conceptions of positionality, in Levinas, and facticity, in Sartre. I substantiate my position by showing that, in the concrete descriptions they use to underscore these formal structures, Sartre and Levinas are more similar than they are different. However, for Sartre, identity is fundamentally an "identity in freedom." As we have seen, even at the level of facticity, what is given over to me is a *meaningful* field of phenomena. This field might not be an *intentional* construction for consciousness, but it is, as the very least, *for* consciousness. Nevertheless, I identify this similarity between Sartre's and Levinas's concrete descriptions as calling for a reading of Sartre's phenomenological analysis through the Levinasian account of "transcendence as excendence." I claim that the vulnerability at the heart of consciousness, to which Sartre's descriptive work points, can be better articulated by supplementing Sartre's formal account of experience (and of identity) with those found in Levinas. Because this Levinasian conception of identity is already built on a fundamental positioning in being, his model of transcendence is, in many ways, better suited than Sartre's model to formalize the concrete analysis found in both thinkers. Said otherwise, transcendence-as-excendence better accounts for the possibility of those experiences, which Sartre himself describes in his work.[6]

Much of Levinas's investigations work along the concrete and formal levels simultaneously. He determines his treatment of these levels of inquiry to be distinct from what, in Heidegger, gives the existentiel/existential divide insofar as he reads Heidegger to be rendering the concrete meaningful in terms of a more formal analysis. Levinas sets himself apart from this strategy in his claim that "a logical contradiction cannot judge a concrete event."[7] He grounds his work in an inversion of this order of priority between the "logical" (or formal) and concrete levels of investigation, and identifies a legitimacy of his formal structures solely in their being concretized in experience.[8] This is the strategy that shapes

Levinas's essay in 1934, "Reflections on the Philosophy of Hitlerism," a work that provides the political-historical formulations of his more theoretical ruminations on identity.

The essay argues for an understanding of our fundamental constitution, which is beyond the ideologies in both Western European liberalism and the National Socialism. Levinas resurrects the problem of Cartesian mind-body dualism to underscore the errors in its founding presuppositions. In an attempt to correct such errors, he asks, somewhat rhetorically, "Do we not affirm ourselves in the unique warmth of our bodies long before any blossoming of the Self that claims to be separate from the body?"[9] Here, he draws on the phenomenological truth that all self-assertion is inevitably embodied and inseparable from a positioned historico-cultural context. To be sure, identity can be understood in abstraction from this, but Levinas points out that this is to surpass that most immediate (and thus most phenomenologically verifiable) encounter with ourselves. He shows that the political tenets of National Socialism originate from this deep-seated "feeling of identity" between ourselves and our *position* in being, and unlike liberalism's counterclaims, which hold that we are, before all else, free-floating rational spirits that are perpetually at a distance from being, such regimes claim that the universal truth of humanity lies in biological positioning, or rootedness to our being. I do not focus on the political implications of this position, but rather trace the consequences of Levinas's reading of them for his formal structure of transcendence.

Subsequently, in *On Escape* (first published in1935), Levinas establishes the roots of that account of identity, which would capture his position in "Reflections." *On Escape* introduces the language of "excendence" that conceptualizes the movement desired by a corporeal existence for its promise of accomplishing a radical exit from the being (the being to which Hitlerism presupposes we are enchained). In this sense, *On Escape* presents the first stages of a philosophy that surpasses both biologism's determined embodiment and liberalism's detached freedom. The exiting of ex-cendence does not disregard that important conviction that we are, indeed, riveted to Being (insofar as we are embodied). Rather, ex-cendence preserves this positionality throughout its accomplishment. But the movement *does* formalize an escape that takes place concretely. In other words, Levinas's account establishes that we do break the chains that tie us to our being, but it is in a sense radically otherwise than the drama involved in liberalism's detached rationalism. Our foothold in being remains throughout the exit constituted in ex-cendence.

On Escape also describes the circumstances under which our position in being is felt most intensely, and which will ultimately bear witness to the subject's desire for a radical exit. Some ten years later, in *Existence and Existents*, Levinas "ontologically" backs up these circumstances (and along with it, his model of transcendence), by giving us an account of an encounter with being without which these circumstances would not be possible. To be sure, it is with reserve that I describe *Existence and Existents* as an ontology, precisely because Levinas's work in the text involves venturing "behind" the ontology born of Heidegger, in order to present a more radical notion of being than the one presented in *Being and Time*.[10] According to his reading, Heidegger claims that we have access to Being only insofar as it is always and already the being of *a being*. *Existence and Existents* claims that we have access to a more impersonal and invasive form of being, which is encountered independently of already meaningful beings. Levinas uses certain concrete experiences to demonstrate the possibility of this encounter, and identifies the term "*il y a*" (or "there is") to distinguish this anonymity from Heidegger's Being.[11]

The account of the *il y a* is clearly inspired by Levinas's concern for alterity. He rejects Heidegger's understanding of Being for the same reason he rejects Husserl's transcendental (intentional) consciousness, which is that they advocate a primacy of thematization that fails to preserve the radically Other.[12] In this vein, one might interpret his conception of the *il y a* as an attempt to better equip ontology (and phenomenology) with the means to account for the disturbance, or (non)-place of alterity. The body of his work is shaped by the conviction that this disturbance conditions the possibility of many of our concrete experiences. In turn, his conception of transcendence as an excendence from being is a direct result of this need to account of alterity.[13]

In his 1981 interviews with Philippe Nemo, Levinas responds to a question concerning the Face as follows, "[The] responsibility for the Other, being-for-the-other, seemed to me, as early as that time, [the time of *Existence and Existents*] to stop the anonymous and senseless rumbling of being. It is in the form of such a relation that the deliverance from the 'there is' appeared to me."[14] Here, the sentiments conveyed establish a clear relationship between the disruptive alterity conceptualized in the "there is," and his notion of an identity that is inseparable from an obsessive responsibility toward the Other. Levinas claims that this responsibility renders the need-based or egocentric drama of being as not yet "good enough," and yet that out of which there is no exit. Signified in the form of the *il y a*, Being likens, in this moment, to a realm of imprisonment.

In this regard, Levinas's analysis in *Existence and Existents* determines that the subject's refusal of its position in existence is inseparable from the proximal approach of the Face. In one sense, the *il y a* just *is* an articulation of the vulnerability of being called to such radical responsibility. Yet in another sense, the Face is the aperture out of which there can be an exit from the senseless monstrosity of existence.[15] However, even in this latter case, an excendence from being would rest on the subject's sacrificial substitution of his- or herself for the Other's suffering.

I discuss Levinas's account of the Other in greater detail in chapter 5. For the moment, I emphasize the advantages of Levinas's model of transcendence over Sartre's in accounting for a significant portion of our concrete experience of disruption and vulnerability. Even though these experiences do not, at surface, appear to have an ethical meaning, they do indicate a displacement of the priority of freedom as it pertains to the subject's primordial constitution. Both Sartre and Levinas give descriptions that oppose the view that human freedom is absolute and uncontested. But it is only in Levinas's account of transcendence that this is conceptualized to the degree insinuated in his (and Sartre's) descriptions. This, I hold, renders the Levinasian model of transcendence phenomenologically valuable to the phenomenologist, or to anyone who considers him- or herself a philosopher desiring to be true to the "thing itself."[16]

I. Behind a Liberal Conception of Identity

Freedom, as it has been formulated by the Western liberal tradition, places us at a safe distance from the world with which we interact. Indeed, we are *with* things (Sartre makes sure to emphasize that consciousness is always "engaged"), but in the midst of that immersion, one manages to hold onto a sense of a cohesive self that remains uncompromised by that into which one is immersed (environmental, historical, and physical factors). If this is not the case, it is precisely because we have chosen to deepen our level of involvement. "I stand in the world and I am part of it," Adrian Peperzak tells us. "But I also face it, because nothing is so sovereign and autonomous in the same manner as I am."[17]

In the essay, "Reflections on the Philosophy of Hitlerism," Levinas sets up the groundwork for an alternative conception of identity as a relationship between the "I" (or *moi*) of liberal rationalism and the "self" (or *soi*) to which the *moi* finds itself attached. He claims that liberalism's position of rational detachment too quickly underestimates the affects of history and culture on human identity. It presupposes that our ability to choose can always be exercised above/independently of these considerations. "The equal dignity of each and every soul, which is independent of the material or social conditions of people, does not flow from a theory that affirms, beneath individual differences, an analogy based on a 'psychological constitution.' It is due to the power given to the soul to free itself from *what has been*, from everything that linked it to something or engaged it with something . . ."[18] In this sense, the past (or history) loses its power to condemn (or to limit).[19] We have a past, but because we are fundamentally autonomous, we are not coincident or identical with our past. Choices are encountered as though independent from this "what has been," and for this reason being is given as an opposing force to be reckoned with in the spontaneous play of possibilities for a free-floating "I."

Levinas reads the political sentiments of a movement like National Socialism as a challenge to these liberal conceptions of identity. These sentiments typically include certain dehumanizing conceptions of race, but Levinas claims that it is possible to understand, in such nationalist movements, lessons pertaining to identity that are other than the insidious ones of racism. He points out that Hitlerism comes from the need to "concretize the spirit," or to recapture the more fundamental (embodied) constitution of nations. Levinas identifies Marxism as a movement directed by these concerns, but like liberalism, Marxism retains the possibility for embodied human beings to overcome their material needs by precisely becoming "conscious" of the material conditions that give birth to them.[20] In Hitlerism there is no such avenue of surpassing since those material conditions of our past, history, and most importantly, our bloodline exhaustively account for who we are.

In this sense, nationality is precisely *not* privy to choice insofar as it is shaped by one's bloodline, which, in turn, is heavy with history. Such factors cannot be abnegated or taken up "arbitrarily" because they are predetermined by a destiny in which individuals find themselves, and which they do not possess the luxury to reject.[21] In this sense, we are more authentically (or more primordially) shaped by our destiny than we are a free charting of our own life path. That we are German, Frenchmen, women, or Jews irrevocably dictate, in an important way, how we understand the world, and the decisions we make across that understanding. Hitlerism locates the possibility of an authentic society in an embrace of this inevitability, instead of "infecting" a person's identity with an abstract sense of liberalist freedom. Hence, it is the responsibility of the individual (the German) who desires to be true to self to recognize this truth.

For Levinas, "certain circumstances" seem to vindicate the sentiments of Hitlerism at the expense of more liberal notions of identity. They render an individual's materiality (the fact that he or she is a physical body) inescapable. In this regard, the body is not simply an obstacle against and over which freedom must work that much harder to reign victorious. Rather, Hitlerism finds, in the body, the very core of our identity—we *are* our bodies. In "Reflections," Levinas cites the experience of suffering (or physical pain) as one concretization that confirms this sentiment.[22] In suffering, a distinction between the "I" and the body is never concretized, and thus remains phenomenologically unfounded. The meaning of the experience of suffering lies in precisely *having to suffer*, or in being imprisoned *as* one's body. In this sense, it reveals to us "an absolute position,"[23] a being held fast to being (to its being). Levinas analyses this event of suffering to show that "[its] content merges with the impossibility of detaching oneself from suffering. . . . It is made up of the impossibility of fleeing [from oneself] or retreating."[24] Fundamentally, one does not choose suffering, and when it commences, one cannot choose to *end* suffering (the way the liberal spirit apparently chooses his or her fundamental attitude toward being, and in so doing, already overcomes it).[25] Physical pain uncovers an "indivisible simplicity" between the "I" and its physical being. It shows that embodiment has a value, independent of what it may or may not be for rational freedom, and lies in revealing our rivetedness to, or position in being. Nonetheless, Levinas recognizes that a free subjectivity is accomplished despite this rivetedness.[26] It is accomplished through an *effort* of existing, which a philosophy like Hitlerism dangerously dismisses in its very biology-based notion of identity.

Levinas only alludes to how Nazism fails to exhaustively account for the nature of identity (he does not explicitly speak of Hitlerism's insidiousness, perhaps taking history to successfully speak for this). It is only in 1935, in his essay on escape, that we see his account of what Hitler's biologism ignores about the human condition. *Of Escape* establishes that an understanding of transcendence as an excendence from being trumps the efficacy of a more liberal notion of spontaneity to capture the structure of identity implied in an experience like suffering. Though an experience of suffering reveals the "absence of any dimension of withdrawal," it is also the case that, as we suffer without reprieve, we also refuse that condition of suffering. I *rebel* against the pain, beyond which I am powerless to go. In reducing the human to its biological form, Hitlerism misses this duality within identity.[27] It misses, "in the depths of this unity [of the individual and the body], the duality of a free spirit that struggles against the body to which it is chained."[28] To be sure, this would refer to a "free spirit" that is already otherwise than what the liberal conception articulates. It would be a conception of freedom that is more nuanced than a spontaneous escape from Being.[29] The refusal at the heart of suffering (the refusal to remain where one must remain) uncovers a structure of human identity, which Levinas refers to as "a duality within a unity."[30] The sentiments of Hitlerism are that we do not have the capacity to remain uncompromised by being. This means that any exercise of freedom must, on a fundamental level, begin with these chains to being. However, Hitlerism misdiagnoses our fundamental condition in its claim that we are not free at all. Levinas demonstrates, in *Of Escape*, that it is possible for us to break free from the chains of our past, history, and embodiment in general. But it is precisely in recognizing that one's position in being is *permanent* that escape is possible. "The transcendence of being takes place *in* being, in the finitude of a finite being, and never leaves this finitude behind."[31] He uses the term *excendence* to distinguish this way of understanding "escape" from a more ecstatic sense.

II. Beyond Liberalism and Nationalism

Levinas's position should be understood as a move away from both the abstract freedom of liberalism and biologism's denial of our concrete sense of freedom. Excendence directs us to that concrete sense by precisely incorporating the value of embodiment and of history into an understanding of human transcendence. Sartre's concrete descriptions of freedom, as a situated freedom, also include this intimacy between transcendence and consciousness's immersion in being, and in many ways, his descriptions of embodiment are indistinguishable from Levinas.[32] Nevertheless, it will become clear in subsequent chapters that Levinas's formal account of identity does these descriptions more justice that Sartre's own account of consciousness and its relation to being. The formal level of Levinas's analysis accounts for the sense in which the subject is one with his or her being, while at the same time, refuses this being, thus breaking the chains that tie that subject to being. The implied duality means that, within the very identity of subjectivity, there exists a primordial opposition.[33] I am my "self," but I cannot rest comfortably in myself, which is to say that, in an important sense, the "self" that is mine is foreign to me. This is already a break away from liberalism's presuppositions of identity, which tell us that the only contention pertaining to our human condition is the one between humans and world (or rather, between the individual and the world). As such, Levinas rejects the notion that "[the] conflict from which the revolt ['between human freedom and the brute fact of being'] arises opposes man to the world, not man to himself."[34]

These presuppositions assume that we are at home with ourselves—that we are capable of "gathering ourselves together" so that we are in the world as a unified and autonomous ego. In contrast to this, *Of Escape* presents a certain "world weariness," whereby this apparently autonomous subject is no longer sure of him- or herself. The subject makes choices, apparently in freedom, but not without a doubling back in self-doubt. In other words, this subject does not exercise the freedom to choose without placing those choices, or rather, the very freedom out of which choice is made, into question. There seems to be something more at stake than subjectivity's ecstatic surpassing of beings toward Being—a "something" that might hold him or her accountable for "being in the world," thus implying that this "being in the world" is, perhaps, not a "being *at home* in the world."[35] This sense of "world weariness" refers to a subject (an "I," or an autonomous ego) at odds with itself, as though its mastery of the world, or its quest for a "better being," were not enough to give it peace. Levinas's employment of the term *excendence* distinguishes his from an understanding of transcendence that refers to a surpassing of those restrictions that pertain to the finitude of our being. Instead, he aims to understand transcendence as a radical "getting out" of being, or an undoing of the supposed precedence of being in general. The world weariness to which *Of Escape* refers points to the sense in which, as it signifies in the human condition, being is no longer an adequate answer to the desire for an exit. If misinterpreted, this desire is reduced to a "false transcendence that does not break with being but only seeks to *be* somewhere else, somewhere better, thus reinstating the notion of transcendence already present in the tradition."[36]

The "moi" and the "soi"

Beyond, or rather, "behind" the struggle between "ego" and "world" lies the struggle between the "ego" and its "self." Indeed, the experience of that unbreakable bond with being is ultimately the experience of "that most radical and unalterably binding of chains, the fact that the I is oneself."[37] What is the "ego" in distinction from its "self," and more importantly, what it a "self" that is not yet an "ego"? To recall, Hitlerism (and other such forms of biologism) recognizes a primordial bond between the subject and Being, for which the spirit of liberalism does not account. This bond seems to animate experiences of physical suffering, as well as the experience of kinship of the blood and body, on which rests certain conceptions of "nation." One is German not because one chooses to be (by taking, for instance, some oath of allegiance). Rather, we are German because of our German blood (and our German ancestors). These biological aspects are not addenda to a spirit that is universally human. Rather, Hitlerism tells us that they *are* the very spirit of humanity. Levinas vindicates this sensibility, but identifies them as indicative of only a certain level of the human condition, a significant level, indeed, which ought to be taken into account by all conceptions of identity, political or otherwise.[38] But together with this feeling of identification with the body, there are also that lived rebellion against one's body. To reiterate, the experience of suffering is marked not only by the impossibility of *escaping* one's physical condition, but also by the impossibility of completely *identifying* with one's body. There is a fissure in identity that renders both biological and liberal notions of identity, by themselves, incomplete.

A thorough account of this fissure is given in Levinas's account of the nonsocial aspect of shame. *Of Escape* points out that, unlike what is conveyed by most social or moral conceptions of this experience, that which is "most stinging" in shame has very little to do with limitation and finitude. "Shame does not depend—as we might believe—on the limitation of our being . . . but rather on the very being of our being, on its incapacity to break with itself."[39] In this description, the significance of embodiment is evident, as is the case in Sartre's understanding of shame. Though both accounts are quite similar, I show in chapter 4 that Sartre's understanding of shame is that it is a manifestation of my being taking on a certain objectification for the Other, or a "fullness of being," which is in turn read as a *limitation* that the Other's look places on me.[40] On the other hand, Levinas claims that that from which I would like to hide (in a moment of shame) is more than a limitation of my being.[41] "What appears in shame is thus precisely the fact of being riveted to oneself, the radical impossibility of fleeing oneself to hide from oneself, the unalterably binding presence of the I to itself [*du moi à soi-même*]."[42] The *moi* takes the liberal notion of identity into account; it is that level (or region) whereby subjectivity, properly speaking resides. The *moi* is a relation with being founded on intentionality, and as such, is a surpassing toward Being. The *soi*, on the other hand, represents the *position* of the *moi* in Being; it is its fact of being (or its "is-ness"). When I am reminded, by certain experiences, of the fullness of my being—of the fact that I am a physical body that occupies a position in Being—I experience the *soi* (or my "self"). Important in this relationship between these "strata" of identity is that the *soi* is felt as simultaneously that which is most foreign and most intimate. I *am* my body (the body that is physically positioned in Being). But I also feel weighed down (or burdened) by my body, or rather, by my position in being of which it is a revelation. Insofar as the *soi* is given over as a burden, there exists a point of nonidentification (or misidentification, if you will) between the *moi* and the *soi*.

In the chapter where he discusses Levinas's conception of responsibility, Francois Raffoul connects what, for Levinas, are similar desires to escape being *and* to escape oneself (*soi-même*). "There is a (viscous) circle between being and oneself that Levinas seeks to break. The horror of the *there is* [which references the Levinasian conception of being in its plenitude] is close to disgust for oneself, close to the weariness of oneself."[43] As such, the phenomenology of shame discloses that elemental need for what Diane Perpich describes as a "break with being that does not merely seek to *be* somewhere else."[44] The burden of the weight of being, and the rebellion against that weight, is at the same time a revolt against the encumberment of having to be (with) oneself. Hence, for Levinas, shame's essential revelation is the of fullness of being, which is also the fullness of *my* being. He determines this to be most significant in the experience of nausea (or malaise) as well. In these moments, the subject is overwhelmed by an uncanny obligation to *be with* his- or herself, despite an adamant refusal to remain in place.[45] *Existence and Existents* describes nausea as a "feeling for existence," and in *Of Escape*, we read that it signals a refusal to remain oneself. In this sense, nausea augments that which is essential to shame—the revelation of an intimacy with ourselves, which we would rather be otherwise.[46] Again, not only do these affective states reveal this intimacy (between the *moi* and *soi*), but they also reveal a *refusal* of this intimacy—a refusal that already "opens a gap in the immanence of identity."[47]

Through the distinction between the *moi* and the *soi*, Levinas attempts to amend and surpass both Hitlerism's and liberalism's conceptions of identity. He presents these levels as inseparable aspects of a genuine unity, so it is not the case that Levinas reinvents the problem of Cartesian dualism, by describing two modes of identity that must then come into communion with each other. "*Moi*" and "*soi*" are but one (personal) existent. However, they are one in a special sense. Instead of mapping neatly onto each other (much like the notion of the autonomous individual at home with his- or herself would suggest), the *moi* and *soi* are out of phase with each other, their march diachronous, with the *soi* dragging behind the *moi*, like a stubborn presence. It is in this sense that we understand the fissure characteristic of suffering. The "I" is ahead of its "self" by only the most infinitely smallest of instants, since the bond between them (that they are, indeed, a unity) only allows for so much. Insofar as the unity indicative of identity consists of this diachrony, it also "amounts to the impossibility of being what one is."[48] Levinas will read the noncoincidence between the *moi* and the *soi* in terms of an *interruption* of the primacy of freedom.[49]

No Exit for "Le Moi"

In the end, Levinas's formulation means that identity is to be understood as the impossibility of identity. This allows him to capture the attitudes of both liberalism and Hitlerism without committing their respective errors and more importantly, to formulate a model of transcendence other than transcendence-as-intentionality, in a model that captures what Levinas demonstrates, which is that our human condition is such that we are riveted to ourselves in a fullness of being from which there is no exit. For Sartre, there is also a relationship between consciousness and in-itself being, which gives to consciousness a certain "anchor" out of which it apprehends the world. Nevertheless, this relationship is a nihilating one, which means that consciousness upsurges as a radical *nothingness* of being, purely empty and purely lucid.[50] Sartre's account of the subject's "position" can account for the fact that human freedom encounters obstacles in being, and in this sense it recognizes a finitude to human freedom. Nevertheless, the meaning of such finitude is always "that which must be overcome, or conquered." In other words, we might understand Sartre's account of transcendence to fall under the Levinasian critique of the West's conception of transcendence, which ultimately maintains the priority of being. In this sense, Sartrean transcendence-as-intentionality would respond to the need to "*be* somewhere else,"[51] instead of the need for a radical getting out of being, or for an escape from "the horizon of being as such."[52] Sartre's account privileges freedom, in the sense that any positioning in or rivetedness to being is signified as a obstacle *for* freedom. This is to already bypass the meaning of positionality that Levinas uncovers in his articulation of identity as a relation between "*moi*" and '*soi*."

The "acute feeling of being held fast" does not spur motivations in the *moi* to fight back. Rather, "what counts . . . in all this experience of being, is the discovery not of a new characteristic of our existence [*not* the fact that our existence is finite], but of its very fact, of the [nonremovable] quality itself of our presence."[53] In other words, to experience the duality between the *moi* and the *soi* is to experience that there is no way out of one's existence. One's choices and fundamental projects may change, but in all this, the "I" *is*, inevitably. In this sense, Levinas radically alters the notion of a finitely free subject, whose woes would lie in the fact that it lacks being (or is in want of a "better being").[54] The permanent quality of existence (the fact of existence, which grounds the tension within the subject) means that these woes rest on the *fullness* of Being itself. It is all around me, and I take my "self" wherever I go. Hence, it is *Being* from which I cannot get away—there is "too much" of Being, and so the problem does not lie in the fact that my being is finite (or not enough).[55] The "limitation" of the subject—of the *moi* enchained to the *soi*—is that, once posited, its existing is without reprieve. On this account, our "world weariness" does not point to a fear of nothingness (of no longer being able "to be," or "to do" or "to act"), but rather, of the horror of how we exist, in a fullness that is without exit or pardon. Our being (or way of being) might be finite, but we are hemmed in by this finite being, from all sides.[56]

Faced with this perfect and absolute fact of self-positing, I aspire to get out of the game of Being. Yet Levinas tells us that insofar as I exist, "I have already embarked," and there is no turning back. One cannot "go back" to the moment in which existing begins (to then loosen its hold), since it is immemorially past, belonging to an "other time." I always already find myself existing in this way. Levinas likens this fundamental condition (our being positioned in Being) with Heidegger's *Geworfenheit*, which captures the sense in which *Dasein* does not get to choose its "being there."[57] Rather, it is out of "being there" that it must subsequently choose. Similarly, the lack of an exit for the *moi* is so radical that it cannot even identify the moment when its horror begins. It always already finds itself burdened by its existence.

In *Existence and Existents*, Levinas locates these moments of pre-choice at the level of the *soi*, where the encounter with an impersonal existence is as though existence has to be "taken up," not yet belonging to a particular existent. At the level of the *soi*, the "contract" with existence is made, such that existence then becomes personalized. But this event is marked with struggle and effort (concretized in those experiences of carrying my "self" with me like a weight). In this encounter, the *il y a* (that impersonal field of existence, or the "there is") threatens to overcome the (not-yet-subjectivized) existent. It is revealed as radically " 'objective,' independent of my initiative."[58] Levinas tells us that this encounter with existence is marked by a feeling of horror, an affective state that points to the radical passivity of the existent as it encounters an impersonal existence. Despite this sense in which existence overcomes and overwhelms by its ambiguous "presence," the existent nevertheless is *there* to encounter this horror.[59] This means that, without yet being a subject, there is a certain immanence of a (personal) existent that has already broken with, or broken up, the undifferentiated field of the *il y a*. To be sure, the immanence of the self in its encounter with existence is not that of the autonomous subject, who can then be either trapped in his or her idealist representation of 'the real,' or spontaneously engage with a transcendent reality. The very signification of the 'originary' interior life of the existent is that of disruption and passivity, and persists in the very ambiguity between where 'existent' ends and 'existence' begins. Levinas's analysis of impersonal existence emphasizes this essential ambiguity surrounding the status of the existent at the level of the *soi*. We see this in the phenomenology of events like insomnia and others, which reveal the *il y a* in its most impersonal 'expression.'[60] By remaining faithful to the ambiguity involved in these concrete descriptions, *Existence and Existents* attempts to negotiate this region of identity that plays between autonomy and passivity. The analysis then grounds what Levinas identifies as the genuine meaning of transcendence (in opposition to the 'false transcendence' of the West) as the pursuit of a radical rupture in Being. To a large degree, the concept of identity as the relation between the 'I' and ;oneself' already attests to this rupture.

III. Before 'Being in the World'

In his forward to the text, Robert Bernasconi describes *Existence and Existents* as a work that "reopens the question of transcendence."[61] Indeed, Levinas traces a relation between beings and Being such that the latter shows up as radically independent of the former. "The *il y a* [is] understood as the paradoxical 'presence' of existence itself, free from all reference to existents."[62] Levinas demonstrates that transcendence is the movement that responds to our urge to "get out" of this impersonal presence, encountered as a region of neutered ambiguity, independent of us. Though indebted to

Heidegger in many ways, Levinas reads his ontological difference as having fallen short of accounting for the meaning of this more "elemental" experience of Being, and this more "elemental truth"[63] of how we encounter ourselves. According to Levinas, Heidegger does not accomplish the radical separation between Being and individual (or ontic) beings, for which his analysis in *Existence and Existents* attempts to account in its distinction between existence and existents (a distinction that is clearly an abstraction, since an existent would already be that which exists and thus would already possess existence). Nevertheless, Levinas conceives of existence apart from existents so as to capture the all-too-forgotten *effort* on which the personalization of existence rests. In other words, to regard existence as not yet belonging to an existent is to bring into focus that instant in which the existent actually *does* begin to exist, and encounters the existence as alien and overwhelming. At this moment, the act of existing requires work on the part of the existent, as that existent takes up his or her position in an unwelcoming alterity. As Robert Bernasconi points out, the encounter with impersonal existence indicates that identity "is not a given, but [rather] arises in being. There is a contract that the human being makes with existence. . . ."[64] This dynamic between existence and the existent concretizes itself in a phenomenology of the passivity of fatigue, vulnerability, and the event of dying, all of which realize the kind of relation with Being that accomplishes transcendence-as-excendence.

According to Levinas, Heidegger determines transcendence to be a surpassing of ontic being to ontological Being. But this journey is concretized only in an authentic attitude to our *own* being. Jean Wahl points out that this is "because the only form of Being with which we are truly in contact (according to Heidegger) is the being of man."[65] This authentic understanding involves an embracing of our "ownmost possibility," or our being-toward-death. Thus, a Heideggarian transcendence toward Being, beyond ontic beings takes place in an embrace of Nothingness, or the truth that "the moment will come when there will be no more possibilities [out of which we choose]."[66] In adopting this authentic attitude of being-toward-death, Heidegger determines that we subsequently relate authentically to other (everyday) beings. In this sense, transcendence toward Being (the Being of ontic beings) ultimately rests on an authentic understanding of our own finitude, or the fact that our possibilities will one day be no more. In experiencing ourselves in light of this mortality, we more genuinely (and actively) choose the possibilities that are ours, instead of allowing them to be arbitrarily "thrust" on us, as though by chance or without any agency on our part.

Levinas reads this formulation of being-toward-death as ultimately reinforcing the supremacy of *Dasein* over Being.[67] Death seems to be given over as yet another possibility for the subject, namely, the "possibility of *impossibility*,"[68] and as such, maintains *Dasein's* triumph over its domain in Being. In this regard, Levinas reads this transcending toward the possibility of my own death as not a real movement *toward*, not a real break in being, or with my being but rather as a return to myself. However, apart from this is Levinas's criticism of the very idea that our fundamental access to Being is through the finitude of our trajectory of choices (or through the fact that the moment will come when I face the end of my possibilities). In his distinction between existence and existents, Levinas shows that a more primordial encounter with the "there is" does not reveal the *finitude* of our being, but rather our existing as *infinitely* endless or without reprieve. One might say that we encounter our existing as "going on infinitely," insofar as the fact of being is everywhere, even when everything else goes away. In *Time and the Other*, Levinas explicitly warns against reducing existence in general (in abstraction from existents) to Heidegger's nothingness: "Let us imagine all things, beings and persons, returning to nothingness. What remains after this imaginary destruction of everything is not something, but the fact that there is [*il y a*]. The absence of everything returns as a presence."[69] The absence of things does not signal nothingness, but rather a strange "something" whose presence is clouded with an essential ambiguity, and indeed, is beyond phenomenality.[70] Being is everywhere, absolutely posited, even as the being of a finite being.

Levinas uncovers this fullness of Being (what he refers to as the plenitude of existence) by returning to those concrete moments that manifest the "inversion" through which existence becomes the existence *of* an existent. These experiences reveal the effort of the existent as he or she enters into, or takes up this contract. That there must be this event of inversion (that existence does not automatically lend itself to becoming personalized) signifies the primordial resistance of anonymous existence. It signifies the sense in which existence "refuses personal form"[71] more originally than it is "the Being of a being."

In his essay, John Sallis likens the characteristic of the *il y a* to nature, "As [the *il y a*] returns, it will appear strange, as if belonging to a region distant from and alien to the human world. In a sense it will have cast off its disguise: it will no longer be the nature that is shaped and formed within the human world in accord with the measures of that world. . . ."[72] Though I reject this comparison between Levinas's *il y a* to nature, Sallis's point does facilitate an accurate understanding of the *il y a*.[73] *Existence and Existents* demonstrates that an encounter with the *il y a* radically breaks with all semblance of familiarity and agency on the part of identity. As such, the very rubric of intentionality breaks down (and perhaps no longer pertains) at this level of pure existence. In a comparison between Levinas's abstraction of existents from existence with Husserl's phenomenological reduction, Iyer writes, "The *il y a*, existence in general, cannot be intuited by the phenomenologist, since it presumes the dissolution of both the phenomenologist *qua* 'stream of consciousness' [or *moi*] and all phenomena. From Levinas' perspective, the existent, in the mode of an intentional relation to the world, does not survive the thought experiment [that abstracts existence from existents]."[74] An exposition of his account of insomnia would make this explicit, and will require us to approach the existent as that duality of *moi* and *soi*, instead of as solely a moment of spontaneous intentionality. Indeed, it is in *Existence and Existents* that we find the phenomenology for which Levinas's account of the *moi* and the *soi* is a formalization.

Insomnia

Levinas's descriptions of insomnia capture the disturbance intrinsic at the level of the *il y a*. Anonymous existence "effaces itself before reflection"[75]; it is simply not open to being captured by thematizing thought. In this regard, it is only very tenuously that we identify insomnia as an *experience*, if, by "experience," one means that which is grounded on the terms of intentionality (in either the Husserlian or Sartrean sense). In remaining awake by anonymous existence, "the ego [what, properly speaking, must be there as proprietor of experience] is swept away by [the *il y a*'s] fatality."[76] But in the midst of the event of insomnia, or of being swept away, the existent remains vigilant against his or her will, watching that which surpasses all comprehension. As François Raffoul writes, "as overturned, the subject is maintained by Levinas, in its very destitute (de)position ... This is how Levinas thinks subjectivity, the *subjectum*—which indeed, is that which is 'thrown-underneath.'"[77] The consciousness who is vigilant in this way is void of all subjectivity, and in this sense, the vigilance of insomnia differs from 'attention to' the *il y a*. "Attention presupposes the freedom of the ego which directs it; the vigilance of insomnia which keeps our eyes open has no subject."[78] For this reason, Levinas tells us that, with insomnia, it is difficult to identify what watches—the existent, or the "night of the *il y a*."[79]

And yet, in undergoing insomnia, "I at least have the experience of being an object" of the *il y a*. In other words, even though the existent is dispossessed of all sovereignty (a sovereignty that might permit the "I think" of the Cartesian ego), there is still some differentiation between his or her interiority and the *il y a*. Insomnia is neither a total annihilation of a personal existent, nor a melding between immanence and exteriority. Indeed, it is imperative that this "reversal" of the subject nevertheless maintains a kind of inverted subjectivity that could then signify in the more subsequent narrative of Levinasian responsibility as the "accusative *Me voici*, 'here I am.' . . ."[80] In other words, insomnia concretizes the sense in which identity is singular (singled out) and uniquely responsible *for the Other* prior to being a spontaneous and intentional reflection of being that then "names" the world *for itself*. Existents are *there* (to be precisely the sufferers of the burden of an absolutely exterior existence), but they are there as precisely not-yet subjects.

Levinas's analysis echoes what he determines to be that fissure within the unity of identity (or the dissonant unity of *moi* and *soi*). Insomnia and other such quasi-experiences of affectivity (like fatigue and suffering), reveal the "limit-point" of the ego's mastery over itself and of impersonal existence, and gestures toward identity as *soi*. In other words, these moments indicate a level of existence more fundamental than the level pertaining to phenomena, "world," and "ego." Insomnia happens at the level in which the contract with existence is made, or at the level in which the burden of existing is taken up *with effort*. For Levinas, this primordiality then makes possible phenomena, "world" and "ego." To be clear, Levinas does *not* regard as false the claim that a subject relates to the world across the movement of intentionality. But before we engage with Being across a freely created network of meaning, we are passive (or vulnerable) under the exteriority of existence in its purest form. This passivity shows up in the radical disturbance or disruption characteristic of such encounters with existence. Consciousness is disrupted enough to be halted in its spontaneity, but not enough to 'no longer be' (or to be *non*conscious).[81] Here lies the ambiguity of insomnia, and of identity's relation to itself in general. Consciousness stands at a limit-point, infinitely separating its triumph over anonymous existence and its vulnerability before the horror of the *il y a*. As a permanent possibility for such a consciousness, insomnia is a reminder that one's position in existence is never a given, but must rather be assumed with effort. Insomnia occurs as an undergoing by subjectivity, but this undergoing can happen only insofar as the subject exists *as an undoing* that is never quite undone.

In other words, the very position of the subject is that "in between" of complete integrity and complete collapse (or annihilation). The event of hypostasis—whereby existence is taken up, so that it takes on "personal form"—is ultimately how existence makes its weightiness felt (in insomnia). In other words, consciousness, as the attestation of a mastery over pure existence, is at the same time, a localized vulnerability at the hands of the horror of pure existence. Levinas describes the "impossibility of rending"[82] this disaster in being, to the degree that it precisely returns at the juncture of hypostasis, that event which should have signaled the disaster's defeat. The experience of insomnia concretizes this ambiguous coupling of freedom and passivity that, on Levinas's account, constitutes the kind of identity that can only be "a subjection for the Other."

Levinas's descriptions of hypostasis (and the concrete circumstances through which it is revealed) illustrate the extent of the effort on the part of the existent, or the effort needed for the *il y a* to be personalized.[83] In this regard, the accomplished personalization signals a sense of triumph over existence, but this triumph is colored with tragedy for two distinct though related reasons. As we have already seen, the very mastery of the *moi* over the *il y a* generates the conditions for the possibility of insomnia. In other words, this victory conditions its own undoing. But more importantly, in establishing its position in existence, the effort exerted by the *moi* results in its unbreakable bond with existence. It is through hypostasis (that event of "mastering" existence) that the subject is riveted in its bond to the *soi*. Herein lies the simultaneous need for an exit from Being *and* the very impossibility of exiting, a dynamic which Levinas uses to locate transcendence-as-excendence.[84]

The Effort of the "Moi" in Hypostasis

Levinas identifies circumstances like fatigue and indolence as those that demonstrate a refusal to act on the part of the existent, and subsequently, the effort intrinsic in the event of existing. In such moments, the event of hypostasis is concretized, insofar as this refusal points toward the exertion on the part of the existent as he or she takes up the burden of existing. Levinas warns, "When we take fatigue and indolence as [mental] contents, we do not see what is effected in them—or of what they are an impotent *nonacceptance* [emphasis mine]. Their whole reality is made up of a refusal."[85] He sets his regarding of these circumstances up against certain "moral considerations," which infer, from any hesitation before acting, a lack of motivation on the part of the subject. These other interpretations identify an indolent subject who chooses to not "rise to the occasion," and settles in futile idleness instead. However, this is to presuppose a subject who is already equipped with a secure foothold in existence, and is already in place with the *capacity* to choose—to take on the tasks of life, or to "remain in bed" and let life go by. Levinas, on the other hand, finds in fatigue and indolence, a meaning that is antecedent to the capacity to choose (to be lazy or hardworking). These moments signal a refusal of being, to be sure, but this refusal is not a *thought* of refusal; it does not concern the intentional movement of a consciousness. This "recoil before existence," as pretheoretical, indicates the event of "beginning to exist"— a beginning that would then make the *thought* of refusal or acceptance possible.

This "recoil" or hesitation before existence, which constitutes the concrete meaning of the instant of fatigue, shows us that the existent has something at stake as it begins to exist—namely, the obligation of bearing the weight of its existence. This paradoxical construction (that I must take up my existence like a weight) again points to the duality Levinas identifies as constitutive of identity. In the event of existing, "it is not just that one is, one is oneself. . . . Existence involves a relationship by which the existent makes a contract with existence. There is a duality in existence. . . . The ego [*moi*] has a self [*soi*] . . . with which it is involved like a companion or a partner."[86] To exist means that I encounter my "self" as that which I have to be, and refuse to be, hence the effort required to be (that self). Nonetheless, hypostasis amounts to an "impossible refusal of this ultimate obligation."[87] This weight of one's existence (the sense in which the *moi* encounters the *soi* as burdensome) captures the ego's original encounter with Being in terms of the vulnerability and passion of what it means to be exposed to a radical exteriority.[88] "[The] liberation with regard to the existent's anonymous existing becomes an enchainment to self, the very enchainment of identification."[89] It is only subsequent to this underlying vulnerability that the ego engages with a world of meaningful objects, across the distance it establishes (between itself and "world") via intentionality. In this relationship, I am engaged in being, though, to a large degree, I remain un-implicated and detached.[90] But prior to this detachment, there is an immersion in existence, to the point of enchainment, which means that I encounter Being (and *my* being) in terms of a "desiring otherwise."[91]

In taking us back to this "deeper drama," Levinas demonstrates that the detachment of intentionality "does not save me [the *moi*] from the *definitive character of my very existence* [emphasis added]."[92] In this sense, the event through which impersonal existence is conquered, or that first articulation of freedom in the existent, rests on a foundation of vulnerability. The free subject (the *"moi"*) "has one foot caught in its own existence":[93] it is fundamentally burdened by these conditions that ground the possibility of its freedom. Hypostasis, as the event of beginning, reveals that freedom is always invested (that it is founded on a prior responsibility to be "oneself"), and as such, makes an *ecstatic* model of transcendence impossible.[94] Given Levinas's understanding of our relation to brute existence, it is clear that an ecstatic model of transcendence cannot respond to the exigency for the escape that Levinas traces in 1935.[95] The triumph of the ego (the *moi*) leads to ultimate disappointment as, once again, it finds itself surrounded, everywhere, by being. In his interview with Philippe Nemo, Levinas tells us that "to escape, one must not be *posed* [as an autonomous subject positioned in existence] but *deposed* [emphases mine]."[96] The meaning of Levinas's excendence is found in this "de-positioning" of the subject.

The Passion and Activity of Sensibility

In his analysis, Levinas resorts to moments of sensibility to capture the passivity at the level of the *soi*, or at the level where we find the existent's initial efforts to take up his or her position in existence.[97] Levinas's thought experiment that requires the reader to think "existence without existents" (the thought experiment that precisely gets us to the *il y a*), is preceded by an account of the relation between sensation and the aesthetic effect.[98] Materiality (or the fact of embodiment) houses the life of sensibility, and as such, Levinas locates this aspect of our humanity in the bond between the *moi* and the *soi*. "Materiality, for Levinas, is not to be conceived of mechanistically, biologically, or physically, as opposed to mind or thought . . . Levinas considers the meaning of materiality in terms of the relationship to existence as the anonymous realm of the *il y a*."[99] Hence, the life of sensibility gets us to the heart of the vulnerability that engenders the need to escape being, which is also the vulnerability that will ultimately be a genuine *transcendence* (as excendence) from Being. Sensibility (or rather, the faculty of sensation) oftentimes indicates the sense in which we receive a raw datum of information from the outside. Hence, it stands for those moments when, at the most immediate level of experience, the *activity* of freedom (the spontaneous creation of meaning, or giving over of signification) is minimal. Levinas employs this understanding of sensibility to underscore the vulnerability through which we encounter pure existence (or more precisely, our rivetedness to existence). In this sense, sensibility functions to capture how the existent (passively) "receives" the *il y a* through a corporeal affection through which the subject not only hesitates under the sheer weight of its existence, but more importantly, lives moments of suffering. The body is open to pain insofar as it is exposed to an exteriority (that wounds), and as we have seen, the essence of suffering lies in our inability to escape the body (our body) at that moment of exposure.

Nonetheless, it is possible to distinguish the sensible life, properly speaking, from what it means to encounter brute existence. In *Otherwise than Being, or Beyond Essence*, Levinas describes the vulnerability of the subject (the subjection of subjectivity, as he sometimes phrases it) as sensibility. "Vulnerability, exposure to outrage, to wounding . . . all this is the self, a defecting of defeat of the ego's identity. And this, pushed to its limit, is sensibility, sensibility as subjectivity of the subject [insofar as it *is* this subjection]."[100] Similarly, in *Time and the Other*, he describes the bond between the *moi* and the *soi* as "the subject's materiality."[101] But elsewhere, Levinas seems to understand sensation as that which already indicates a kind of mastery by the subject, since it sustains the "for the mind" characteristic of our relationship with objects in the world.[102] On this account, sensibility does not render the subject passive enough to capture the existent's undoing in the face of the *il y a*. In 1982, Levinas argues that receptivity of the sensible life actually retains a sense of activity, which would position it at the level of the autonomous *moi*. "The passivity of suffering is more profoundly passive than the receptivity of our senses, which is already *active* reception [emphasis added], immediately becoming perception. In suffering, sensibility is a vulnerability, more passive than receptivity; an encounter more passive than [sentient] experience."[103]

These two different ways of understanding sensibility serves our purpose here, insofar as the existent is given over as both "active engagement with being" *and* "passive positionality in existence." To understand that sensibility partakes in the vulnerability of an encounter with the "there is" *and* signals a certain triumph over and against this encounter is to understand the precise nature of the relationship between the *moi* and the *soi*. It is to understand what Levinas intends as the slippage between spontaneity and vulnerability, which structures human identity. Levinas's account of enjoyment aptly captures this ambiguity, since he locates the life of enjoyment within the spectrum of sovereignty (over the elements) and dependence (on the elements).[104] In this sense, the life of enjoyment seems to account for the passion *and* activity that can be identified (with equal legitimacy) in sensibility. As John Drabinski writes, "The sense of Enjoyment issues from the outside."[105] In this regard, what we enjoy is not yet an objectivity (in the epistemological sense). So though what we enjoy is a modality of being that is "for us," pointing to (active) attempts to step beyond the level of the "there is," it also retains the passivity belonging to "behind the world," precisely because it originates in sensibility (the very life of materiality).

Enjoyment

The body provides the locus for both the freedom of enjoyment and the passion of sensibility. Insofar as its foundation is in the sensible life, enjoyment is already an indication of an immersion in being.[106] As such, the sense of freedom achieved is not (or rather, not yet) the freedom characteristic of intentional models of our "being in the world." Levinas has accused Heidegger for passing over this initial freedom from being by moving too quickly to an approach mediated by instrumentality.[107] Under this Levinasian interpretation, our primary engagement with ontic being is always already colored with meaning pertaining to our fundamental projects, and in this sense, Being shows up as belonging to beings that are of *use* to us in those projects. However, before beings are situated into this instrumental matrix, and given to us across a distance of detachment, the *moi* is bathed in being, and thus already attests to its rivetedness to the *soi*.[108] Before the food on my table is an object of consumption, I enjoy it, through consumption, as I "become one" with it. Similarly, I enjoy the spectacle before me prior to establishing a theoretical distance from it (to then examine it "objectively," perhaps), and in that moment of enjoyment, I feel myself part of the beauty of the spectacle I see.[109]

For these reasons, Levinas tells us that the world is constituted as a "technical finality" only after it "nourishes [us] and bathes [us]."[110] To be sure, the immersion in being that provides the conditions for enjoyment is different from the sense in which the existent is overtaken by the *il y a*. The wakefulness of insomnia is given over as dreadful precisely because existence disturbs and invades with its strangeness. On the contrary, the "elemental" is familiar, and it is *as* familiar that it is enjoyed. But similar to the *il y a*, the elemental is also a "reversal of reality," equally void of objective meaning. Nevertheless, the elements that "show up" for enjoyment presents itself with a familiarity that is precisely impossible in the case of the *il y a*.

Enjoyment then presupposes an essential immersion in Being—it is "as though we were in the bowels of being."[111] But insofar as enjoyment renders being familiar, it accomplishes that "first victory" against the anonymous horror of the *il y a*. To reiterate, the *il y a* has this power to overcome the subject insofar as it (*moi*) must support the weight of its "self" (*soi*). The subject has a foothold in existence, which renders it susceptible to circumstances like insomnia, fatigue, and suffering. Consequently, there is a victory in enjoyment precisely because the subject manages to veil (though temporarily) the chains that tie it to its "self." In other words, the familiarity through which enjoyment relates to existence results in an "instantaneous transcendence," in which there is, at least momentarily, liberation from the self, or from the foothold that anchors the *moi* in existence.[112]

This liberation (or "self-forgetfulness," as Levinas calls it) happens through the dialectic of need, which is inseparable from the life of enjoyment. We enjoy objects because they satisfy some preexisting need we have for them. In this sense, we depend on the object of enjoyment for precisely that satisfaction. However, as Levinas's analysis of pleasure demonstrates, on this *dependence* lies the *independence* achieved from the *il y a*. Characterized as "the most primordial phenomenon of need's satisfaction," Levinas shows how pleasure breaks up the density of our being and of Being in general.[113] The existent feels itself dissipated throughout the instant of pleasure, such that "it grows lighter, as if drunk."[114] In this moment, existence is no longer encountered as a fullness that is concentrated within the instant of hypostasis, precisely because pleasure signifies an abandonment of that position. There is "a loss of oneself, a getting out of oneself, *an ecstasy* [emphasis added]."[115] In this sense, enjoyment realizes a certain liberation from self, or postponement of the "anonymous night of the *il y a*."[116] In devouring the object that ultimately satisfies its needs, "the subject is absorbed in the object it absorbs,"[117] thus experiencing a "getting out of itself." Nonetheless, transcendence through enjoyment is only "instantaneous" because the very needs that open up the "exit" from self also signify a return to self through the structures of work and physical pain. Before my needs can be satisfied, I must work to attain the terminus of that need. These objects are other than me, and as such, I must actively reduce the distance that separates me from them, constituting them in terms of an accessibility for me.[118] In this sense, any kind of escape is met with disappointment. For Levinas, this also applies to the abandonment of pleasure, when as subjects, in shame, we find ourselves with ourselves once again.

However, what is noteworthy in Levinas's analysis is that enjoyment does signify those first attempts at transcendence, insofar as there is that first rupture in the totality of being (of the subject's being). Most importantly, this quasi-liberation does not signify independently of the sense in which we are bodies or the fact that we are *there*, rooted in Being. Rather, it is very explicitly rooted in an exposed body, and as such, a more genuine transcendence-as-excendence is promised across the affection of embodiment. "The vulnerable skin of the subject bears the trace of the hither-side."[119] Hence Levinas articulates a glimpse of an exit that begins in the exposure of being-a-body (of being riveted to ourselves). In this sense, enjoyment opens up the possibility of an excendence that might take place through the underlying passion of an existent riveted to existence.[120]

IV. Excendence Takes Place Prior to Freedom

In the essay, "Without Identity," Levinas reminds us that "[no] one is at home [in Being] . . . precisely because no one remains comfortably in himself. [There] is a divergence between the ego and the self, an impossible recurrence, an impossible identity."[121] In contrast to the primordial kinship between Being and *Dasein*, which grounds the Heideggerian account of being-at-home, Levinas names the ego's failure to coincide with itself. He establishes our fundamental homelessness in Being, citing the psalmist prayer to the Holy to reveal His instructions to him, since he is "a stranger on the earth."[122] It is precisely out of this strangeness in Being, or out of the ego's inability to rest comfortably in itself, *despite* its rivetedness, that excendence ultimately takes place. To reiterate, transcendence occurs as a *de-*positioning of the existent, and *not* in terms of the supremacy of a free subject. It is precisely out of the vulnerability of being without a home that Levinas finds the signification of the rupture in being that would be an excendence. This would mean that excendence cannot be an *act*, in the proper sense, since it takes place at a level prior to the possibility of all action.

Excendence is Concretized in Absolute Passivity

The transcendence of need, on which the escape constitutive of enjoyment rests, fails not only because the need to work forces the subject to return to his or her position in being. More importantly, escape through enjoyment is carried out in *isolation*, which is to say that the life of enjoyment persists in an enclosure of self, such that the subject encounters only itself.[123] It is *I* who attempt to liberate myself in enjoyment, and for this reason, it becomes a movement that reinstates the supremacy of the subject, reducing that which is other to (her) interiority. To be sure, the subject's supremacy in enjoyment is "tamed" by an original immersion in the elemental. But this sense of vulnerability is quickly replaced with activity on the part of the subject, as he or she approaches Being with an "as for me." To be sure, this "as for me" (what palpitates through the relation of enjoyment and need) is more sincere or engaged than the approach across intentionality. The subject is significantly more compromised by the sincerity of his or her hunger, relative to the detachment on which a more cognitive relation to being would rest.[124] Nonetheless, the transcendence of enjoyment inevitably gives us a subject *satisfied at* the terminus of his or her needs and, as satisfied, has conquered the alterity of the object of need.[125] The subject has ultimately reaffirmed him- or herself, alone (in the isolated and not solitary sense) once again.

However, we have seen that the immediacy of enjoyment does point us toward the *affectivity* of being open to that which is radically other. Levinas points out, "The morality of 'earthly nourishments' is the first morality, the first abnegation. It is not the last, but one must pass through it."[126] Here, "morality" indicates the alterity of which the rupturing of Being will offer expression, and signals the interruption of the closed immanence of (an isolated) subjective life. The subject is taken out of him- or herself, with no possibility of return. But for this to take place, this "taking leave" must *happen* to the ego, irrespective of any effort or activity on its part. Levinas identifies the elemental as this "first morality" because, despite the return into immanence that characterizes the satisfaction of needs, there is exposure of interiority to physical pain and suffering.[127] This mode of exposure intensifies in the alterity of death, which is, for Levinas, the most extreme point of vulnerability. When physical suffering is at its peak, death shows up as a salvation. In other words, when I suffer to the degree that my rivetedness to my (corporeal) self is immeasurable, my death appears as the possibility of an escape. In these moments, if only death would come, it would grant me the exit from myself (the exit whose impossibility captures the essence of suffering). But it is precisely when I desire my death that I encounter the impossibility of *willing*, or actively bringing about my death.[128] This conception of "death as the impossibility of all possibility" replaces what Levinas reads as Heidegger's understanding of death as the "possibility of impossibility." Levinas reformulates death to signify as radically otherwise, always approaching from elsewhere. Hence, it is in the passivity under which the subject faces an approaching death that the avenue for excendence opens up.[129]

Death as the Ultimate Depositioning

When suffering is at its peak, as with the approach of death, the ego faces the limit of its powers as an ego (as a locus of agency and spontaneous creation). The desperate desire for refuge, along with the end of all capacity to bring that refuge to fruition, indicates that the will is dethroned absolutely. As such, death approaches at the moment in which interiority is no longer in terms of the *moi*, but must be understood in terms of the *soi*, the existent who encounters his or her very existence as a radical alterity. Levinas acknowledges that someone can *choose* a state of affairs that would impose physical pain, but insofar as it is chosen, this pain does not yet constitute the most extreme passivity of suffering, which is a suffering onto death. In other words, Levinas's point is that the intensity of the most severe instant of pain is severe *insofar as* it is given over, and not chosen.

I am no longer able to choose an end to my suffering, and hence, I am also unable to bring about the death that would precisely put an end to that suffering. In this sense, death signifies as something that is about to *happen to* me, always coming from elsewhere, as "[threatening] from beyond."[130] Even apart from the moment of absolute suffering, when the ego may not be concretely facing its death—even when death is not *literally* near, but rather, is like an inevitability that we manage to push to the backdrop of our existence—it bears this essential quality of unassumability. "The unforeseeable character of the ultimate instant is not due to an empirical ignorance, to the limited horizon of our understanding, which a greater understanding would have been able to overcome. The unforeseeable character of death is due to the fact that *it does not lie within any horizon* [emphasis added]. It is not open to grasp."[131] This is why Levinas defines suffering (and by extension, death, in its elusiveness) as essentially monstrous. "The evil of pain, the deleterious per se, is the outburst and deepest expressions of absurdity."[132] The disruption that is essential to suffering is precisely radical insofar as it deflects all attempts to make it meaningful. In this sense, an interpretation that would reduce death to either "a passage into nothingness" or "a passage to another existence"[133] is ultimately frustrated by death's unassumability.

It is insofar as death constitutes this proximal approach from "elsewhere" that the ego, in suffering onto death, breaks with the density of being. Herein lays the aporia in Levinas's conception of transcendence. I am rendered absolutely passive when confronted with the radical alterity of an approaching death, at which point I am most riveted to myself.[134] But it is at this precise moment (of absolute rivetedness) that excendence is realized. When the subject looses all capacity to make an exit *on its own accord*, or when the only option is resignation, the aperture of excendence appears. Absolutely vulnerable, the subject does not (cannot) constitute the proximity of death in terms of an "experience" of the proximity of his or her death, and this is precisely because, at the moment of transcendence, subjectivity is a (nonautonomous) "subjection."[135] The singularity of identity is maintained in this excendence, which solves what Levinas regards as the problem of transcendence whereby "[the] subject that transcends is swept away in its transcendence [and therefore] does not transcend itself"[136] Instead, transcendence as an excendence from being would made bare (or would expose) the very identity of the subject as a primordial passivity.

To recall, excendence ought to get the ego out of *being*. Levinas understands this in its radical sense, which is in opposition to philosophy's persistent "obedience to Parmenides."[137] The modalities of being seem to be all around us; we barely enter language before we employ them in some form. We thematize, identify, bestow meaning, seek meaning and discard as meaningless, all of which are borrowed tools from all encompassing Being. But the absurdity in death (the suffering onto death) ruptures these modalities. "[Death] places me before a category that does not enter into either term of [the] alternatives [of being and nothingness]."[138] It is almost as if, in the most vulnerable of vulnerabilities, the subject does indeed resign to his or her rivetedness, but the very signification of that station in being is altered. No longer able, no longer able to be able, the subject "is" outside of ontological modalities ("is" in a sense other than a conjugation of the verb *to be*). In the impossibility of all possibility, interiority nevertheless palpitates, since "the death agony is precisely in this impossibility of ceasing, in the ambiguity of a time that has run out and of a mysterious time that yet remains."[139] In this sense of dead time, or of "coming to an end while not coming to an end," being is ruptured in excendence. Most importantly, transcendence as excendence is not ecstatic, since it is in extreme rivetedness that the aperture, through which escape takes place, is given. In this regard, Levinas's conception of the existent who is positioned in existence at the level of the *soi*, grounds the possibility of genuine transcendence. Contained in his notion of positionality is this fundamental vulnerability, openness or exposure that would rupture the totality of volition, for which a system of ontology is equipped.

In the following chapter, I argue that the temporality coming out of this account of positionality demonstrates that solitude is fundamentally implicated in Levinas's sense of alterity. Not only is solitude a primordial structure of an identity configured in terms of the *moi* and *soi*, but it is included in the very meaning of an encounter with (Levinas's understanding of) radical alterity. Said otherwise, to be exposed to the radically Other is to be precisely left alone in that exposure.[140] I identify a similar dimension in Sartre's concrete descriptions of nausea, and argue that his descriptions are one of a subject who is radically *un*constituted in his or her position in existence. From Sartre's descriptions, nausea reveals a realm of subjective life which, I argue, is vulnerable in a solitude very much like the existent is in Levinas, as that existent encounters the *il y a*. I use these findings to support my claim that Sartre's formal account of consciousness, as exhaustively an encounter with Being across the thematizing powers of intentionality, does not account for the entirety of the human condition.

CHAPTER 3

Levinasian Positionality in Sartre's Account of Nausea

Positionality, as conceived by Levinas, refers to what is oftentimes felt as the unyielding obligation to be with one's "self," despite not being completely identical with that "self."[1] As positioned, the existent feels herself abandoned to the alterity of the *il y a*, and I read, in this abandonment, an inevitable solitude that pertains to the existent's condition. In Sartre's concrete descriptions of nausea, which emphasizes the sense in which embodiment captures the obligation to "be oneself," I identify resonances with these (Levinasian) notions of positionality and solitude. On Sartre's account, consciousness's encounter with existence is founded on an obligation to exist that, I hold, exposes a level of vulnerability on the hither side of radical freedom.[2] To be sure, this reading of Sartre is explicitly Levinasian. But this is only because it is informed by similarities that I identify between Levinas's conception of the *il y a* and his (Sartre's) concrete descriptions of nausea. I establish that not only do both thinkers portray a level of vulnerability that is more primordial than (spontaneous) subjectivity, but also that they recognize a correlation between this vulnerability and the radically solitary condition of the self.

For Levinas, the disruption that is brought on by the obligation to be with my "self," *along with* my inability to identify with that "self," births an existential forlornness such that I am left alone to carry the burden of existence.[3] Chapter 2 presented phenomenologies of insomnia and fatigue to show that this encounter with the burden of existing happens outside the parameters of an intentionally constructed network of meanings. Sartre's descriptions of the experience of nausea are similar in this regard, since they too capture a nonintentional encounter between consciousness and being. My claim is that, in such moments, consciousness's experiences are no longer those of a world (*any* world), but rather exist in what can only be described as an ambiguous "in-between" of pure being (void of all meaning) and the meaningful totality of beings constitutive of a world.[4] In this disintegration of "world," there is also a similar disruption, or dissimulation of the subject's position as a spontaneous flight from being.[5] This would support my claim that Sartre recognizes a region of positioned solitude within the structure of consciousness, despite its movement of intentionality. Since they seem to indicate "an identity in disruption," much like what sustains Levinas's conception of transcendence-as-excendence, I read Sartre's descriptions of nausea as calling into question his formal account of an absolute freedom that was outlined in chapter 1. In other words, given the similarities I presently trace, between these concrete descriptions of nausea and the phenomenology grounding the Levinasian notion of the *il y a*, the event of nausea seems to call for an understanding of human identity that is simply absent in the Sartrean structures of consciousness.

In tracing these similarities, a fair reading of both Sartre and Levinas requires that one also takes note of the important differences between their accounts. Levinas identifies, as the conditions of an encounter with the *il y a*, the existent as already troubled with a certain modulation of alterity. Sartre, on the other hand, locates, in the breakdown of signification found in nausea, consciousness's responsibility to create meaning, and as a consequence, its world. In this sense, the monstrosity of an undefinable field of existence is given over to the Sartrean consciousness as the template out of which it must freely make itself what it must be.[6] Nevertheless, Sartre does explicitly recognize a marked forlornness that comes as a consequence of this radical responsibility.[7] As such, when immersed in the horror of nausea, consciousness encounters itself as radically alone, supporting the burden of having to choose its world, in solitude. In Levinas's account of the *il y a*, he identifies this primordial solitude as the promise of an excendence from being. The *il y a* "shows up" only through a positioned existent that, across its hypostasis, occupies its position alone. In this regard, both Levinas and Sartre understand the condition of the subject to be one of solitude, even though Sartre explicitly determines that a consciousness condemned to such solitude is subsequently free, while Levinas employs this solitude to found the passivity (or *non*freedom) of the existent. Nonetheless, the trajectory of this book's analysis lies in reading the "concrete" Sartre against the "formal" Sartre. In this chapter, this will result in identifying a similar passivity in the solitude of the Sartrean consciousness as well.

I. Positionality and Beginning

We have seen that the relationship Levinas describes between the "*moi*" and the "*soi*" makes possible his aporetic account of transcendence. The "world weariness" portrayed in *Of Escape* replaces the account of a confident and autonomous subject with one who is no longer in ownership of his- or herself. In this regard, intentionality, though it accounts for a certain aspect of identity, leaves out this drama of beginning that we see in the way in which existence is taken up at the level of the *soi*. Hypostasis captures the existent's active manipulation of existence, insofar as she conquers the anonymity of the *il y a*. However, this conquering brings with it the obligation of having to exist, or of supporting the burden of one's existence. In this sense, hypostasis is both a moment of freedom *and* an infliction with the passivity of "having to be oneself." "The [free] relationship with Being [through which the subject sets up a position in being] is only remotely like [a relationship]; it is called a relationship only by analogy. For the Being which we become aware of when the world [of meaningful phenomena available to the *moi*] disappears is not a person or a thing . . . it is the fact that one is, the fact that *there is*."[8]

As the condition for freedom *from* impersonal existence, hypostasis brings with it "a weight and a responsibility . . . a positive enchainment to one's self [the *soi*]."[9] In Rudi Visker's words, "That bond [between the *moi* and the *soi*] is, so to speak, the ransom of being: to be, means to be me, not to be able to not conjugate the verb 'to be' in the first person singular."[10] There is an inevitability or fatefulness at the foundation of the existent's triumph over existence. This is not to insert an ossifying essence, which would then make static the fluidity of the stream of consciousness. Rather, Levinas's formulation of the *soi* means that, underlying and despite the dynamic freedom of intentionality, the subject rests on an "unassumable passivity"[11] that already calls for a radically different understanding not only of passivity, but also of the freedom of intentional life.[12]

Positionality contains the aporia of an existent's upsurge on a base that is ultimately unassumable. This means that I am unable to claim the foundation of my existence, despite my upsurge, since my very position in existence is like a *de*positioning.[13] It is in this sense that, at the level of the *soi*, identity is a fundamental vulnerability, perpetually on the verge of its undoing. It is not the case that the existing of the subject merely connotes some struggle for the maintaining of existence. More severely than this, the idea of positionality points to an "*unassumability* of position." "[The] adherence of existence to an existent appears like a cleaving,"[14] through which the challenge is more than sustaining the existing of the existent. "Preservation *of* existence" would already orient this struggle in terms of the *moi*, where a certain coincidence with self is already presupposed of identity. Rather, the existent's struggle for its existence is a struggle for its very *position* in existence (as an existent). It is an effort, exerted at the level of the *soi*, directed toward *beginning*, or toward that moment of taking up the obligation to be a self, despite the absence of all coincidence with that self. "When taken at the level of the time of the economic order, as it ordinarily is envisaged, [this struggle] appears . . . as the care that a being takes for its endurance and conservation . . . It is not a continual birth, understood as a distinct operation by which an existent takes over its existence, apart from what it may do to conserve it."[15] To put this otherwise, it is my very position as a personal existent that is at stake in this event of birth. Before the battle with the unknowns of the future, there is that threat, which faces the existent, of the impossibility of entering into the present.[16]

In this primordial beginning, Levinas portrays a non-Heideggarian temporality, insofar as the unraveled subject opens up a dimension of diachrony.[17] "Positionality," as the "unassumability of position," means that the freedom to exist is likewise an exposure to the usurpation by existence. The way in which I take up a position in existence, such that "I" have a "self" that I must be, indicates a "mis-identification," nonconstitution, or radical unraveling of identity. Instead of mapping neatly onto each other, the *moi* and *soi* are out of phase with each other. This is unlike the synchronous time marking the life of consciousness (or "economic time"), whereby all of being is, in a sense, brought together in one temporal scheme, or understood in terms of a futuricity (of care). The diachrony constitutive of the Levinasian subject "amounts to the impossibility of being what one is."[18] In other words, it amounts to that very impossibility of belonging to the time of intentionality, since the event of birth at the level of the *soi* is a performance outside of that time.[19]

For this reason, a life of consciousness cannot exhaust the structures of subjectivity, through which is enacted the ontological event of "making present" in a theme. I am "there," in existence, as positioned, but as a consequence of the diachronous relationship between my "fact of existence" and the origin on which my existing stands, my presence is a "not yet" of presence. The subject never quite "gets to begin," since it neither "exists" this beginning nor begins in (the time of) existence. Hence, when Levinas determines that hypostasis occurs prior to a time of subjectivity, he determines that by the time of intentionality, something has already occurred, which can never appear in, or be temporalized in terms of intentionality.[20] It is precisely its origin that the subject can never own or make present. For this reason, this origin comes to the existent from an 'elsewhere,' and is encountered as a locus of obsession and not as a condition of autonomy.[21]

Because the event of "beginning" is categorically maintained outside of and irreducible to the temporality of subjective life, I "begin" as the very disruption of my identity. Nevertheless, this origin is mine, despite its foreignness and unassumability. Hence, without being annihilated by it, the *moi* houses its own undoing.[22] His depiction of positionality reveals that which is both *of* subjectivity, and *other in* subjectivity. It is in this aporia—of a disturbance within interiority, without the annihilation of that interiority—that he locates the condition for the possibility of radical transcendence.[23]

II. The Time of Alterity as a Time of Solitude

Before I develop a distinction between the "time of alterity" and the "time of solitude," I address the charge that Levinas's position undermines the solitude that necessarily plagues our human condition. In place of this critique, I assert the *importance* of solitude for Levinas's account of alterity, and ultimately transcendence.[24] An implication of his project is that the existent's "being alone" is maintained throughout its encounter with radical alterity. Again, I read this as reinforcing the similarity between Levinas and Sartre, insofar as the latter also describes the existential condition of the human being as a radically solitary one. Sartre grounds this solitude on the extreme responsibility to which a radically free subject is abandoned. Though his formal ontology does not indicate, in this solitude, an interruption of the free movement of intentionality, my claim is that his descriptions do. In this sense, these descriptions are quite indistinguishable from where Levinas describes the existent's being disrupted by an immemorial beginning (that abandons the existent to the forlornness of solitude).

As already demonstrated, the temporality coming out of Levinas's notion of transcendence is such that the time of subjective life is diachronous to that of the subject's origin, which is "of another time." The subject has been left alone, or left behind by this origin, in the sense that I encounter my beginning as immemorially gone-by. However, this radical absence *affects me*, since its being "never there" signifies as a disruption. Hence, it is not the case that, phenomenologically, identity is self-contained, none the wiser to its missing moment of birth. Rather, what abandons the subject has, in absentia, this power to *disrupt* the subject, such that identity is constituted *as* this very disruption.[25] In the works post *Totality and Infinity*, Levinas employs the notion of the trace to capture this sense in which a radical absence nevertheless "presents" itself in ways other than *appearing to* (consciousness). This signifies as an interruption of the very core of a phenomenological method that prioritizes (or regards, as the sole conditions for the possibility of "making present") the activity of intentionality. Diachronous time means that an alterity presents from, or as, "elsewhere," and as such, interrupts as "the nonrecuperability of the trace."[26] This radical inversion (of identity, of spontaneous subjectivity, of the priority of presence) presupposes the solitude of the existent. In other words, on this formulation of diachronous time, to be radically disrupted by that which is other means that I am alone precisely when I enter into relation with that "other." This is because, for Levinas, alterity is encountered in terms of the trace, or as what has "always already gone-by."

"First-" and "Second-"Order Solitude

Featured in Levinas's analyses of transcendence are two "orders" of solitude. One such order points to the heart of intentionality's odyssey. This unanchored[27] trajectory of intentional life does not qualify as a radical exit, since the intended "object" ultimately sits in a light originating from the "subject." For this reason, consciousness's journey is one of a boomerang, inevitably ending with itself. As subjects, we fail to leave ourselves when we project toward the "world." Instead, that toward which we project is reduced to a signification *for* us, thus failing to remain "other." Ultimately, the subject continues to be alone, closing in on him- or herself and reducing, in that closure, all exteriority to modulations of the "same."[28] In light of my bringing Levinas into dialogue with Sartre, I note that Sartre's formulation of the transcendence of consciousness would fall under this narrative, which I categorize as a "first order" solitude. The implications of this are more fully developed in chapter 5, in my account of the Sartrean Other. However, for the moment it should be noted that what I subsequently uncover in Sartre's concrete descriptions of nausea seem to explicitly call into question his more formal account of a transcendence, the implication of which is the impossibility of a consciousness to be radically disrupted by an (absent) alterity.

A different kind of solitude is revealed in Levinas's account of the subject's encounter with the *il y a*, and in the diachrony that ensues from that encounter. Not yet intentional in structure, the *soi* relates to the *moi* as that to which it is irrevocably tied. The temporality of such an encounter indicates that the *moi* discovers the *soi* in an immemorial past (as that which is forever gone-by). Consequently, this order of solitude is concretely lived as a radical disturbance of subjective life. I find myself inevitably tied to that which is "never there," perpetually open to, implicated in and disrupted by a radical abandonment. Unlike the solitude founded on the privileging of the movement of intentionality, the relationship between the *moi* and the *soi* reveals a solitude that rests on the very impossibility of interiority, and as such, the very impossibility of the closure of identity.[29] I title the solitude of this exposed life a "second-order" solitude. Though both orders capture an existential aloneness, their difference is clear. With intentionality, *despite* its solitude, the subject remains untroubled and somewhat confident in her reductive practice over exteriority. However, with that "second-order" solitude, it is precisely this exteriority that troubles the subject (*moi*), in its relation with itself (*soi*). The existence, which the subject takes up, to ultimately *be* a subject, is encountered as an absolute and irreducible alterity, interrupting in its "coming from elsewhere."

"Identity in Intentionality" and "Identity in Recurrence"

In *Otherwise than Being*, Levinas introduces the term "recurrence" to capture the kind of diachrony that is portrayed through the relationship between the *moi* and the *soi*. As such, recurrence captures the way in which hypostasis demands a renegotiation of identity to include the disturbance of alterity *without* undermining the solitary nature of that identity. "In the hypostasis of an instant," Levinas writes, "we can discern the return of the *there is*. The hypostasis, in participating in the *there is*, finds itself again to be a solitude."[30] To reiterate, hypostasis has a triumphant aspect to it, since the event makes possible the "subjectivization of a subject."³¹ But if, through hypostasis, the goal of struggle is personalization (to set up oneself as a uniquely singular articulation of existence), then on hypostasis, the struggle continues *precisely insofar as* there is a unique and personal existent. In other words, hypostasis is "not yet spontaneity," since the event of becoming a personal existent generates the burden of facing, in the very structure of that uniqueness, the recurring threat of the *there is*.

Subjectivity retains its triumphant "preeminence over being," only insofar as it can push into the background of awareness its participation in the anonymity of pure existence, or its *fact* of existence. "Consciousness appears to stand out against the *there is* [in dominance] by its ability to forget and [subsequently] interrupt [this anonymous field]. . . ."³² By adopting a certain oblivion to its "self" (to its fact of being), the *moi* is positioned to enjoy the spontaneity of intentionality, "world and light." However, as its condition of possibility, this dominance over existence rests on a lived forgetting of that very event of existing. In this sense, hypostasis births an intimacy between consciousness and the *there is*, or between *moi* and *soi*, such that the burden of existence can be forgotten but never undone. It is across this ambivalence—of dominating existence by forgetting the vulnerability into which one is embroiled as the condition of that dominance—that I locate the difference between "first-" and "second"-order solitude. Hypostasis awards me the basis on which I can withdraw from myself, in a forgetting of my materiality, or of my being positioned, without a foothold, in existence. In the world of (intentional) light, I ultimately return to myself, insofar as I am mirrored in the objects of my experience. However, these intentional projections rest on a merciful oblivion of self, which would then cover over the irrevocable return of these projections, or keep hidden the fact that they ultimately begin and end with me.

This forgetfulness is sustained only insofar as my rivetedness to myself is not yet problematized. In other words, throughout the movement of intentionality, my anchor in existence remains concealed precisely because this inevitable solitude does not yet signify as troubling or disruptive. Rather, it rests in that cloak of security that shelters in an (intentional) sense-making. More importantly, Levinas's analysis shows that it is *only* as disrupted or troubled that the existent can encounter its condition as one of solitude. In other words, I come to "see" myself as "being with myself" only because I am already radically disrupted by that which is sufficiently exterior to bring about this disruption. Hence, the alterity at the heart of transcendence-as-excendence amounts to a rupture in (solitary) existence by precisely reinforcing that existence as *painfully* solitary.[33] The existent finds herself all the more riveted to a position in existence despite her encounter with a trace from "elsewhere." In other words, the experience of being disturbed by alterity would be the very experience of solitude.

Of these two orders of solitude ("intentionality" and "recurrence"), the difference is lived at the level of the concrete. It is a lived difference between two kinds of encounters with (or relations to) Being. "First-order" solitude is solitude as hidden insofar as my "being with myself" operates in invisibility. In turn, this invisibility presupposes that my "being with myself" has not yet been problematized. "Second-order" solitude would then be solitude unveiled as a consequence of the disturbance conditioning that revelation. This reinforces that, on Levinas's account, the central role awarded to alterity does not *undermine* our metaphysical solitude, but rather indicates a *reinforcement* of that truth. Beyond (or behind) intentional life, I find my "being with myself" showing up as severely inadequate. In this sense, solitary existence reveals itself as already infected with an obsession that makes it impossible for me to rest easy in myself. My fact of being, or of my being positioned in existence through hypostasis, is unveiled as a "not enough." This is because the affair to which I must respond does not belong to the "world and light" of intentionality. Hence, despite the successes and triumphs of that world, made possible through my forgetting of this primordial condition, I discover myself, in radical solitude, as always already inadequate and alone.

By describing the bond between the *moi* and *soi* in these terms, recurrence indicates that condition at the heart of identity, which troubles the very distinction between interiority and exteriority that would then make identity possible. Elisabeth Louise Thomas describes recurrence as "inequality beyond consciousness where the self is out of phase with itself," which underscores that the "without identity" of recurrence is less a violent annihilation of being (or of the being of the subject) and more a persistent "gnawing away of identity."[34] In this sense, the ego persists, or continues even though it does not continue "to be." It is most alone, or most extremely with its "self" in this precise moment of the rupturing of being (of its being) by radical otherness.

In this renegotiation of identity, Levinas does not separate the priority of the plague of solitude from his account of the radical obsession of alterity. Said otherwise, his "phenomenology" of the Other does not succumb to Rudi Visker's critical view, which states that, "In Levinas's universe, it is impossible not to hear the Other's appeal, [and thus] this view ignores the existence of a dimension of selfhood that cannot be absorbed into intersubjectivity."[35] Visker reads, in Levinas's portrayal of the Other's appeal, or rather, in the inevitability with which we hear that appeal, a disregarding of "a metaphysical loneliness" that, on his view, more realistically reflects our fundamental human condition. In other words, he interprets what Levinas develops as the disturbance through which solitude signifies as a *reprieve* (and as such, an outright denial of the primordial character) of solitude.[36] However, it is only in excluding Levinas's account of positionality, whereby identity is founded in recurrence, that readings such as these can be sustained. When he identifies the *moi* and the *soi* as terms in recurrence, Levinas describes the "oneness without any duality of oneself, from the first backed up against itself . . . twisted over itself in its skin . . . *in itself already outside of itself* [emphasis added]."[37] To recall, the aporia of the ensuing formulation of transcendence is that an exit from Being happens precisely when exiting is impossible. In a similar vein, the existent is disrupted in an encounter with radical alterity precisely in a revelation of its being abandoned to be "with itself," either in the passivity of an enchainment to Being, or in the "gnawing sensibility of remorse," with which the suffering of the Other is received.[38] In other words, the interruption tantamount to the face's expression would not be possible outside of what Visker's accurately identifies as the metaphysical solitude of our human condition. To determine, along with Levinas, that this disruption lies at the very heart of identity, is not to undermine the truth of a solitary existence. Rather, his analysis of the structures and meaning of positionality shows how the existential condition of an identity in recurrence rests on this truth.

In the following section, I trace Sartre's descriptions of nausea as described in the novel, *Nausea*. My account of this novel uncovers intersections between its analysis and what I have already established as the disruption constitutive of the Levinasian subject. Most importantly, and against many standard readings of this novel, I argue that Roquentin, the novel's protagonist undergoing the experience of nausea, is severely contested in his position as a subject, which is evidenced by the breakdown of his "world." In this sense, a moment like this, consisting of an undoing of both the subject and her constituted world, rests on an encounter with the radical alterity of pure existence. As in the case with Levinas's account of an encounter with the *il y a*, the Sartrean subject who undergoes this moment of nausea is more vulnerable than she is free. The ensuing weight of her solitary position in existence interrupts those constituting powers needed to project *as* a subject into a meaningful world.

III. Roquentin's Journey in *Nausea*

It should be noted that Levinas seems to explicitly set himself apart from Sartre's account of nausea when he writes, "In horror [before the meaninglessness of existence] a subject is stripped of his subjectivity, of his power to have private existence . . . [But] 'Nausea,' as a feeling for existence, is not yet a depersonalization."[39] The implication here is that, were nausea only a "feeling for existence," the experience would presuppose an integrity on the part of the subject, which would persevere despite the apparent disruption of the subject's intentional relation with the world. For Levinas, it is precisely this integrity that is undermined in an encounter with the *il y a*. He seems to understand nausea as an experience of existence whereby the subject ultimately continues to enjoy, despite his or her subsequent disquietude, the privilege of an inner life. I argue that, in subjecting the concrete descriptions of Roquentin's misery to these Levinasian standards, the account in *Nausea* does qualify as one that depicts a radical interruption of interiority. Said otherwise, Roquentin's turmoil is insofar as he no longer occupies the position of "subject." So despite the above intimations of a direct criticism of Sartre, Levinas would identify, in *Nausea*'s concrete analysis, a sufficiently severe disruption of interiority to qualify as an account of an encounter with brute existence.[40]

In Roquentin, Sartre portrays an individual whose moments of instability hardly resemble the sovereignty of a subject who purviews the world as from a distance. His trauma clearly denies him the possibility of apprehending an object across a relation of knowledge, which means that it is impossible for him to freely withdraw from being, to then view it from an (engaged) distance. Hence, in the experience of nausea, consciousness no longer seems implicated in an intentionally constituted *world*, but rather lost in a field of pure existence that is void of meaning. Though Sartre's portrayal of Roquentin poignantly captures the horror of pure existence, his ontology of a transcending consciousness (even that aspect of the ontology that accounts for the inevitability of an *engaged* transcendence) cannot adequately account for the gravity of moments such as this.[41] For this reason, a strictly Sartrean analysis of Roquentin's journey would understand the protagonist's relation to Being like every other relation between consciousness and exteriority as already, or at least potentially, a relation between "subject" and "world." In this sense, Sartre's work *would* fall prey to the above Levinasian critique. Nevertheless, I argue that Sartre *describes* the radical meaninglessness of pure existence, as well as its effect of interruption on consciousness. There is clear evidence for this throughout the trajectory of Roquentin's journey.

Roquentin's Horror

Nausea traces the academic adventures of Antoine Roquentin as he collects the material he needs to complete his research on Marquis de Rollebon. Sartre paints a picture of a man in utter and inner disarray. Nothing in his world appears to hold the explanation of his peculiar ailment; nothing seems to be able to explain Roquentin's inner turmoil—nothing, except the feeling of having lost his ground in being. This can be likened to Levinas's conception of positionality as a *de*positioning in existence, since, for Roquentin, things and people lose their significance at the blink of (his) eye. Even his thought patterns are void of meaning—"[through] the lack of attaching myself to words, my thoughts remain nebulous most of the time. They sketch vague, pleasant shapes and then are swallowed up . . ."[42] More often, the symptoms of his predicament are far from pleasant. From the strangeness of his own reflection, to the overpowering swarm of meaninglessness at the park, Roquentin's "world" disintegrates to an insignificant yet ominous swarm of stubborn existence. In other words, nothing that can be called "world" remains, in light of Roquentin's symptoms. "I draw my face closer until it touches the mirror. The eyes, nose and mouth disappear: *nothing human is left* [emphasis added] . . . An entire half of my face yields, the left half of the mouth twists and swells, uncovering a tooth, the eye opens on a white globe, on pink, bleeding flesh. That is not what I was looking for. . . ."[43]

In all this, Roquentin discovers himself to be mobilized despite himself, and unstable, as if on fluid ground. "I hesitated . . . and then there was a whirlpool, an eddy, a shadow passed across the ceiling and I felt myself pushed forward. I floated, dazed by luminous fogs dragging me in all directions at once."[44] Bernd Jager writes, "[In] elevators, on trains, at sea, the everyday, mundane instances of nausea appear when we feel ourselves not simply in motion, but more importantly, in motion *despite ourselves*."[45] In *Of Escape*, Levinas describes the moment of nausea in terms of "a refusal to remain there," with oneself.[46] This is interestingly juxtaposed to Jager's reading of nausea as a moment in which one *moves*, despite oneself. Though appearing to be opposed, these accounts echo quite similar sentiments. There is a sense in which, overcome by nausea, the subject encounters a loss of the ground or foothold out of which he or she can possess control. In other words, to be mobilized despite oneself is to no longer be in control of oneself. Levinas's description of nausea as a refusal to remain in place is subsequent to his conceiving of the experience as a manifestation of "[being] revolted from the inside."[47] Overcome by nausea, the existent longs for an escape from itself, which it would bring about was there *not* a disruption of ownership, control, or both over itself. However, Levinas's analysis is similar to Jager's exposition insofar as the work in *Of Escape* presents the moment of nausea as a moment of marked powerlessness. To be sure, Levinas couples this powerlessness with a certain resolve, on the part of the existent, to refuse the inevitability of its entrapment to its being. But "this effort [to refuse] is always characterized as desperate."[48] Hence, in the end, the lack of freedom portrayed at the heart of Roquentin's turmoil, and on which Jager comments, is also embedded in Levinas's conception.[49]

Quite against his will, Roquentin is "pushed forward" and "dragged." In his own words, "I am no longer free, I can no longer do what I will."[50] The freedom that Roquentin laments to have lost is the freedom with which consciousness organizes its world into a system of instrumentality *for* it. Out of this organization, things show up in light of their capacity to bring about the projects we freely constitute for ourselves. As David Detmer puts it, "[We] generally look at things under the color of our interests and projects.... When consciousness intends objects in its normal ways, it encounters *meanings*, not *existence* ... We see the *whatness* of things, rather than their *thatness*."[51] However, overcome by nausea, Roquentin is engulfed in an undeniable presence that no longer possesses "sense," utility or meaning. Rather, presence stands in its "thatness," radically independent of the "whatness" that existed *for* him. "You use [objects], put them back in place ... they are useful, nothing more." Roquentin seems to remind himself in desperation, but to no avail, "But [these objects] touch me, it is unbearable. I am afraid of being in contact with them as though they were living beasts."[52] Sartre's use of metaphors of monstrosity suggests that objects are not merely useless, but more strongly, they burst through the confines of utility altogether. All the indications of intentionality appear to fall away in Roquentin's experience. The loss of control, his overwhelming instability, all point to a replacement of his world by a superfluous existence.

Nevertheless, Roquentin does feel himself to be quite separate from the field of senselessness making itself present to him. Said otherwise, he "knows" himself to be distinct from this undifferentiated existence, so it is not the case that this experience of being engulfed amounts to a complete annihilation of the consciousness undergoing nausea. In other words, there is still that singularity of the self, very similar to what we find in the Levinasian account of the existent in her encounter with the *il y a*. In both cases, there is a personalization that does not yet qualify as subjectivity, insofar as it is a personalization grounded in a vulnerability (and not in spontaneity). Quite frankly, there are aspects of Roquentin's condition whereby he is overwhelmingly aware of himself. To borrow from my earlier analysis of Levinas's conception of solitude, the moment of nausea indicates a most extreme "being with oneself." Roquentin feels himself as "not being" the chestnut tree, yet he also feels himself immersed passively in what is no longer a world. "I am in the midst of things, nameless things. Alone . . . defenseless, they surround me, are beneath me, behind me, above me."[53]

To recall, Sartre tells us that, as a movement of intentionality that is inevitably embodied, consciousness is an "engaged surpassing" in the world.[54] As it transcends toward objects of experience, it is simultaneously *there*, in the world. However, this sense of being-there, or of "being in the world" is precisely not what Roquentin describes of his immersion in the meaningless swarm around him. I return to my earlier distinction between "first-" and "second-order" solitude, and locate, in the former, Sartre's conception of nonthetic consciousness. This is insofar as first-order solitude rests on a "forgetting of oneself" that is typical of an intentional relation to "world." As subjects, we experience ourselves in terms of the objects of our experience, oblivious to our "selves," since our self-awareness really *is* an awareness of the objects in the world.[55] It is for this reason that Sartre emphasizes, in his account of intentionality, that "consciousness" and "world" are in one stroke, inseparable at the level of concrete experience. However, in Roquentin's case, self-awareness looses this ecstatic nature. He is no longer *outside* himself and "in the world," but rather, finds himself irrevocably riveted to himself, or to his being. He does not apprehend himself "from a distance," precisely because the world out of which this act of withdrawal takes place has disintegrated.

In *Being and Nothingness*, Sartre defines nausea as the "perpetual apprehension on the part of [the] for-itself of an insipid taste which [it] cannot place, which accompanies [it] even in [its] efforts to get away from it, and which is *[its]* taste."[56] One "cannot place" the taste characteristic of nausea because it indicates that which is too close, namely, one's self. As a result, there is no room to withdraw. I encounter myself through this insipid taste that is my nausea, but that self (*my* self) is precisely that from which I "cannot get away." Echoing this sentiment, Roquentin writes, "[Existence] is there, around us, in us, it is *us*, you can't say two words without mentioning it, but you can never touch it."[57] That this alterity is resistant to touch is quite telling, insofar as it underscores what I determine to be most significant in Sartre's novel. It is clear that Sartre intends his reader to understand this encounter with existence as something *suffered* by the consciousness involved. As I have already shown, Levinas conceptualizes suffering to signify as precisely the impossibility of escaping that moment of suffering. There are no avenues out of which one might establish the distance that would lessen the intensity of the subject's obligation to be with his- or herself. We might utilize this analysis here, to capture the sense of Roquentin's proclamation that "existence, though all around, can never be *touched*." In the extremity of his nausea, there is no distance between Roquentin and himself that could provide the condition for any kind of active apprehension on his part, such as one in the mode of touch. Monstrously "other," the alterity of pure existence is, all the same, Roquentin himself, wholly foreign yet wholly intimate. This brings to mind Levinas's conception of the subject's relation to itself, and the passivity that is characteristic of that relation.[58] In nausea, we no longer find ourselves through a recognizable world of meaning, but rather as vulnerable to a strangeness that is other *in* us. It is at this point that intentionality appears as a flawed exit, and that the "forgetting of self" of first-order solitude is replaced by the "I must be with myself" of second-order solitude. On this account, Roquentin's nausea is an event much like what Levinas understands of insomnia. Both moments point to an inevitable impossibility of escaping ourselves.

IV. Transcending despite "Nausea"?

Nonetheless, given the dominance of his conception of transcendence-as-intentionality, it comes as no surprise that readers of Sartre understand nausea within the parameters of a consciousness that *does* escape itself through intentional projections. I set my reading of *Nausea* alongside these more standard interpretations, showing that because nausea reveals the subject's positionality in brute existence, it falls outside of an intentional reference to things. In other words, the encounter with existence that happens in a moment of nausea signifies more positively than a failed intentionality, or as the unyieldingly infinite possibility of meaning-giving for consciousness.[59] Roquentin's positioning shows up insofar as he must always be "with" himself more fundamentally than he surpasses being toward objects of experience. In this sense, the argument that transcendence-as-intentionality describes our *primary* relation to being is flawed. More prior to a relationship with being across intentionality, subjectivity is a rivetedness to being (or a positioned immersion in being). In this sense, I situate Sartre's concrete description of nausea alongside the Levinasian phenomenologies of insomnia and fatigue as all moments of affectivity that demonstrate this rivetedness in being. Hence, in his phenomenology of nausea, Sartre seems to have portrayed an *undergoing* on the part of consciousness, which is something radically beyond the parameters of intentionality. In this sense, an account of a consciousness that autonomously constitutes a network of meaning, through which a realm of transphenomenal being shows up as a world, does not quite formalize what Roquentin lives through.

Nausea as a Revelation of Facticity

I identify Thomas Busch's commentary as a fair representation of those analyses of *Nausea*, which I currently call into question. Thomas Busch points out that "[the] reason for this neglect [that is typical of intentionality] of existence is that, while engaged in projects, consciousness is outside of itself, preoccupied with the world."[60] Preoccupied as such, consciousness is able to keep in the background its most immediate bond with existence itself. Busch interprets *Nausea* as Sartre's way of articulating this "forgotten existence," and as such, of affirming the facticity of consciousness. To this end, the novel is presented as a Sartrean critique of Husserl's phenomenological reduction. To recall from chapter one, Sartre understands, and is consequently wary of, the *epoché* as that which demolishes all belief concerning the actual world. For Sartre, not only does this leave unexplained the actual existence of the world, but also the value of the facticity of consciousness. According to his critique, the *epoché* cannot account for the "motivation" behind the different ways in which real and imaginary objects are intended. Hence, on Thomas Busch's reading, Sartre uses *Nausea* to correct this shortcoming, and presents those concrete descriptions that *would* give "evidence" for such motivation. In the end, it is pure and actual existence that explains the difference in intentionality between the imaginary and the real, and it is this pure existence for which (according to Sartre) the *epoché* cannot account. Summarizing Sartre's position on the phenomenological reduction, Busch writes, "For Husserl, subjectivity consists of *acts* of consciousness, of which perception is the foundation. Sartre sees an irrational specificity here . . . Intending acts can break down into their "stuff." The body can "sense" its facticity and is more than simply an intentional system."[61]

In this regard, Busch interprets Sartre as identifying, in the experience of nausea, an aspect of consciousness that cannot neatly subscribe to the structures of intentionality. In other words, his reading of Sartre determines that nausea is, indeed, not yet an *intentional* encounter with being. However, he understands this "not yet intentional" aspect of consciousness in terms of facticity, or in terms of a relation to being that is ultimately captured by the Sartrean structures of facticity. I discuss facticity at length in chapter 4, but chapter 1 lays sufficient ground to establish that, within Sartre's formal account of experience, facticity does not undo the primacy of freedom that sustains his formal ontology. On the contrary, Sartre's account of facticity maintains that consciousness's relationship with being is exhaustively one across the spontaneous projection of intentionality. My argument is that the experience of nausea reveals a loss of stability that voids all possibility of these projections. The threat of "being mobilized" without notice, or of being riveted against one's will, indicates the very absence of ground that would enable a free movement of intentionality. As something that *happens* to us, nausea reveals a passivity in our being, rather than, or prior to the active constituting on the part of consciousness. Busch is correct in reading *Nausea* as an account of what it means to encounter the pure and undifferentiated existence that "stands behind" our meaningful world. He is also right to identify Sartre's descriptions as gesturing toward what is "not yet intentional." However, in equating this purity of existence with consciousness's facticity, his interpretation of Sartre's descriptions of nausea maintains the absolute freedom of consciousness. Furthermore, for Sartre, facticity is "the fact of not being able not to be free."[62] Hence, insofar as facticity shows up as such, it is always already meaningful, and therefore always already the consequence of a freely surpassing consciousness. In describing Roquentin as being able to "sense" his facticity,[63] Busch leaves unanalyzed that level of identity at which consciousness *is no longer* an intentional system. If the brute existence encountered by Roquentin is indeed his facticity, it is that "given" from which he has already escaped or surpassed, and which possesses meaning *for* him.

"Existence is a fullness which man can never abandon," are Roquentin's words, as he agonizes over his destabilizing experience.[64] Michael Brogan successfully identifies the similarities between this description of brute existence, and the ones employed by Levinas in both *Existence and Existents* and *Time and the Other*.[65] There is a sense in which Sartre, in both *Nausea* and *Being and Nothingness*, presents being-in-itself with a fullness that cannot simply be reduced to the negation of consciousness, since it possesses a positivity all its own.[66] Nevertheless, his explicit intention is for any such positivity (in a transphenomenal being-in-itself) to signify differently from the presence of the Levinasian *il y a*. Unlike the plenitude of the *il y a*, which Levinas overtly employs in his formalization of the subject's passivity, the fullness of being-in-itself is quite complicit with Sartre's formalizations of the structure of consciousness as absolutely free. So though Roquentin's exclamation concerning the fullness of existence bears similarity with Levinas's descriptions of "the irremissibility of pure existing,"[67] the implications of this fullness differ for Sartre and Levinas respectively. The "irremissibility of pure existence," for Levinas, means that it is impossible to exit being, though, quite aporetically, this impossibility grounds the possibility of transcendence-as-excendence. For Sartre, the fullness of existence, "which Roquentin can never abandon," means something entirely different.[68] The positivity of being-in-itself does not affect the absolute *negativity* of consciousness, and in this sense, supports the idea of a subject as always already exiting being.[69] To recall, an important distinction for Sartre is the one between "being" and "existing"—consciousness is an essential escape from *being*, but it cannot "*not* exist*." Hence, when Sartre claims (either explicitly or implicitly) that existence is inescapable, he refers to the necessity with which consciousness must be empty of all being. Said differently, the impossibility of escaping existence for Sartre just *is* the necessity with which the self "is always at a distance from itself by virtue of its conscious, projective activity."[70]

In this vein, Sartre's "rivetedness to existence" is meant in a sense that is completely opposed to the work in *Existence and Existents*. Levinas holds that we are riveted insofar as we are "full of being,"[71] whereas in *Nausea*, Roquentin is riveted insofar as he is radically free, or is an absolute nothingness of being.[72] My bringing Sartre's account of nausea under a Levinasian scrutiny maintains these significant differences in what I regard as their formal enunciations of identity. In light of these differences, it is all the more striking that Sartre's concrete phenomenology quite successfully underscores the formal account developed in Levinas's work.

Nausea as the Groundwork for the Phenomenological Reduction

In another commentary, Thomas Busch also advocates for a reading of Roquentin's character as representative of consciousness taking leave of the "natural attitude" that precedes Husserl's *epoché*. "With the break-up of the life-world, it is possible to discern the beginnings of the reduction, of a disengagement from the life-world in order to thematize it."[73] One also finds this reading in Bernd Jager's essay, in which he understands Sartre's descriptions of nausea to "[bespeak] a . . . radical break within our environment, a loss of what has been taken for granted, a sudden departure from known and trusted ways, an alienation from our ground . . ."[74] Interpretations such as these find, in the agony of nausea, the subject coming to terms with his or her responsibility to support the justification and value of which his or her "world" is comprised. Prior to this realization, the subject treats as absolute all belief and meaning of which that world is constituted. On this reading of Sartre, Roquentin's anguish is that inevitable passage through which consciousness passes as it finally accepts that every object is ultimately a noematic correlate of a free *noema*. To use a mundane but nonetheless pointed example, while I apprehended the rose in front of me as *intrinsically* pleasant, nausea prepares a subsequent (and more phenomenologically accurate) apprehension of the "rose-as-pleasing" as an intentional construct of my consciousness.[75]

In this regard, the experience of nausea reinforces the absolute existence of consciousness. Even as the world dissolves into anarchy, the subject finds herself positioned triumphantly, to create out of the monstrosity of pure existence, a coherent and meaningful world. Prior to Roquentin's crisis, the things that he encounters as utilizable are marked with a certain permanence. Interpretations like Busch's and Jager's would say that he does not yet realize these "tools" to be noematic correlations of (his) noetic acts of intentionality. His nausea rests on a revelation of this truth, which then sends Roquentin whirling into an abysmal appropriation of his responsibility. For Sartre, this abyss reflects none other than the absolute extent to which consciousness is free. The implication of these readings is that Sartre employs *Nausea*'s phenomenological descriptions to demonstrate that, without Roquentin, there is no world. He is the sole and ultimate source of value and meaning.

I argue that though this reading of Sartre is reasonable, nausea's ordeal is not necessarily exhausted by this explanation. In Sartre's concrete analysis, nausea reveals pure and undifferentiated existence. "The thing which was waiting was on the alert, it had *pounced on me* [emphasis added], it flows through me. I am filled with it. It's nothing: I am the Thing. Existence, liberated, detached, floods over me."[76] Existence is clearly described as *overcoming* the consciousness to which it is "revealed," and this should not be undermined so as to favor a formal account of consciousness as an absolute freedom. Of this overcoming, Busch writes, "[Existence] reveals itself as nauseating to a certain type of consciousness, a certain *noesis* [emphasis added]."[77] If we understand the consciousness that encounters existence as (still) an intentional act, and the "revealed existence" as (merely) a noematic correlate, then we ultimately miss what is clearly described in the novel's phenomenology. This amounts to ignoring an aspect of identity that is precisely *not* free to engage in a reflective exercise like the phenomenological reduction. To say this differently, a necessary condition for Husserl's *epoché* is that consciousness is already free to disengage itself from the natural attitude, a disengagement that could be nothing other than a spontaneous *act*. However, Roquentin is not *described* as a subject who "actively mentally destroys the objectivity of things," and a reading of Sartre should be wary to *formalize* the character in this way. Both Roquentin's position as "subject" and his world disintegrate *against his will*, such that he *suffers* this event.

To this end, I argue that nausea is a revelation of a more primordial positioned and *affected* solitude, on which free subjectivity then stands. Roquentin does experience himself as an existent, already differentiated from an anonymous field of existence. However, Sartre's descriptions point to a level whereby "existing" is not yet tantamount to the freedom of consciousness. In other words, "Roquentin the existent" seems anterior to "Roquentin the intending subject of experience," very much like Levinas's *soi* is anterior to the *moi*. Though this conception of identity is not part of Sartre's formal ontology, his concrete description of nausea clearly resonates with this idea of a passivity underlying the work of freedom.[78]

My reading of Sartre's concrete descriptions "on their own terms" is explicitly Levinasian, since, on their own terms, they *are* indistinguishable from Levinas's analysis. To be sure, unlike the conception of identity included in the account of hypostasis, the Sartrean consciousness is an *emptiness* of being. The implication of hypostasis, on the other hand, is that transcendence (as excendence) rests on a *fullness* of the being of the existent. Nonetheless, the similarity between Levinas's account of the *il y a* and Sartre's description of nausea must be noted. I understand Sartre's formal position as one that comes from a commitment, in advance of his phenomenology, to grounding an emancipatory philosophy. In this regard, his is an ontology that conditions the claim that the human subject is absolutely free to give meaning to her situation. Nevertheless, his concrete descriptions of nausea point to a more Levinasian understanding of how we encounter ourselves as corporeal and positioned in an existence that comes to us as radically "other." In chapter 4, I present a similar reading of those descriptions in Sartre, which I broadly construe as descriptions of affectivity. Insofar as they reveal a passivity similar to the one I have uncovered in Roquentin's encounter with pure existence, these descriptions further align the "concrete" Sartre with Levinas's articulation of a primordial vulnerability in identity. I have given Sartre's work on nausea its own treatment, to the degree that it (implicitly) recognizes a relation with being within which the structures of intentionality do not yet belong. In this regard, the analysis of nausea sets the ground for a more positive articulation of what my analysis in chapter four regards as a region (in identity) of affectivity. The ides of consciousness as riveted or positioned implies a relationship between the self and being that is more disruptive of subjectivity than intentionality would suggest. Chapter 2 presented Levinas's explicit articulation of such trauma in his concrete descriptions of moments like insomnia, fatigue, and suffering, whereby the immanence of the self does not yet constitute a free subject. In chapter 4, I establish that Sartre intimates a similar (nonintentional) anarchy in his descriptions of embodiment and affectivity, in general, even though he maintains, in light of this phenomenology, a formal account of an exclusively intentional relation between consciousness and being. To reiterate, this formal account compels a reading of the descriptions in *Nausea* as depicting its protagonist encountering his radical responsibility to freely create a meaningful world.[79] However, the next chapter's analysis of affective experience shows that such moments are marked by a significant interruption of those distinctions that designate the "subject" apart from his "world." In employing the resources found in Levinas's understanding of identity, we see that, in these moments of affectivity, consciousness's primary relation with being is across a vulnerability.

CHAPTER 4

Levinasian Positionality Implicit in Sartre's Affective Experiences

Throughout Sartre's ontology, all experiences are interpreted as belonging to a consciousness whose entire relationship with being is one of intentionality. This is no different for the lived moments that are discussed here. According to Sartre's formal account of transcendence-as-intentionality, the significance of this phenomenology of positionality is negative. In other words, they are described in terms of what they are *not*, namely a spontaneous projection toward being. However, I argue that outside of this formal account, and in prioritizing the level of the concrete, they point to a primordial level of positionality, since they all feature consciousness encountering the limit of its freedom. This is the premise on which I presently reconstruct Sartre's account of facticity and its relation to embodiment, pain-consciousness, as well as shame in being-seen. I argue that they signify an originary positionality of consciousness that is otherwise than a limitation to spontaneity. While transcendence-as-intentionality reads, from this limitation, an *opposition* that freedom must reduce, the idea of a consciousness that is originally positioned in being would require us to find, in this limit, a challenge to an already-unjustified spontaneous freedom. In other words, it gives the Levinasian picture of a freedom that is "always already" invested. Upon this interpretation, consciousness is not called to conquer in these instances when freedom is limited. Rather, it would be called to give an account for its freedom, or for projects that are grounded by that freedom.

It was shown in chapter 1 that Sartre's formulation of consciousness as transcendence-as-intentionality means that consciousness just "is" a complete surpassing of being, *toward* being. As such, consciousness is a pure emptiness, or "nothing at all." This transcendence *toward* being is an ecstatic relation that frees consciousness from all "ties," including those to its "self." Nonetheless, Sartre's descriptions of "conscious body" and "pain consciousness," like the concrete descriptions contained in *Nausea*, suggest a relation with being other than this ecstatic surpassing. To be sure, many of Sartre's analyses do support a consciousness that transcends toward being (his descriptions of temporality is one such example). Hence, I reiterate that it is *not* my claim that transcendence-as-intentionality is not an applicable account of consciousness's relation to being. Rather, I argue that intentionality is not its *only* relation, and it is certainly not its most fundamental one.

This chapter's discussion begins with Sartre's notion of facticity, as revealed in his phenomenology of the body. Though facticity was introduced in chapter 1, this chapter more fully develops the claim that Sartre's concrete descriptions of facticity expose a subject who is dense with being. For Sartre, embodiment is revealed as being "given over" to us, since we neither choose to be a body, nor do we choose the fundamental type of bodies that we are. This counts as a revelation of the facticity of consciousness, insofar as it includes aspects of consciousness that precludes its spontaneous acts. Sartre explains that consciousness is necessarily embodied, and for this reason an experience of the world is always "situated." However, his explicit conception of "being in situation" does not in the least limit the free transcendence of consciousness. Rather, it further supports Sartre's claim that intentionality exhausts consciousness's primary engagement in being. It is *as* embodied, or in situation, that consciousness ecstatically surpasses being.[1] I discuss Sartre's interpretation of the phenomena of physical pain and sensation, showing that, despite the affectivity he describes in these experiences, he still recognizes them as belonging to a consciousness that surpasses being absolutely.

The following section argues that Sartre's formal ontology is also less equipped than Levinas's conception of identity when it comes to accounting for his own description of shame. Both identify shame as a "revelation" of an aspect of ourselves that we would "like to hide." Sartre describes this aspect as "degraded," while Levinas describes it as a mode of "ourselves as diminished beings."[2] The similarity in descriptive language suggests that both find a similar modification in the subject living that event of shame. Nonetheless, despite his concrete descriptions, Sartre never articulates what we find in Levinas, which is the structural passivity of an imploded subject. I claim that this is the case because, when it comes to this locus of vulnerability in the subject, Sartre's formal structures betray the concrete descriptions to which they should be accountable. As such, I read his descriptions of shame as a continuation of what I understand to be a calling into question of his formal ontology of a radically free "I," void of all being.

In the end, although Sartre ultimately identifies an ecstatically transcending consciousness in them, the experiences discussed show an aspect of the subject captured in Levinas's notion of positionality. To recall from chapters 2 and 3, hypostasis, for Levinas, is that event in being, whereby consciousness establishes its position (or foothold) in being, to then be able to transcend freely in the movement of intentionality. This "base" in existence is precarious, insofar as it grounds both the victorious conquering of existence *and* the existent's vulnerability under the weight of that very existence. In this sense, hypostasis characterizes that event through which consciousness is ambiguously *both* "autonomous subject" and "passive existent." Levinas's conception of transcendence-as-excendence is able to account for this event, because he understands transcendence *not* as an ecstatic movement toward being, but rather in terms of a desire for an exit *from* being. It is precisely in the anarchical vulnerability before existence that this exit is accomplished. Even though Sartre's formalizations of the affective moments of consciousness include an account of consciousness's rootedness, my reading finds it deprioritized to a more privileged account of an unlimited freedom.

I The Body as Facticity

Through his account of facticity, Sartre gives a concrete understanding of human freedom. He emphasizes that, though consciousness is a nothingness of being, it is ultimately always situated. The implication of its being situated is that, at all times, the subject faces certain "coefficients of adversity" against which he or she must exercise her freedom. Sartre's argument is that it is only through freedom that these coefficients of adversity show up as such, since it is ultimately *for consciousness* that certain aspects of being-in-itself appear as resistance to be overcome.[3] Hence, despite the account of "being in situation," consciousness is understood as fundamentally free. The concrete meaning of freedom is that consciousness encounters resistance in the world, as it projects itself toward the future. But this resistance does not come as a limitation of freedom. The very *meaning* of our facticity—that there are obstacles to our freedom—is grounded in freedom. Indeed, the world that resists consciousness is *its* world, since meaning is always *for consciousness*. In this sense, even in the midst of those factical aspects, consciousness has already transcended, absolutely, toward certain possibilities. In other words, facticity already "fits" into a world that is constructed in light of my free choices.[4]

Sartre's locates the significance of the body within the parameters of facticity, and as such, understands embodiment to support the conception of an absolutely free subject. Against the misguided mind-body problem, his is not an account of consciousness and "its" body as two distinct substances, whose relation must subsequently be established. Rather, Sartre holds that consciousness is always embodied, and bodies are necessarily conscious. Concretely, we *are* our bodies, and any distinction would be on a level of formal abstraction only. The very possibility of experience is conditioned by embodiment. "[By] the mere fact that there is a world, this world can not exist without a univocal orientation in relation to me."[5] In other words, objects in the world are necessarily experienced spatially, and this means that consciousness must have a spatial position, from which it can apprehend the spatialized objects of experience. Outside of this orientation, the phenomenon of the world cannot signify. Hence, consciousness is such that it is always "to the left or right of" that of which there is consciousness. In other words, intentionality happens in terms of this spatial orientation.

The body is therefore the point through which consciousness is situated in the world. I am necessarily "there with objects," immersed in a common spatial network. However, it is also always the case that consciousness intends objects across a distance. "To come into existence, for me, is to unfold my distances from things and thereby to cause things 'to be there.'"[6] Hence, the body is both a point of immersion *in* the world and a withdrawal *from* the world. Sartre tells us that we apprehend our body as that which we have already escaped. It "is never a given which I can know . . . it exists only in so far as I escape it by nihilating myself."[7] Hence, my body has already been transcended by the time it shows up (as meaningful). This transcendence of the body means that consciousness's embodied immersion in the world is in the form of a "nihilating escape from being." The body just *is* the original upsurge in and withdrawal from being, facilitating the free and creative projects of consciousness. In this sense, Sartre's account of embodiment and "being in situation" supports an account that understands intentionality as the original relation between consciousness and being. Intentionality necessarily occurs as a body, which is precisely why the body does not compromise the primacy of freedom. "[We] have laid down as the foundation of the revelation of the body as such our original relation to the world—that is, our very [free] upsurge into the midst of being."[8] The revelation of my body means that I have already escaped it, or transcended, toward my possibilities.

Sartre's treatment of the instrumentality of objects of experience further demonstrates this. Fundamentally, objects in the world are experienced according to the functions they fulfill (the hammer does not show up as oddly shaped pieces of wood, glued together, but rather, as a hammer), insofar as I know of its use beforehand. Sartre carries this analysis as near to us as our own hands. I pick up the hammer, I also employ my hands as instruments. Nonetheless, the difference between the hand and the hammer is that, unlike the hammer, I *am* my hands (along with my body in general). This means that my hand does not show up for me explicitly, but rather disappears into the background of the experience of using the hammer (to, perhaps, drive a nail into a wall). To be sure, my approaching the hammer is "confined" (as it were) to begin from my hands, just as my relation to the world in general is confined to happen as my "being a body." But that "confinement" makes possible a transcending toward possibilities, which is to say that the body does not limit, but rather facilitates, an ecstatic movement of transcendence.

Sartre's treatment of the phenomena of affectivity and physical pain is no different from his analysis of the body (for-itself). We have established that the body is the necessary condition for the free being of consciousness, insofar as it offers that standpoint from which I then transcend the past, in order to freely project toward future possibilities. In other words, "body" provides a ground on which there can be that primary relation of intentionality (or transcendence-as-intentionality), without in any way compromising, or making less free, this transcending engagement in being. Thomas Anderson's analysis successfully uncovers certain inconsistencies surrounding this issue in the Sartrean analysis.[9] But he also determines, quite correctly, that the cards ultimately fall on the side of a consciousness whose radical spontaneity is *despite* its embodiment. Consequently, it is important that readers of Sartre also negotiate this conception of consciousness with those descriptive moments in his work, where he presents the body as a locus through which consciousness feels itself a passive recipient of being, or what I determine to be his (concrete) phenomenologies of affectivity. In such accounts, there are aspects of experience that are beyond the powers of my manipulation in the sense that I must resign myself to something that has *happened to* me. For instance, we suffer grief over the loss of a loved one, or on the opposite end of the spectrum, we are overcome with joy at the birth of a child. In both cases, it is improbable that we can identify (through introspection, perhaps) the instant in which we *choose* to grieve, or *choose* to be happy, precisely because these are affective states that we apprehend as being "given over to."

Physical pain is a significant instance of this kind of affectivity, since it belongs to that region of embodiment, which, according to Sartre, is the source of spontaneity. Additionally, Sartre's descriptions of the phenomenology of pain features what has already been seen in Levinas's account as a union between consciousness and its "self." In those moments of grief and joy, I find that I cannot tear myself away from myself-as-grieving, or myself-as-joyful, precisely because of this union. Despite Sartre's claim that such experiences retain a fundamental surpassing of consciousness, this impossibility to withdraw from "self" indicates the impossibility to *will* the end of the affective moment. So even though Sartre reads, in the experience of physical pain, evidence that the "pained body" has already been transcended, it is also the case that, unique to such moments is an unwilled attachment to one's position in being, which must also be accounted for.

Given that Sartre determines the body to be that point of engagement with being out of which consciousness upsurges as a radical nothingness of being, he holds that we do not have an explicit experience *of* the body. This is because the body provides this *condition* of experience. Put otherwise, it is impossible to take a withdrawn point of view on the body, precisely because our point of view *is* the body. "[It is] impossible to withdraw in order to 'give oneself plenty of room' and to constitute a new point of view on the point of view [that is our bodies]."[10] This means, according to Sartre, that there is no consciousness *of* the body in the way that there is consciousness *of* objects in the world. The body is given over to consciousness in a similar sense in which signs are given over, hidden and indicating something beyond itself. The stop sign at the intersection performs its function because it is apprehended as "to be surpassed" toward the meaning "behind it." In a similar sense, Sartre tells us that the body is revealed to consciousness in its being surpassed toward that which it conditions, namely, the experience of a spatialized "world."

Yet, the body must be given over in some way, "since I can be nothing without being the consciousness of what I am. . . ."[11] For Sartre, this is the function of affectivity in general, and physical pain in particular; they result in a nonpositional consciousness of the body.[12] "Consciousness (of) the body is a lateral and retrospective consciousness of what consciousness is without having to be it (i.e., of its inapprehensible contingency [and by contingency Sartre refers to the fact that consciousness *must* be a body without having 'to be'], of that in terms of which consciousness makes itself a choice) and *hence it is a non-thetic consciousness of the manner in which it is affected* [emphasis added]."[13] It is through the affective aspects of experience that consciousness apprehends its body, but because this is always done prereflectively, the body is never a known object for consciousness. Nevertheless, Sartre holds that the affective acts themselves have correlate transcendent objects (even though the body is not given as one such object). In this sense, Sartre regards affective experience to be no different from experience in general, locating it under that umbrella of an intentionality (between consciousness and a region of a transcendent world). "All hate is hate of someone," which means that, in being affected by an emotion like hate, "a transcendent 'intention' is directed toward the world and apprehends it as such. Already therefore there is a surpassing. . . ."[14] These affects are ultimately *acts* of consciousness, taking consciousness outside of itself and into the world.[15]

The Affectivity of "Pain Consciousness"

There is a sense in which Sartre recognizes that the "whole" of the manner of the body's revelation for consciousness is not captured in its pointing beyond itself to some transcendent object in the world. He distinguishes between "pure pain" and "pain-consciousness," and emphasizes that his analysis does not pertain to the former. "Pure pain as the simple "lived" cannot be reached; it belongs to the category of indefinables and indescribables which are what they are."[16] Here, Sartre indicates an aspect of pain's affectivity that refers to the manner in which consciousness "exists" its pain. Unlike pain-consciousness, which is shaped by intentional acts that allow transcendent objects in the world to show up, "pure pain is totally void of intentionality."[17] In this sense, pain is on *this* side (the side of consciousness) of the relation between consciousness and world, and hence, there is nothing transcendent about it. Unlike the affective states of grief and joy, pain does not allow for a cognitive grasp of an object in the world, precisely because it does not come to consciousness "from a distance." Pure pain, or what, under the Sartrean account of consciousness, remains "indefinable and indescribable," means that physical pain *is* consciousness. It is "the translucent matter of consciousness; its "*being-there*," its attachment to the world."[18]

It is interesting that Sartre brings together the terms "translucent" and "matter." In his ontology, the translucent character of consciousness typically grounds its nonbeing, accounting for the fact that consciousness is all lightness and lucidity. Matter, on the other hand, is what Sartre assures us could never be an aspect of consciousness. As pure density, matter would be the "germ of opaqueness" that is banished from the structure of the for-itself.[19] Any such opacity would destroy consciousness's "nonbeing," making it "heavy and ponderable." Hence, in describing consciousness in terms of "translucent matter," Sartre seems to be articulating the very paradox of affectivity, whereby the body positions both subjectivity *and* a self who is not yet free to withdraw from her embodied position. A similar paradox is described in Levinas's conception of an identity that is both a transcending subject *and* a riveted existent. Though Sartre's formal account of consciousness never comes close to this Levinasian "identity in recurrence," it is important to recognize what remains on the outside of that Sartrean account, as implicitly acknowledged but not formalized.[20] This becomes even clearer in the following example that Sartre cites. While reading, I may find that my eyes become painful. To reiterate, my "eye-as-painful" is not an object transcendent to my act of reading. On the contrary, I carry out this act *through* my pained-eyes (they are "not distinguished from my way of apprehending transcendent words"[21]). Insofar as I *must* now carry out the conscious act of reading *through* painful eyes, I am reminded that my sole means of relating to the world is as (or through) a body. To be sure, outside of my experience of pain, this inevitability slips into the forgotten background of my spontaneous projections. But pain gives my body over to me as that which I must be, or as that to which I must be attached. In this example, one reads Sartre's attempt to present the paradox of "translucent matter," or the paradox of a spontaneous field of ecstatic projections that is nowise dense with being as a consequence of embodiment.

These descriptions reveal a rivetedness in being that is also a noncoinciding with that position in being. "Pain-consciousness . . . exists its pain—i.e., itself—as a wrenching away from self. . . . [it] is a project toward a furure consciousness which would be empty of all pain."[22] In this account, Sartre seems to read the sense in which consciousness "is not" its pain as a transcending or surpassing (of that pain). However, might this not be akin to the phenomenology found in Levinas's analysis of the revolt characteristic of moments of suffering? In 1935, some ten years earlier than Sartre's descriptions in *Being and Nothingness*, Levinas also attempts to account for an autonomous "I" that is nevertheless riveted to being, or to its position in being. "[This] revelation of being [as that to which we are attached without reprieve, especially evident in the experience of suffering] . . . is at the same time the experience of a revolt. Such a revolt no longer has anything in common with what opposed the 'I' to the 'non-I.' "[23] What Sartre describes in his analysis as the refusal of pain is very similar to what Levinas describes as a refusal of *one's own being*. As such, they both describe an imprisonment in oneself that is nonreducible to the reification found in a materialistic account of identity.[24] Of such moments of pain/suffering, Sartre writes, "the inexpressible which one wishes to flee is *rediscovered at the heart of this very wrenching away* [emphasis added]."[25] To be overcome by a pained corporeality is, indeed, to live as a rejection of that pain, or more precisely, to live as a rejection of my present being as painful. However, that rejection is haunted, and perhaps even fueled by the steadfastness with which consciousness is "held on to" by its pain.

Sartre is right to identify, in this rejection by consciousness, a projection toward a "better" consciousness through which there can be a more pain-free way of transcending toward the world. In a similar fashion, Levinas identifies, in this "revelation of being," a definite revolt, or refusal to resign to "things as they are." But to say that this aspect of pain-consciousness (in its most immediate sense) is a surpassing, or an "internal negation of the world," is to undermine the sense in which pain is a revelation of *my being*. The decisive difference between those acts of consciousness that are an actual transcending toward objects in the world, and those moments of affectivity (or *non*acts) that are the underbelly of *pain-consciousness*, is that the latter signify as a relation between consciousness and its "self" ("pain does not exist anywhere among the actual objects of the universe"[26]), and not as a relation between consciousness and "world."

Hence, notwithstanding the ramifications of his formal account, Sartre's descriptions read as descriptions of that most immediate bond between consciousness and its "self." This stands alongside other portrayals in his work, of events in which we encounter our "selves" without, or rather, *before* we possess the freedom to surpass our embodied position in being. In such moments, consciousness encounters its body across what Levinas rightly regards as a fissure, since, as pained, the body is both what one must be, *and* that with which one cannot completely identify. Here, the language of "fissure" is pertinent for capturing the significance of the noncoincidence between consciousness and "consciousness in pain," without reducing that noncoincidence to the distance typical of consciousness's intentional movement.²⁷ In other words, by employing this Levinasian language, it possible to recognize the body as that from which we are separate, but to which we cannot relate across intentionality (*despite* that separation).²⁸ This is because despite (or one might say, by virtue of) this fissure, it is precisely this pained body to which we find ourselves riveted.

The Inadequacy of Intentionality

My claim is that, because Sartre has at his disposal only that formal account which understands all experience in terms of intentionality, he is unable to maintain this paradox of "translucent matter," or of a fissure, that is not yet a distance, between consciousness and itself. All the same, this paradox comes through to the reader in his concrete analyses of such moments of conscious life. For this reason, I argue that Sartre's work would benefit from a more Levinasian approach to the structures of identity, insofar as it quite successfully accounts for the relationship between pain-consciousness and its body. I reiterate the analysis from chapter 2, as a reminder that Levinas understand identity as a diachronous duality within a single term precisely because he uncovers a relationship between consciousness and being that is nonintentional, or rather, intentional in a radically other sense.²⁹ On this account, consciousness-as-intentionality remains a valid structure of consciousness that allows us to account for its relation to the world. However, there exists that duality within identity across which the subject relates to itself, and for which intentionality does not account. Intentionality is concerned with those experiences whereby consciousness freely surpasses itself, or its position in being, toward the object, or that which is "not-consciousness." As such, it is unable to account for the relationship between consciousness and its "self" precisely because, in that relationship, consciousness is unable to make itself the kind of "other" that it would surpass toward itself. It is *as that which it is unable to surpass* that consciousness would encounter its self, very much the same way the Levinasian *moi* would encounter the *soi* during moments of fatigue and insomnia. In Sartre's description of the experience of pain, we encounter our bodies "with no space in between." We *are* this pain, since we "exist" it *and* we reject it equiprimordially.³⁰ To be certain, there is that positing of a pain-free future state, which Sartre identifies. But to then say that such a positing is consciousness already "not being" its pain is to disregard the exigency and immediacy within Sartre's concrete account. In giving our *rejection* of physical pain priority over our existential rivetedness to that moment of suffering, the meaning of "pain consciousness" is reduced to the formal structures of "consciousness-as-transcendence," which, I have argued, fail to allow the truth of this paradox to come forth.

An important claim in Sartre's ontology is that consciousness is never privy to being in its purity. Instead, being is always-already encountered across a meaning-bestowing relationship with consciousness. It is for this reason that, even in those moments of affectivity, Sartre understands being to be given over to consciousness in terms of a constituted world, organized with meaning and significance. On the contrary, the Levinasian conception of the *il y a* functions to recognize such an encounter (with being in its purity).[31] In this regard, this conception of pure existence positions Levinas to recognize a signification in affective moments (of vulnerability) that resides outside the scope of intentionality. He can read, from his phenomenologies of embodiment, "evidence" of an existent (of a self who is not yet a subject) that is both noncoincident with *and* riveted to its "self," or its position in existence. Said otherwise, Levinas understands identity in terms of an imminent *disruption* of that identity, which then calls into question the possibility of the kind of subjective coherence conditioning an intentional relation with being. This notion of an identity in disruption clearly informs Levinas's analysis of the experience of shame. I hold that it stands in a telling relationship to Sartre's analysis of such an experience, insofar as the latter's concrete descriptions underscore what one finds at the more formal level in Levinas. As is the case with his analysis of pain-consciousness, Sartre finds, in shame, the possibility for consciousness to freely reappropriate (in a pseudo-intentionality) its objective being-for-others, even though this interpretation stands alongside a concrete analysis that would suggest otherwise. To further demonstrate this betrayal (of Sartre's formal analysis by his concrete descriptions), I present his and Levinas's accounts of the event of shame.

II. Finding Levinasian Passivity in Sartre's Descriptions of Shame

In both thinkers, shame is identified as a "revelation" of an aspect of ourselves, which we would "like to hide." Sartre describes this aspect as "degraded,"[32] while Levinas describes it as a mode of "ourselves as diminished beings."[33] The convergence between descriptive language suggests that both find a similar modification in the subject living that event of shame. Nonetheless, Sartre never articulates the overarching theme of Levinas's analysis of shame, which is the structural passivity of an imploded subject. I claim that this is the case because Sartre's formal structures betray the concrete descriptions to which they should be accountable. Missing in his formal account is that level of the Levinasian *soi*, which would explain the passivity characteristic of both moments of shame and "pain-consciousness."

In this sense, I read Sartre's descriptions of shame to understand what I have revealed in his descriptions of embodiment, which is that it calls into question his formal ontology of a radically free "I," void of all being. Sartre's analysis of his description of the look of the Other is done through the lens of a formal ontology that interprets consciousness in terms of either reflective or prereflective experience. As such, shame, much like all moments of affectivity in Sartre, would retain the structure of intentionality. I demonstrate that by Sartre's own standards, the event of shame escapes the parameters of this ontology, insofar as it is neither reflective nor prereflective. This positions an event like shame to call into question the fundamental presupposition of intentionality, which is that, as subjects of our experience, we are in full ownership of ourselves, and return to ourselves despite the (transcending) projection of intentionality. Under the Other's gaze, consciousness finds itself with itself in a relation which, very similar to the Levinasian "*moi-soi*" relationship, does not constitute one of identity. This means that, in addition to the trajectory of intentionality being turned inward, consciousness is held hostage to the "self" with which it must identify. In this vein, I argue that shame, insofar as it fits into neither categories of reflective nor prereflective experience, would more adequately articulate that region on the hither side of (intentional) experience founded in Levinas's account of transcendence. Levinas's formal structure of the self recognizes shame as "not yet" an experience in the real sense, but nevertheless belonging to the self. I argue that what is positively signified in Sartre's description is better recognized when read through this Levinasian formalization of identity, which understands the subject to be dense with him- or herself despite its intentional projections.

Sartre's Descriptions of "Being-Seen"

Unlike the claim in Levinas, Sartre determines that it is only in front of the Look that the revelation constitutive of shame happens. "[Shame] . . . is shame of *self*; it is the recognition of the fact that I am indeed that object which the Other is looking at and judging. I can be ashamed only as my freedom escapes me in order to become a *given* object."³⁴ Sartre's ontology of an absolutely transcending consciousness requires that one reads, in these descriptions, a challenging of the primacy of freedom. However, the intersection between these descriptions and Levinas's suggests that the event of shame might fall outside of an ontology of an absolutely free consciousness. In this sense, the Look's interruption is less of a challenge to a freedom that is justified beyond reproach, and more of a calling into question of that very position of justification. I trace this possibility, determining that Sartre's descriptions of what shame concretely reveals point to a region of subjectivity that is "otherwise than" free, or to a subject who is called to accountability. To reiterate, this is not to say that the Husserlian bent of Sartre's analysis, which presents consciousness as an intentional projection in being, is misguided. Rather, I argue that consciousness-as-intentionality should not exhaust a formal account of identity, given the possibility of shame.

Christine Andrews writes of Sartre's analysis, "My shame is a confession of the fact that I am indeed an object which the Other is looking at and judging."³⁵ Facing the Other's look, the nothingness of consciousness undergoes the most radical of changes, insofar as it becomes a reified "something." The emptiness that would typically condition the reflection of a meaningful world gets converted into an interiority. In this sense, consciousness takes on an "inside," identifiable by something other than a pure translucent exteriority. Of this transformation, Arne Vetlesen writes, "[The] modification is not something I welcome as an enrichment of my being; on the contrary, it is something I *suffer* as imposed upon me."³⁶ He makes sure to note that the word "suffer" is his choice, and not Sartre's, but from the latter's description of being-looked-at, suffering would be an adequate depiction of the scenario of being-looked-at. It indicates a fullness of *being* at the depths of consciousness, which precisely compromises the essential emptiness of the for-itself.

Outside of an encounter with the Other, I am prereflectively aware of myself through my experience of a transcendent world. It was established in chapter 1 that, at this level of self-consciousness, there is no "I" in the experience. This means that I am aware of my being as a pure exteriority, always already beyond myself, in the world that I project *for* myself. The "I" only appears subsequently, in *reflective* acts, whereby it is posited as an aspect of a transcendent ego that unifies conscious states.³⁷ That there is no "I" at the most immediate level of experience means that consciousness is never "there" with itself. It is an outward-pointing "directionality" toward objects of experience. Sartre writes, "Let us imagine that . . . I have just glued my ear to the door and looked through a keyhole. I am alone and on the level of a non-thetic [or prereflective] self-consciousness. . . . This means first of all that there is no self to inhabit my consciousness. . . . I am *my* acts and hence they carry in themselves their whole justification. I am a pure consciousness of things. . . ."[38] The unity of the phenomena that appears to consciousness suffices to unify consciousness throughout the duration of the experience, hence the gratuity of the "I" at this prereflective level.[39] More importantly, at this level of self-consciousness, experiences are given over as *belonging to consciousness* (the experience of eavesdropping behind the closed door is *my* experience). As such, there is an unthematized and immediate sense of self, which yet rests on the pure translucency of consciousness, empty of an "I." This self-awareness is not in the form of a unifying ego, but rather, in the form of the unity of the objects before me.[40]

However, in front of the Look, my immediate experience is made to emanate from an "I-object" that is not a spontaneous creation of a reflective act of consciousness. To put this otherwise, the Look *gives* me an "I," for which I am responsible and to which I am riveted. According to Sartre's descriptions, I am seen very much as a part of the Other's world of objects, oriented in terms of and constituted by my relation to those objects.[41] So whereas, in solitude, I can intentionally refer to the world without "touching" the objects of my projection, my being-seen bestows on me a body with which I touch the world, and of which I am now a part. As we have already seen, my embodiment typically resides at the backdrop of my experience, as that invisible stance from which there is visibility. Now, in front of the Look, I am "there," for the Other sees that I am there. In this sense, I find myself *in* my body, unable to transcend it. To revisit Sartre's example of the snooping consciousness, "What I apprehend immediately when I hear the branches crackling behind me is not that *there is someone there*; it is that I am vulnerable, that I have a body . . . [and that] I occupy a *place* [emphasis added] . . . that I can not in any case escape from. . . ."[42]

Hence, through its being-for-others, consciousness finds that it is *there*, with itself, and no longer ahead of itself in the object of experience. Recall a similar rivetedness in Sartre's concrete descriptions of pain-consciousness. My body becomes a point in the world whose reference is "me," but all the same, a reference with which I can never completely identify.[43] Sartre's descriptions demonstrate that, on encountering the Look, I am *with* my body, without *being* my body, or without being able to completely identify with my body. Again, this is the case in the lived experience of one's body as "pained." In both cases, consciousness must take ownership of a "stranger-self" to which it is forever riveted.[44] It is of interest to understand this in terms of Sartre's own analysis of experience. What does one make of the sense in which shame situates consciousness with itself, but across a distance that makes impossible a relation of identity? To ask this otherwise, what type of self-awareness does shame constitute?

Situating Shame Beyond Reflective and Prereflective Experience

As a movement of intentionality, consciousness simply *is* its experience; its being resides completely in the objects of experience. Except when under the gaze of the Other, every experience is coupled with this type of self-awareness. As I have shown, there is consciousness of "self" prereflectively, which means that consciousness is aware of itself *not* as an explicit object, but rather *in* its awareness of the objects of (its) experience. Self-awareness can also move to the reflective level, which would mean that consciousness makes itself an object *for* itself, much like the objects of its experience is an object for it. We have seen that, for Sartre, this reflective self-awareness consists of creating and projecting an "ego object," with which I identify. However, as Sartre points out in *The Transcendence of the Ego*, by the time of this projection, I would have already escaped the confines of that reflected self-object. In other words, just as in the case of prereflective self-awareness, consciousness is *in* its object of experience, at a distance from itself. The difference is that in the latter case, the object of experience is constituted to represent consciousness itself. Nevertheless, in both instances of reflective and prereflective self-consciousness, consciousness is directed completely toward the world of its experience.

However, under the gaze, the directionality of this reference turns inward. No longer solely a reference to the world, consciousness, as it is looked at, becomes a "pure self-reference." "I suddenly hear footsteps in the hall. . . . I now exist as *myself* for my unreflective consciousness."[45] The Other, in "giving" consciousness a "self" (which the Other uses to identify that consciousness as an object in his or her world), causes consciousness to turn back into itself. Instead of having its entire being in an intentionally constituted world, consciousness finds itself *with* itself, trapped in the physical body-object that the Other sees.[46] This purity of reference opposes what would constitute a prereflective self-awareness, the latter being self-consciousness through a pure reference *to the object of experience*. On the contrary, in being seen by the Other, consciousness purely refers to itself. To be sure, I am never my being-for-others in the sense that this book is "this book." This is the difference between the two modes of being identified in Sartre's ontology (being-for-itself and being-in-itself). Amidst the purity of reference to its objectified seen being, there is still that distance between consciousness and the objectified "self" that it is for the Other. There is also a distance between consciousness and the ego-object into which it projects itself during reflective self-awareness. Nevertheless, there is a fundamental difference between the distance across which I am *shamefully* self-aware of by objectified seen-being, and the distance across which I am *reflectively* self-aware. Consciousness is able to recognize itself in its ego in a way that is precisely impossible when it comes to its being for-the-Other. It is the precise nature of this difference, and the sense in which there is a pure reference between consciousness and an essentially alien "self," which is of issue.

According to Sartre's account of the inevitability of bad faith, I can never disown my "self," in order to then apprehend it as an object from which I remain unimplicated or detached. Hence, the strangeness of consciousness's being-for-others does not rid it of its responsibility to *be* this "seen self." I must identify with this "self" across a strange distance of nonrecognition. It is in this sense that consciousness's reference to its objectified being is unmediated, or pure. I *am* this self, without reprieve, despite my being a stranger to myself. Hence, the type of self-awareness involved in this pure reference to my being-for-others is precisely *not* the self-awareness of reflective experience. My objectified being for-the-Other is imposed on me, and though there is a distance of nonrecognition between my "being-for-itself" and my "being-seen," an encounter with the Other compels both to map onto each other in a dissonant yet undeniable identity.

Insofar as consciousness's objectified being does not replace its being-for-itself, Sartre describes "being seen" as "a solidification and an abrupt stratification of myself *which leaves intact my possibilities and my structures 'for-myself'* [emphasis added], but which suddenly pushes me into a new dimension of existence. . . ."[47] Consciousness does not dissipate; it is still there, as a reflection of being, albeit in a "new dimension." How then, must we understand this "new dimension"? It is clear that shame is not a reflective experience; consciousness does not (and cannot) apprehend its being-for-others across the distance necessary for reflective experience. "Shame is an immediate shudder which runs through me from head to foot without any discursive preparation. . . . I am unable to bring about any relation between what I am in the intimacy of the

For-Itself, without distance, without recoil, without perspective, and this unjustifiable being-in-itself for the Other."[48] This explains the sense in which my being-for-others is beyond my cognitive grasp; I am "with" my "self," and as such, cannot withdraw from my being, so as to regard it cognitively.[49] Nevertheless, there exists a "fissure" of noncoincidence between consciousness and its being-for-others, despite this failure to withdraw.[50] It is precisely this fissure that captures the angst of the responsibility to acknowledge that what the Other sees is *me*.

Sartre's explanation of the lived noncoincidence between consciousness and its being-for-others is that the origin of its objectified being is in the Other, and not in the spontaneity of consciousness itself.[51] My view is that this account too hastily assumes consciousness to be nothing other than an intentional projection in being, which, in turn, reads shame as an *experience* belonging to consciousness. However, the immediate significations in the event of shame render both prereflective and reflective self-awareness obsolete as a viable explanation of the event. Said otherwise, on Sartrean terms, shame would fall outside of the parameters of *experience* in the proper sense. To summarize, my being-for-others is that from which I cannot withdraw, so it is unlike the "I" of reflective experience, the possibility of which depends on the withdrawal of the reflecting consciousness. However, neither is the awareness of my objectified being at the prereflective level. Sartre writes, "consciousness of self [in the prereflective sense] is not dual. . . . there must be an *immediate* [emphasis added] non-cognitive relation of the self to itself."[52] In shame, consciousness is aware of itself immediately. Nevertheless, there is an important difference between what it means to be aware of oneself prereflectively, and to be aware of oneself as "looked-at."

Commentaries on Sartre's theory of intersubjectivity recognize that the "tragedy" in the experience of being-seen lies in the inability of the seen-consciousness to cognitively grasp its objectified being.[53] Again, this would be the result of the *Other* being the origin of my objectified being.[54] Though it is the case that the cognitive capacity of consciousness finds its limit in the event of shame, this interpretation does not yet capture (because it has already gone beyond) what is most essential to the event. As in the case of shame, prereflective self-awareness does not bring about a knowledge of self. But *unlike* the case of shame, the individual who is prereflectively aware of herself is not inflicted with, as a consequence of this cognitive block, anguish or "instability."[55] At the prereflective level, *in isolation*, consciousness is unable to grasp itself cognitively because it is never *there to be* grasped. It exists as an ecstatic movement toward being, and as such, has always already surpassed its "self." However, in shame, I *am* there, for the Other. This is the difference between the prereflective experience of oneself, and shame of oneself before the Other. Before the Other, I have a "self," which I am no longer able to surpass, the way I would in prereflective self-awareness. Before the Other, I am directly aware of myself in the mode of what I *am*. Prereflectively, I am directly aware of myself in the mode of what I am *not*.

Ultimately, there are aspects of both reflective and prereflective levels of experience, from which shame "borrows." Like reflection, consciousness encounters a fixed identity that "represents" its being, and as in prereflective experience, consciousness relates to its seen-being purely and immediately.[56] Nonetheless, there are also structures properly belonging to shame, which place it beyond both reflective and prereflective modes of experience.[57] Levinas's analysis of the formal structures of shame makes available a language that is better suited to this "new dimension," opened up by Sartre's concrete descriptions. Again, this is insofar as Levinas more successfully allows his formal explanations to unfold from the concrete peculiarities of the event of shame. In so doing, he includes, in the very meaning of identity, the internal trauma of having to identify with a "self" that is forever other. This is in opposition to the implication in Sartre, which underscores this discordance to be a dethroning of an autonomous subject that is particular only to the experience of being-seen.

III. Passivity in Levinas's Reading of Shame

By situating Sartre's phenomenology against Levinas's, it becomes clear that the intricacies involved in the event of shame call for something other than a Sartrean sense of reflective and prereflective self-consciousness. Neither of these modes of experience accounts for the sense in which consciousness is burdened with the being it *has to be* before the Other. This is because, in terms of the reflective or prereflective, one must resort to a negative understanding of shame as a cognitive *failure*. We are left with an account of what shame is *not*, and not what it *positively* is. The noncoincidence between my "for-itself" interiority, and my exterior "being-for-others" does indeed have these cognitive ramifications. Since I am an object that is valued with reference to the other's possibilities, my seen-being is outside of my cognitive grasp, and remains entirely inaccessible to me. My being-for-the-other is not an object of my own reflective act, which is why, under the Look, consciousness can be assured of its existence as a physical person.[58] However, apart from these epistemological effects, this noncoincidence might signify on its own terms.[59] It is in the hope of finding a more positive reading that I return to Levinas's analysis in *Of Escape*.

In Christina Howells's discussion of the similarities between Sartre's and Levinas's account of the Other, she also points out that they both identify an essential noncoincidence in subjectivity. She determines that, while Levinas identifies this noncoincidence as "good, precious and better than self-coincidence," Sartre often focuses on the freedom this noncoincidence represents.[60] For Sartre, it is precisely insofar as consciousness is forever *outside* itself, in a condition of noncoincidence or nonidentity, that it is structured as the freedom of intentionality. From Levinas's exposition on the event of shame, one understands subjectivity in terms of nonidentity with self, *not* insofar as the subject is beyond him- or herself in a free transcendence. Instead, the moment of shame reveals a nonidentity *despite* the "I" being irrevocably *riveted* to itself. As such, the subject apprehends his or her being as a plenitude that, in the midst of its intimacy, is absolutely foreign.[61] Hence, for Levinas, shame demonstrates the vulnerability of an existent who is invested in that which is absolutely exterior, or in what approaches from a radical "elsewhere."

His descriptions of shame begins as follows, "[Shame's] whole intensity, everything it contains that stings us, consists precisely in our inability not to identify with this being who is already foreign to us. . . ."[62] As the analysis proceeds, it becomes clear that this "inability" is not *essentially* a failure on the part of the subject. Indeed, it does uncover the limit point of cognitive ability.[63] However, Levinas does not reduce the primary meaning of our inability to identify with ourselves with any limitations of our being. "[Shame]," he says, "is more attached to the being of our 'I' than it is to its finitude."[64] In other words, it is not the case that I am unable to identify with myself because I lack the necessary cognitive powers. Rather, this inability is featured *positively* in the analysis, instead of merely indicating a lack in the structure of the subject.

On the issue of what shame reveals, both Levinas and Sartre seem to agree. Sartre finds in original shame a "state of nakedness,"[65] very much like Levinas's determination that "shame arises each time we are unable to make others forget our *basic nudity* [emphasis added]."[66] Nudity, he determines, signifies the "sheer visibility" of our being—it points to our inability to hide both from ourselves and from others, precisely because our being is such that it is wholly *there*. Sartre echoes this sentiment when he claims that, in putting on clothes we actually seek to hide our "object-state." Though for Sartre, it primarily points to an epistemological defeat, this state of nakedness is, for both thinkers, the *"thereness"* of our being. In this sense, they both recognize a connection between the way in which shame signifies and the subject's exposedness or visibility.

Levinas's formalization of subjectivity underscores his concrete descriptions in general, and those of shame in particular. His conception of positionality allows us to read the nudity associated with shame as an exposure to the brute fact of existence, or to the brute fact of *my* existence. To find myself exposed, despite my desire for invisibility, is to face the underlying conditions of my freedom, which is the "thereness" of my being. Beneath a movement of intentionality that would render consciousness "never there," always ahead of itself, and empty of being in the Sartrean sense, the subject is full of being, with itself irrevocably. Levinas reads shame as a revelation of this dimension of the "I." In this sense, the concrete moment of shame is possible insofar as the "I" is rooted in a position in existence, and lives in a passivity (or non-freedom) before the sheer weight of taking up this position. On this account, shame reveals an aspect of the subject of which it has no real ownership. The *thereness* of the "I," or its position in existence is beyond the span of its free movement of intentionality, a region to which Levinas refers as the "hither side" of intentionality. Shame would then be a revelation of this primordial "thereness."

We find this in Sartre's account as well, when he indicates the necessary noncoincidence between the "for-itself" being of consciousness and the being it is called to take up, in shame, before the Other. Similarly, for Levinas, that aspect of my being from which I would like to hide is part of my lived unity. I *am* this being that is most foreign to me. Though Levinas's conception of identity, as a unified duality, is never developed in Sartre's ontology, the latter's descriptions resonate with the picture of a subject who is riveted, vulnerably, to her position in existence. Levinas identifies this "rivetedness to being (to *our* being)" as that which underlies our intentional engagement with the world. "What appears in shame is precisely [this] fact of being riveted to ourselves."[67] As in Sartre's account, the shameful "I" encounters itself as exposed, or naked, bound to a "self" that is simultaneously strange and intimate.

The reference to visibility in both Sartre's and Levinas's accounts of shame makes embodiment a significant aspect of the event. Sartre does not hesitate to point out that it is my *body* that the Other sees, and with which I must identify. In Levinas's descriptions of the nudity of our being, the body also plays a crucial role. The subject (or *moi*) experiences its body as though enchained to it; it is given over as burdensome, or as a weight that is "suffered." In this sense, the fullness of our being, unveiled in both Sartre and Levinas, is indicated through the intimacy of the body.[68] I am my body without distance, even though I cannot completely identify with it. We see this in Sartre's descriptions of the affectivity of physical pain and in his concrete analysis of consciousness's shame on encountering the look of the Other. Though his account of facticity includes the sense in which the freedom of consciousness must take into account certain "coefficients of adversity," I have shown that Sartre does not account for this region of nonfreedom as adequately as Levinas's conception of identity does.

The analysis that follows in chapter five compares Sartre's conception of alienation with Levinas's conception of substitution. Respectively, these structures account for the alterity of the Other, and in their own right, take the reader into more ethical and political considerations in their broaching of the question of the subject's responsibility for the Other. As I engage this question, I focus on the difference between Sartre's and Levinas's signification of nonfreedom, particularly in an encounter with the Other. As I have shown in my analysis of Sartre's account of shame, he identifies a reification or substantiation of the subject's spontaneity. This reification will ground his more political conception of alienation. In Levinas's account of substitution, he inscribes my "being for the Other" with a passivity that is *other than* an object-like reification. This, among other significant differences, will inform their respective accounts of what it means to be responsible for the Other.

CHAPTER 5

Levinas and Sartre on the Question of the Other

The preceding chapters have argued in favor of minimizing the distance between Sartre and Levinas from the vantage point of concrete analysis. It is clear that both describe, in several lived experiences, a primordial level of subjectivity that calls for an interruption of the primacy of freedom. For many of the lived experiences that demonstrate this resonance, Levinas's formal account of identity and transcendence-as-excendence provides a more adequate basis on which these moments of nonfreedom can be explained. Sartre sustains the claim that such experiences ultimately manifest appearances *for* a consciousness that continues to be an absolute spontaneity in Being. In other words, he holds that the structures of freedom remain in place in such concrete moments.

This chapter brings into dialogue Sartre's and Levinas's analyses of the Other[1] in a way that exceeds my previous discussion of their accounts of shame.[2] As is the case in other descriptions, their (concrete) phenomenologies of alterity are similar in many respects. However, there is significant divergence in their interpretations of this alterity of the Other. As previously done, I identify descriptive language in Sartre that, for the most part, is indistinguishable from Levinas's descriptions of the Other. But in so doing, I make clear that, despite this similarity, the explicitly political commitments through which Sartre formalizes his phenomenology of alterity are quite absent in Levinas's work.[3] To be sure, there are significant political implications in Levinas, and I will present Sartre's analysis as a way to bring those implications to the forefront. Nonetheless, Levinas's approach toward alterity is motivated by a pursuit of the meaning of the metaphysical that, he claims, disappears throughout the trajectory of Western thought.[4] In this regard, we will see that Levinas understands alterity as a radical aperture in human identity, which then makes it difficult to determine what it might mean to act, politically, in the name of others. Sartre's work takes this question (of committed action) head on. In this vein, my analysis maintains Sartre's and Levinas's formal conceptions of the Other in their own distinct spheres of relevance. More importantly, I evaluate the strength of their respective conceptions in terms of the very different questions for which they are designed to address.

Both thinkers identify a moment of vulnerability that is undergone on encountering the Other. Sartre formalizes this vulnerability in the concept of alienation, while Levinas captures it in his account of substitution. Given the different conceptions of identity from which these are formulated, the contents of alienation and substitution vary in essential ways. So even though both notions refer to a sense in which the "presence" of the Other troubles the free movement of the subject, Sartre presents alienation in a significantly more negative light than Levinas does with substitution. In the end, Sartre's notion of authenticity shows how consciousness might have a more positive encounter with others in a sociopolitical space. This difference aside, this conception of authenticity is like Levinas's substitution insofar as they both advocate for a level of ethical responsibility toward the Other, which then obligates me to make him or her my concern. Although Sartre never articulates an account of transcendence-as-excendence, it is clear that, beyond the pages of *Being and Nothingness*, his exposition of authenticity does recognize a sense in which a free consciousness must positively value the freedom of others. It is not sufficient to then attribute to Sartre the claim that the subject is otherwise than absolutely free, since this would imply that my valuing the Other's freedom puts me in an asymmetrical relation to him or her. Sartre's (more political) account establishes that individuals who are radically free must also be *equally* free. On the other hand, Levinas's conception of substitution identifies asymmetry as the only rubric that adequately captures my relation to alterity.

Furthermore, Sartre's *Notebooks for an Ethics* makes a clear case against the use of notions of duty and obligation in formulating an ethics of authenticity. In other words, he very precisely refers to a duty-bound consciousness as a slave-consciousness, or as one that has internalized the violence of the Other. However, my approach toward Sartre's account of authenticity employs an understanding of "obligation" very much like the one found in Levinas's account of substitution. In that account, my obligation before the Other is not of the order of servitude, since this would presuppose that my freedom and the freedom of the Other reside "on the same" plane, and as a consequence, can come into the kind of conflict espoused in Sartre's discussion of an ethics of duty. Because Levinas's project is one of metaphysics, he explicitly establishes that alterity "manifests" itself through an encounter with the Face. The Face then becomes a locus of metaphysical desire, or "height." In this vein, the plane on which my obligation encounters its indebtedness toward the Other is *vertical*, and not horizontal. I describe, in greater detail, Levinas's exposition of this. But for the moment, suffice it to say that, in Levinas, any mention of obligation is already *not* that toward which Sartre's critique is geared. In the end, despite this critique, I determine that Sartre's position is similar to Levinas's insofar as they both attack the assumption that, because consciousness is absolutely free, it is also free to remain ambivalent to the Other, or to the Other's fundamental projects.

The work in this chapter does not identify Sartre's formalization as more (or less) problematic than Levinas's. It is also not my claim that Sartre's narrative of committed (political) action requires him to subscribe to the more Levinasian notion of substitution. I do determine that, barring the different conceptions of identity that support these accounts, both thinkers substantively ground a philosophy of ethical responsibility for the Other.[5] Sartre's conception of authenticity and Levinas's notion of substitution open onto the idea of a subject being called "to do something" in response to the persecution of the Other, or to commit to bringing about the Other's freedom. But it is in Sartre that we find a more robust account of what it means to *take action* on behalf of the Other. Though never completed before his death, his ethical position includes the argument that an (authentic) ethics must explicitly be a "praxis." Whatever responsibility I might have toward the Other, it must manifest itself in action that comes out of the immediate contingencies of my situation. By contrast, we find, in Levinas, the absence of such explicit articulations of committed political action. However, it is important to note that this does not indicate a shortcoming, since Levinas's question is not one of responsible political action, but rather a question of what conception of identity would account for the possibility of encountering radical alterity. As such, I do not include in my main arguments that Levinas needs to subscribe to a Sartrean account of authenticity in order to pursue what is peculiar to his own project. To a large degree, substitution better accounts for the obsessive vulnerability that is concretized before the face of the Other, insofar as it brings to completion the conception of a disrupted identity with which Levinas works. But for a different project (one that seeks out the possibility of responsible praxis), Sartre's analysis seems to point toward a more fruitful account of responsibility.[6]

To this end, I identify Sartre's position on authenticity to be supportive to the Levinasian scholar. Given its resonance with the conception of substitution, authentic praxis is a viable option for the reader of Levinas who wants to move into a more politicized notion of responsibility without significantly undermining Levinas's radical conceptions. To reiterate, this is not to say that Sartre's account *needs* to be supplemented by Levinas's analysis of substitution. Rather, given the similarities of both conceptions, Sartre might provide that gateway into the political for as radical a notion as Levinas's.

A point of reminder is worthwhile, regarding my overall reading of Levinas. Throughout the preceding chapters, radical disturbance has been identified as most pivotally shaping Levinas's conception of transcendence. Hence, even though Levinas is significantly committed to the ethical moment, transcendence is not localized (reductively) in the face of the Other. In a footnote in *Otherwise than Being*, he explains that "[ethical] language, which phenomenology resorts to in order to mark its own interruption, does not come from an ethical intervention laid out over descriptions. It is the very meaning of approach, which contrasts with knowing. No language other than ethics could be equal to the paradox which phenomenological description enters when, starting with the disclosure, the appearing of the neighbor, it reads in it . . . a diachrony which cannot be synchronized in representation."[7] In my bringing together Levinas and Sartre around the question of ethical responsibility, it is importance to remember that Levinas identifies himself as "resorting" to this ethical language, in order to then articulate the moment of phenomenology's waning, in its attempt to account for as singular a moment as an encounter with alterity.[8] So though substitution concretizes his conception of transcendence-as-excendence, it is insofar as the obsession of this "pre-experience"[9] indicates that the subject is primordially structured as "not yet," or radically interrupted.[10]

I. The Other is "Extramundane" for Both Sartre and Levinas

Sartre approaches the question of the relationship between two consciousnesses through the problem of solipsism. Both realism and idealism, he tells us, fail to adequately address this problem because the relation between the "I" and the "Other" is given by both as an externally negative relation. "For both idealism and realism, therefore, since the other is revealed to me in a spatial world, there is a real or an ideal space which separates [us]. Consequently [idealism and realism] are forced either to bridge this gap by invoking God, or to fall back on probable certitude and ultimately solipsism."[11] In this sense, the question of the other's existence is erroneously presented as a question of *knowledge* of the Other. It is against this error that Sartre guards himself as he formulates his solution to this problem. He shows that the certainty of the other's existence does not come from knowledge, but rather from the "prereflective awareness" that we have of his existence. This type of awareness gives us unmediated access to this absolute alterity, but it is not the case that we *know* of his existence. That the Other is "beyond the world" is precisely that which makes him immediately accessible to consciousness. To put this differently, it is through the failure of knowledge that Sartre solves the problem of solipsism.

This unmediated awareness of the Other, given at the prereflective level, is opposed to the sense in which awareness of all else is given through the constitutive power of consciousness. As was discussed in chapter 1, Sartre's analysis of "situation" shows that the world is not a simple given—"that the mind is not a camera,"[12] but rather that it is an intentional construction. To be sure, included in consciousness's "situation" are the concrete limitations encountered by its free projections, as a result of the fact of being.[13] We find ourselves having to negotiate these brute "givens" of existence, because they do not seem to be of the sort that can be subject to our choice. Yet, Sartre determines that our very appropriation of these "givens" is already a constitution. He uses the relationship between the ambitious rock-climber and the "crag" before him to demonstrate this inseparability: "Here I am at the foot of this crag which appears to me as "not scalable." This means that the rock appears to me in the light of a projected scaling—a secondary project which finds its meaning in terms of an initial project which is my being-in-the-world. Thus the rock is carved out on the ground of the world by the effect of the initial choice of my freedom."[14] Sartre does identify those aspects of the crag that are radically independent of the climber's choice (independent of "human existence"). But at the same time, the individual encounters such a crag as either "climbable" or "not climbable"; outside of these two alternatives, it is not *there* for the rock climber. Hence, despite its characteristics that are apparently independent of any human presence, this crag belongs to a world (the world of the rock-climber) insofar as it appears in terms constituted by (his or her) consciousness. Its shape, size, and texture all contribute to its unscalability. But it is precisely because it is unscalable *for* a rock-climber that these given features show up in light of a free and transcending project.

The Other does not "show up" in this sense, but rather eludes all attempts at knowing him or her. We *can* encounter the Other as a physical object, because he or she is embodied. But the Other qua physical body is not yet the Other as *another consciousness* or a "lived body."[15] His or her "being other" has no noetic correlate, since it is not an object for an intentional act. When encountered as *another consciousness* (and not simply as a physical body with spatial dimensions similar to my own), he is given over as beyond constitution. The Other is radically beyond the "world" insofar as his or her fundamental meaning cannot be *for* a consciousness.[16] In the attempts to situate the Other's physical body within the matrix of already-meaningful objects, the Other "refuses himself and flees."[17] Unlike the rock-climber's crag, which belongs to the world, the Other is "extramundane," or "beyond the world."

Nevertheless, Sartre determines that my relation with the Other is given negatively, much like my relation with everyday objects. In this sense, he is that which is "not me." But this negation is an "internal one" and a "reciprocal one," originating neither solely in myself nor solely in the Other. "[A] positive theory of the Other's existence . . . envisages my original relation to the Other as an internal negation; that is, as a negation which posits the original distinction between the Other and myself as being such that it determines me by means of the Other and determines the Other by means of me."[18] Hence, it is not that the being of consciousness is constituted *first*, so as to then encounter the Other. Rather, the presence of the Other is part of the being of consciousness. "The Cogito (subjective ego) is one dimension of self-consciousness. Being-for-itself is equiprimordial to being for others."[19]

That this "self-Other" relation is internal signifies, for Sartre, "a primary absence of all relation."[20] "Relation" works across a distance between two terms that are fundamentally exterior to each other. But insofar as the Other is implicated in the very being of consciousness, the internal negation does not support the distance across which a true relation might stand. Does this mean that Sartre's is simply a reiteration of Heidegger's *Mitsein*? In an important sense, he does borrow heavily from this formalization. For him, Heidegger's analysis is insightful insofar as it recognizes that though he cannot be known, the Other is given to me most immediately. However, Sartre is also explicitly critical of *Mitsein*. It is not insofar as the Other is "with me" that I encounter him immediately. He is "not me," has no affiliation with me, nor what comes from me (namely, my world). Hence, I encounter him as an immediate absence.[21] He is given "without concealment or mystery," but it is precisely as alien that he is unconcealed. The Other is wholly and immediately encountered as a radically foreign existence. For Sartre, this is insufficiently accounted for by Heidegger's *Mitsein*.[22]

Hence, Sartre interprets the radical otherness of the Other as that for which consciousness is never equipped ontically, and definitely never ontologically. The modifications undergone by the being of consciousness, resulting from the Other's look are real modifications, "at the deepest ontological level." In this sense, they could not be precluded in consciousness "in isolation." My being-for-the-other cannot be derived from my being-for-itself.[23] The Other is "internal" to consciousness, but as a radical negation (or a radical absence) of "self." Sartre aims to preserve the Other's transcendence in describing our relation to him as a "primary absence of relation."[24] He recognizes the importance of the fact that the Other is beyond the world, or beyond constitution. Hence, his use of negativity is precisely an attempt to capture the sense in which consciousness cannot constitute the Other in encountering him. This is important to remember as we approach Levinas's treatment of alterity, which recognizes a similar focus on radical absence.[25] Sartre's purpose in describing the "self–Other" relation as both internal and negative is to recognize, like Levinas, that the Other is "not there" for consciousness. So even though Sartre's use of negation as the structure of transcendence would fall under Levinas's critique, it remains the case that Sartre's and Levinas's analysis align to the extent that they employ a phenomenology of absence in their negotiations of the Other.[26]

The Non-Manifestation of Levinas's Other

From a Levinasian perspective, to claim that the Other is the negation of consciousness is to lock the Other in absolute immanence. Terms that relate across negation require each other, and are thus included in a single totality. If the negation is external, then that totality is one of meaning. If it is internal, then the totality is one of being. In both cases, Levinas understands negation to be a reduction of all otherness to participation in the realm of the same. By contrast, Levinas holds that the otherness of the Other is infinitely and absolutely distant from the "I." Indeed, Sartre is right to note that there *is* an absence of relation between the "I" and

"Other." But there is also an infinite distance between them, which is ultimately destroyed in a negative relation. Whereas Sartre's other is given *in terms of* an "I" (the other is "non-I"), Levinas presents alterity as an absence that signifies beyond the dichotomies of "I" and "non-I" (or of being and nonbeing).

While Sartre's work is, overtly, a phenomenological ontology, Levinas's project rests on an explicit rejection of ontology (and, to a degree, phenomenology) altogether.[27] No comparison of their work would be fair without acknowledging the implications of this significant difference. Sartre is directed toward developing the relation between consciousness and being that would establish consciousness as the absolute foundation of experience. In this regard, his exegesis accesses alterity through the structures of consciousness, and ultimately in terms of its intentionality and meaning-bestowing (or constituting) activity. In contrast, Levinas's agenda is metaphysical, and searches for the "how" of exteriority's signification. Even though he employs the tools of phenomenology, his work renders these tools defunct on their encounter with what signifies as beyond being.[28] As such, Sartre's account is simply unable to articulate, at the formal level, the exteriority to which Levinas's metaphysical descriptions alludes.[29] This is because Sartre's formalization of his concrete descriptions take place through the categories of being, which in turn calls for an accounting for alterity (or for its absence of meaning) in terms of negation.

How is Levinas's metaphysical analysis equipped to avoid the reduction of radical alterity through the use of negation? One way of addressing this is to understand Levinas's employment of the Cartesian formulation of the infinite to demonstrate this proper signification of the Other.[30] The idea of infinity is one that the *cogito* does have, but the content of this idea is such that it could not have originated in the *cogito*. The infinite is never fully captured in its corresponding idea, and in this sense, "the Cartesian notion of the idea of the Infinite designates a relation with a being that maintains its total exteriority with respect to him who thinks it."[31] In this way, Levinas formalizes a "relation" that keeps intact the absolute distance between the terms that relate, which is essential in a relation with radical exteriority. We think the infinite without actively contributing to the idea's constitution. Hence, it is more accurate to say that the infinite is thought in us.[32] It is on this essential "passivity" on the part of the *cogito* that the alterity of the Infinite is made manifest without being destroyed in that manifestation. The thinking of the *cogito* "is [aporetically] conditioned by what it constitutes, [giving rise to] a thought that overflows itself or that thinks more than it thinks."[33]

In this sense, infinity reveals itself, but *as surpassing* the idea that thinks it, outside of all theme, concept, or representation. "The *intentionality* [emphasis added] that animates the idea of infinity is not comparable with any other," because thought aims toward, without capturing.[34] Yet, it is not the case that this modality of thought fails. Rather, "[in] this rupture of representational adequacy and mastery," the *cogito* precisely succeeds in thinking what it would wish to think (namely, the infinite).[35] This formal structure—of a relation that maintains the distance between its terms—finds its concretization in an encounter with alterity. In that encounter, it is *not* that the other is "not me," much like the sense in which the infinite is not merely "not finite." Like the relation between the idea of infinity and the infinite, the Other overflows any and all possible conceptualizations of him or her, including that which determines the Other negatively.

Levinas uses the Face to capture this way in which alterity, or that which is radically exterior, is given over.[36] In place of a theme or manifestation, the Face *expresses* in its alterity. "The way in which the other [expresses] himself, exceeding *the idea of the other in me*, we name here face."[37] Not only is it possible to encounter this alterity *without* reducing its expression to a theme, but it is precisely in the failure of consciousness to think this otherness that, in the words of Sartre, "absolute immanence opens up to absolute transcendence."[38] Alongside Levinas's employment of this notion of the Face, there is Sartre's identification of the Look as that which captures, most fundamentally, an encounter with alterity. For Levinas, the Other as "face" already signifies the radical rupture of the identity of the Same. Conversely, Sartre's conception of the Look understands the Other as an invasive alterity that alienates a (looked-at) consciousness from its interiority (an interiority that would otherwise be an uninterrupted transcending toward "world") This difference, between the "Other as a Look" and the "Other as a Face" will play a critical role in both understanding Sartre's and Levinas's respective projects, as well as how those projects come into dialogue with each other.

II. Sartre's Alienation before the Other

In *Being and Nothingness*, Sartre tells us that, "I do not choose to be for the Other what I am, but I can try to be *for myself* [emphasis added] what I am for the Other."[39] At this stage in his work, consciousness's objectified being-for-others is a momentary "fall" of its freedom to carry out its own projections.[40] To recall, consciousness is a gap in the density of being-in-itself, which means that its (non-)being rests in its withdrawal from being, or its remaining separate from beings that "are" something fixed and definite. This is the sense in which consciousness is free, spontaneously surpassing any reified identity. All else, by contrast, is an absolute fullness of being.[41] In placing the encounter with alterity within these parameters, one consciousness remains a transcendence toward a nothingness of being, while the other "attains" the fullness of an object *for* the Other. In this sense, the problem of intersubjectivity, for Sartre, is the problem of how two ontologically and necessarily free "beings" might remain free throughout the experience of looking at each other. In this regard, the Look is problematic insofar as it is the source from which I am alienated from my freedom.

Along with David Detmer and other Sartrean scholars, Joanna Pier reiterates Sartre's claim that "I come to know the existence and freedom of the Other because of my experiencing being made an object by [him]."[42] Indeed, this experience of objectification is the *only* source of verification of the Other's existence.[43] Hence, for Sartre, the moment I encounter that which does not become an object *for me*, but rather makes *of* me an object, is the moment in which I have encountered radical alterity. "As soon as a freedom other than mine arises confronting me . . . it is not a question of my conferring a meaning on brute existents. . . . It is I myself who see a meaning conferred upon me."[44] Sartre is like Levinas in the sense that he not only places the Other beyond the intentional grasp of consciousness, but more importantly, recognizes this "beyond" as essential to this alterity. The consequent reversal of the direction of meaning-bestowing indicates to consciousness that it has encountered a radically free transcendence who will deflect all signification imposed on it, and remain forever "on the outside" of such attempts to make it present in a theme.

Alongside this seemingly conflict-ridden account of what it means to encounter alterity, Sartre establishes an important distinction that, at least concretely, presents this experience of alienation in terms that are less oppositional. Said otherwise, there is another sense, in Sartre's concrete descriptions, whereby I discover, in the Other, a limit-point to my spontaneity without necessarily being called to overcome the source of that limitation. This distinction, between the resistance inherent in the Other's actions, and the resistance of his very *existence*, operates as early on as *Being and Nothingness*, and acquires full exposition only later, in the *Critique of Dialectical Reason*.[45] The actions of another consciousness impose a limit on me, but insofar as I encounter these limitations as such, I have already woven them into my own projects.[46] The actions of others are encountered as a resistance that means something, for consciousness, and in this sense, do little to undermine the structure of spontaneity. My freedom ultimately perseveres against any potential reification I might face under the Other's actions.

However, the fact of the Other's *existence* reveals a significantly different truth. According to Sartre, it places consciousness in a "new dimension,"[47] in which the experienced resistance is precisely *resistant* to taking on a meaning whose origin is in consciousness. Confronting the Other's existence, "something of myself . . . exists in the manner of the *given* . . . it *is* without *being existed*."[48] The (brute) existence of the Other, unlike his actions, deflects all signification whose origin is my world, and remains on the outside as that which is absolutely exterior. In this analysis, Sartre appears to be describing a relation to a pure exteriority, in the sense that the Other "shows up" independently of the projections of the consciousness that encounters it, which is really to say that it shows up as absent *for* that consciousness. In this sense, Sartre's development of the alterity of the Other's existence is very much like the Cartesian idea of the infinite, from which Levinas borrows in his articulation of metaphysical exteriority. To be certain, Sartre ultimately formalizes this concrete phenomenology in terms of his ontology of a radically free consciousness, which is to say that the Other's existence is understood as a point of theft of my freedom, and the source of my alienation to which my proper response is a kind of self-determination. Nonetheless, I situate such a formalization of this phenomenological description at a "later" level, already removed from the lived moment of finding, in my world, that which is an "absolutely outside" alterity. More importantly, despite its being "outside," or its approaching from elsewhere, this absence of the Other is very much my concern. Said otherwise, the alterity of the Other's existence makes itself felt in its very deflection of all meaning. It enters into the world of consciousness *as* "an outside," or as a strange and unknowable absence that is very much "there" in its "not being there." At this level of the concrete, this alterity is not (or is not *yet*) another freedom at odds with my own. Rather, it is that which I encounter as radically resistant to my capacity to bestow meaning in such a way that my freedom no longer takes precedence and priority.

Sartre describes this "present absence" as alienating. The existence of the Other separates me from myself, by "sectioning off" my interiority from what would have been my freedom to project meaning into the world. Sartre writes, "I find myself as something which I have not chosen to be."[49] To be sure, the conflict against my choices, encountered in the Other's actions is also not my creation, in the same way the steepness of the crag's gradient is not created by the rock climber.[50] However, such factors are ultimately domesticated, becoming an integral part of *my* situation, the components of which are all accessible insofar as they exist *for me*. By contrast, an encounter with the Other's existence signifies that, prior to and throughout my situation, I *am, for* someone else. Even more severely, my entire situation takes on this character of a "given" for this radically alterity. "The true limit of my freedom [is] the fact that my situation ceases for the Other to be a situation and becomes an objectified form in which I exist as an objective structure."[51] This is the extreme objectification that Sartre describes as my being-for-others, and it necessarily alienates me from myself. It does not merely indicate a givenness of certain aspects of my situation, but rather, inscribes in my very existence an inertia, such that I "am it without existing it." According to Sartre's analysis, the very meaning of "being in situation" already precludes this fact of alienation, or of having to undergo an objectification for the Other. Hence, at the base of "being in situation," there is that "essential characteristic" of the Other's existence, which gives that situation an "outside." So although Sartre's formal account of "situation" underscores the priority of the freedom of consciousness, "situation" simultaneously testifies to a (nonfree) alienation. "[From] the fact of the Other's existence, I exist in a situation which has an outside, and which due to this very fact has a dimension of alienation."[52]

In this regard, Sartre determines that consciousness will *invariably* encounter the alterity of the Other across an experience of alienation. In other words, I can avoid alienation (by the presence of the Other's existence) with as much success as I can take myself out of situation (that is, with no success at all). In this vein, it seems as though alienation inevitably belongs to the structure of consciousness, insofar as that structure includes the truth that freedom is always a "situated freedom." My situation, which is freely constituted by and for me, will always have an exteriority that is *beyond* my constitutive reach. Thomas Busch writes, "As a structure of human reality, this alienation [before the Other] is *ontological and unavoidable* [emphasis added]. . . ."[53] The alienation of consciousness before the Other is part of what it means to *be* consciousness, which seems to be why Sartre describes this unavoidable alienation as "the passion [or affective *nonfreedom*] of freedom."[54]

In the *Critique of Dialectical Reason*, Sartre articulates this radical interruption of spontaneity in explicitly historical terms. In this later text, he understands the freedom of consciousness to be in a situation that is always historical and social in nature. As a consequence, his analysis is not strictly one of intersubjectivity, but rather of the web of relationships that exists within and throughout history. To be sure, Sartre is of the position that history is produced out of these relationships, very much like consciousness freely creates the meaning of the situation out of which it engages with Being.[55] However, sustained in the *Critique* is the claim that the relationship between the individual and history is dialectical. "[Man] . . . is the product of his product."[56] It is out of this dialectic that we read the fullness of Sartre's conception of alienation by alterity, and ultimately, the responsibility for the freedom of all individuals, which comes out of this experience. Sartre understands alterity, or the source of freedom's radical interruption, to refer to the sense in which the material world absorbs the intentions of consciousness, transforming them into intentions that are *against* the agent.[57] This underscores what was established in *Being and Nothingness* concerning the Other's existence, insofar as the violence of materiality is an indication of this existence. The matter with which I inflict my free projects is already layered with meaning and signification that originate in a world of others. In this sense, I am always engaging in a *praxis* that will take on a trajectory independently of the one I carve out, obliging me to be the author of intentions, the scope of which I am not fully aware. I experience alienation as the Other steals from me my freedom, insofar as I must act on a materiality that already realizes meaning that pertains to an Other's project.

These alienating effects of the materiality of history provide the basis on which the following, from *Being and Nothingness*, makes sense, "[Alienation] is therefore ultimately not an head-on obstacle which freedom encounters but a sort of centrifugal force in the very nature of freedom, a weakness in the basic 'stuff' of freedom. . . ."[58] Might this way of describing alienation be an insinuation of a less-than-absolute freedom of consciousness? This "centrifugal force," which Sartre describes, can be read as a burdensome responsibility for a (meaningful) world, despite its not being in full ownership of the intentions that result in the manifestation of that world.[59] As such, there is that ontological weight, which I must bear, and subsequent to which there is the "lightness" of my spontaneous projections toward being.[60]

We can also read, from this account, another kind of weight at the heart of consciousness. It seems as though Sartre's account identifies an alterity that is irreducible to the order of intentionality. On the contrary, the trajectory of intentionality *refracts* on encountering the alterity of the Other, which would suggest that consciousness undergoes a modification of its very *being* in that encounter. In this regard, the resonance between Sartre's analysis and Levinas's is unmistakable. These descriptions of the alterity of the Other can be likened to what, in Levinas, indicates an inflicting of the freedom of consciousness with a burden of unassumable vulnerability. The passion of alienation (through which, for Sartre, the Other's existence "signifies") seems to articulate a type of vulnerability that is prior to or behind the stage on which I engage in a "battle for transcendence." This passion is unlike the objectification brought about through the Other's actions, whereby my freedom is already primed to reclaim its position as the source of signification (for both my world *and* for the Other's). The vulnerability through which I meet the Other's "pure" presence stands for the exteriority of my situation and is "ontologically inevitable," which implies that the Other's existence conditions the very possibility of consciousness (or the very possibility of my being free). Levinas's conception of identity, as a unified duality between the *moi* and the *soi*, explicitly formalizes this level of vulnerability out of which there can be free projections into an intentionally constructed world. But for Levinas, because this vulnerability signifies that to which my freedom is indebted, it is concretized in my obligation to support the being of the Other. To refer to Michael de Saint Cheron's summary of Levinas's position, "[My] freedom, in what is fundamental to it, begins with [a passivity that is] my obligation to the Other."[61]

Can we make a similar claim with regard to Sartre's analysis? It is clear that he recognizes the sense in which the freedom of consciousness contains a certain "passion," or underbelly of nonfreedom. It is also clear that this is, in a very direct way, a consequence of the "presence" of alterity (or more specifically, the alterity of the Other). However, Sartre is very critical of a language of obligation and duty, particularly when it comes to questions of ethics.[62] His critique is clearly a consequence of his formal account of identity, and the role that freedom plays in that formal account. Nonetheless, his relationship to Levinas, across this question of how a certain structural vulnerability might then reflect a subject's responsibility for the Other, is in need of much investigation. This is because, alongside Sartre's contempt of the notion of ethical obligation is his claim that I must be an advocate for the freedom of all men.[63] We find this claim in several of his more politically motivated writings, where he describes relations among others that are not merely conflict-ridden, or driven solely by the need to transcend the Other in order to avoid alienation.

Sartre's criticism of an ethics founded on obligation suggests that these more positive ethical relationships should never be *obligatory*, but he does recognize the *possibility* of such relationships.[64] For this reason, I claim that Sartre is already in dialogue with Levinas, and that his position on obligation is not sufficient to justify a pitting of the two thinkers against each other. At this juncture, as I trace Sartre's position on an ethics of duty, it is important to note that he is just as committed as Levinas is to determining the meaning of the ethical, and to articulating the possibility of the concretization of that meaning.

Sartre on Obligation

In this Sartrean account of alienation, there are implicit intimations of something having slipped into the being of consciousness, after which its only option is to "cope," or bear the burden of having (or being) this passion of existing. My claim is that one can find, in this vulnerability, a relation to the Other that looks less like the conflict described in the pages of *Being and Nothingness*, and more like the radical responsibility described by Levinas. However, the viability of this claim hangs on a proper assessment of Sartre's position in his "less than complete' sketch of an ethics in *Notebooks for an Ethics*.[65] In his commentary, Thomas Anderson advocates for the value of this text, despite its incompletion, insofar as it represents "one of the most coherent attempts to respond to Dostoyevsky's challenge."[66] We are faced with this challenge every time we attempt to articulate the possibility of transcendent values against which we might regard our fundamental choices (and their ensuing actions) in normative terms. However, questions like "what *should* I do," or "which path *should* I pursue" encounter an impasse, since Dostoyevsky's revelation is that God is dead. Anderson's assessment of *Notebooks* is right, insofar as it harkens toward an existentialist ethics that seriously considers the ramification of Dostoyevsky's proclamation, which is the radical absence of justification for the freedom of consciousness.[67] To be sure, Sartre's argument for the contingency (or unjustifiability) of consciousness already shaped his earlier ontological positions in *Being and Nothingness* and in *The Transcendence of the Ego*. But these earlier works were relatively individualistic accounts of what it meant to freely create a meaningful world. By contrast, Sartre's sketch of an ethics tries to bring this absence of justification to a more intersubjective and social account of consciousness and its relation to "world." In other words, the radical spontaneity coming out of his ontological position is analyzed through the lens of a world that has already been constructed, implicitly and explicitly, by infinitely many others.[68]

In *Being and Nothingness*, Sartre writes, "[There] is no compulsion that can get a hold of freedom."[69] We find an echo of this sentiment later on, in *Notebooks*, where he identifies the "oppression of man by man" as that which is "originally unjustifiable."[70] He rearticulates the ontological structures of consciousness, which depict a radically free subject who realizes ends that are created by and for him or her. This means that when I pursue a course of action, it is so that I can bring about a version of the world that reflects the network of value that I spontaneously create. In this regard, any suppression of my creative power is described by Sartre as "originally" unjustifiable, since this creativity is primordial to the being of consciousness. There is no sense in which a consciousness can *be* consciousness without subscribing to this formal structure. More importantly, human freedom remains as the *sole* source of value (and ultimately, the "world") subsequent to the death of God. Hence, to undermine the freedom of consciousness, or to choose or act as though consciousness were less than absolutely free, would be to simultaneously recognize certain values *and* disregard (or leave unacknowledged) their source.[71]

This structure is fundamentally violated when I pursue a version of the world on the realization of ends to which I consider myself *duty-bound*. In other words, when I find myself realizing ends that I am *obligated* to realize, these ends show up for me as "what I have no choice other than to pursue." The *Notebooks* describes this consciousness as being in a "spirit of seriousness," very much like the consciousness of *Being and Nothingness*, who, in veiling from itself all that is implied in its situated freedom, exists in bad faith. "The spirit of seriousness," Sartre writes, "is voluntary alienation, that is, submission to an abstraction that justifies [that] one . . . man is a slave who has his master in the world, *outside of himself* [emphasis added]."[72] Hence, I minimize as "inessential," or of little determinative force, those real, concrete conditions out of which I act, to then negotiate the legitimacy of my choices in terms of a "duty" that predates the immediacies into which I am immersed. These concrete factors would be valued (as either worthy or not worthy of consideration) relative to an abstract and nonlived ideality. In this sense, my choices would derive their normative worth from that which is not only "other than me," but also more essential than me, or more essential than my freedom. Sartre describes this kind of morality as one in which "man is the inessential and the abstract the essential," and as such, one that is no longer applicable to the structures of *human* freedom.[73] Maintained throughout the trajectory of Sartre's work is the sense in which the freedom of consciousness is solely a freedom that unfolds "in the motion proper to existence."[74] Outside of that motion, as in a transcendent realm of fixed and objective ideals, freedom can no longer be this existential unfolding.

Human freedom is always a freedom in the concrete, or in situation. Hence the value that I place on my choices, projects (and ultimately, my world), must be a product of, and directly mirror, the content of my situation. These values come into existence spontaneously, and have being only insofar as the concreteness they reflect continues to persist. Faced with a sufficiently alternate concrete situation, consciousness must author and give legitimacy to a different set of choices, values, and actions, which would be equally as justifiable as (even though entirely different from) what preexisted them. In this sense, Sartre determines that ethics must emerge from a lived world, and is a product of a creative spontaneity very much like "world" is. However, when a consciousness justifies its acts in terms of a duty, "value" is no longer derived from the concrete (or that which is lived), but rather, from a point of *abstraction from* that which is lived. Freedom finds itself no longer realizing ends whose existence is, genuinely, a *spontaneous* existence, but rather bringing about ends that are encountered as already existing through an abstract will. In this sense, my freedom can either be creative and constituting (and, thus, really a freedom), or it can be used toward the realization of an end that is not mine, constituted by an essence that predates my existing. Insofar as an end is of the latter in kind, "it no long has as its task to bring about the world of ethics, but just to maintain [that which has already been constituted independently of my freedom]."[75]

For Sartre, "obligation is the presence in me of Freedom [and not *my* freedom]."[76] This "Freedom" refers to ends that are unconditional and atemporal. He describes such obligatory ends as that which "transcends me toward its own end: [they pass] through me [insofar as] the end of an obligation is a *real* and alien bumper over against which I will have to give way. [Its] value is not a *real claim on me* since I cannot realize it directly."[77] It is in this regard that the subject who is motivated by duty no longer finds him- or herself in those acts whose justification comes from this "atemporal Freedom." The world that I am called by duty to bring about is an alienating force that steals my real and concrete freedom from me. The agent of this theft is, somewhat paradoxically, Freedom itself. But because this is in the name of an abstract ideal of freedom, Sartre describes it as a "Freedom behind my freedom," or "a back door kind of transcendence [that] lies behind the very source of my [free being]."[78]

This language of "that which lies behind my freedom," or that which is more prior to my freedom, takes us back to the formulation of identity that Levinas derives in *Existence and Existents*. Subjectivity, captured in the upsurge of the *moi*, has, as its source, the position of the *soi*, a level of identity in which existence is encountered as an alterity, burdensome and heavy. To be clear, Levinas does not couch the "relationship" between the *moi* (the free subject) and the *soi* (the subject's self) in terms of clashing wills. Sartre's account very clearly intimates this kind of violation, as he identifies those obligatory ends as belonging to "the will of the other behind me."[79] In this sense, the projects that I am called to pursue (because I am duty-bound) are a violation of my freedom insofar as they are legitimized by an alien "for-itself." "Duty," in this regard, would be "the violence of other people but internalized."[80]

In pursuing this dialogue between Sartre and Levinas, across the question of alterity, it is important to make clear why Levinas's conception of obligation does not fall under this Sartrean critique of duty. It will be shown that when Levinas identifies, in my substitution, a call to respond to the Other (or be responsible *for* the Other), it is not the case that that to which I respond is the Other's *will*. Very specifically, he determines the encounter with absolute alterity to be something other than an encounter between two wills, or two freedoms (or my freedom, on the one hand, and the ideal of Freedom, on the other hand). The Other is proximal insofar as he or she is absolutely vulnerable, not yet a freedom that is equal and opposed to mine. Levinas says that my being substituted opens me up onto a "passivity more passive than the passivity of a stone." I develop this in the subsequent section on Levinas's notion of substitution, but we might read, from this declaration, a kind of passivity that is more prior to what Sartre describes as the alienating effects of an ethics of duty. For Sartre, any sense of obligation refers to the other's will, which, in turn, refers back to the Look. "[The] other's will is a *look* (the eye of God, the eye of conscience) . . . [and it] constitutes the world that I see. . . ."[81] However, to return to a question raised at the end of the first section of this chapter, the "other as a Look" is something different from "the other as a Face."[82] In his conception of the Face, Levinas emphasizes a notion of alterity that cannot be reduced to a source of oppositional violence. In this regard, what Sartre describes as a submission to the other's will, or to the Freedom that "transcends transcendence," is something entirely different of my being substituted for the other's being. In that substitution, there isn't a violation of my freedom insofar as the Face, for which I substitute myself, is not yet the kind of "violator" that could initiate the slavery described in Sartre's conception of duty. Quite the contrary, it is *I* who discover myself in the role of "violator," in lieu of the radical vulnerability of the Face. To say this otherwise, this Face accuses in a way that is not presupposed in Sartre's formal account of the Look.

Hence, even though both employ a language of obligation, it is not the case that the content of their accounts allow for a direct comparative analysis. In light of Sartre's formal conception of consciousness, his criticism of founding interpersonal relationships on the notion of ethical (or moral) obligation is only fair. A Sartrean understanding of the primacy of freedom would imply that out of duty is derived "an ethics of slaves." In this regard, a mode of existence committed to the realization of duty would be one in a mode of bad faith, and in alienation from its freedom. Levinas does not recognize the structures of freedom to be exhaustive of or fundamental to identity, and it is on these terms that we read his determination that the subject, through substitution, is under an obligation to be "for the other."

Despite his admonitions against the notion of obligation, it still remains that Sartre recognizes the possibility of positive (and even ethical) relations with the Other. To say this otherwise, as early on as *Being and Nothingness*, Sartre gestures toward certain conditions under which the alterity of the Other does *not* signify as a theft of my freedom, even though he or she is a point of transcending spontaneity.[83] Instead, under these conditions, the Other signifies as a source of freedom that is equally as valuable as my own spontaneity. Hence, as I realize the value of *my* freedom throughout the course of my projections, I acknowledge that the freedom of the Other signifies in a similar way. The *Notebooks* outline Sartre's attempts to develop an ethics out of this kind of recognition, alongside the claim that the aforementioned ethics of duty is essentially incompatible with this more positive mode of intersubjectivity. In other words, the analysis is driven by the claim that, in promoting the freedom of all others, I am precisely not using obligation as the source that justifies my ends.

III. Freedom as the source of all value

In *Being and Nothingness*, Sartre discusses, at length, the unavoidability of bad faith. His account describes the sense in which consciousness will always exist along some point of a pendulum-swing between an erroneously emphasized transcendence and an overly emphasized rootedness to

Being. In so doing, consciousness hides from itself the real structures of its freedom, which is a twofold unity of a "situated transcendence." Always free to transcend, I am also always transcending certain (given) factical aspects of my condition, whose meaning I must then be responsible for. At the pinnacle of this self-deception, Sartre identifies the "God-project" toward which a consciousness in bad faith typically projects. In flight from the absolute contingency of my existence, I desire to be the kind of being who is self-caused, or the kind of being who *gives itself* its reason for being. In other words, in appropriating for itself this God-project, consciousness pursues a version of existence that would exclude the possibility of its nonexistence.

Sartre identifies this pursuit as a "useless passion," insofar as it is destined for defeat. Nevertheless, it presides over our human condition as that screen that protects us from the contingency of our radical freedom. The truth of my being is that all meaning and justification, particularly that which applies to *my own* existence, is (or rather, must be) my spontaneous creation, and sustained as such. The implication of this is that my existing (or what I determine my existence to mean) is quite unnecessary. In every sense, it is "for no reason," other than, of course, that which I give to myself, and it is this radical contingency that consciousness desperately wants to evade. Thomas Anderson writes, "[Man] rebels against considering his existence to be a mere accident or freak of nature, a mere chance occurrence that could have just as easily not happened. He will be content only with a reason or meaning that shows him to have a right to exist."[84] To this end, I evade the truth of my existence (namely, its nonjustification), and pursue a kind of existence that *does* have a reason. However, was this reason to come to me from the outside, it would mean that the ground of my being would be beyond the scope of my control. In other words, to be justified externally would be to reencounter another level of contingency, since there would be no way for me to ensure that that justification remained. For these reasons, consciousness pursues the project of "being God," insofar as God is, categorically, that kind of being whose justification is included in (presupposed by) its existence.

Sartre details much of the inconsistencies and contradictions of a fundamental project such as this. For my purposes, I focus on those contradictions that contain ramifications for our relations with others. In other words, how does this desire to be God signify in the relationship between one such consciousness (pursuing self-causation) and another? In the section of *Being and Nothingness* titled "First Attitude Toward Others," Sartre identifies both love and masochism (as well as all possible in-betweens) as modulations of an original conflict that categorizes the experience of my being-for-others, but which arises only on the grounds of my having a God-project.[85] Before the Other, I find myself with a meaning that originates from the Other. Insofar as that meaning pertains to me, or more specifically, to the being I must own despite my not being its author, my encounter with the Other gives me a reason for being that is "on the outside," or beyond my freedom.[86] If it is the case that I desire self-causation (that I have taken on this fundamental God-project), then my being-for-the-Other appears to me as a violent compromising of my freedom. I must now negotiate some "cause" of my existence that is alien to me, and which is in direct conflict with my desire to be *self*-caused. In other words, insofar as I hold on to the fundamental project of being in-itself-for-itself, the Other shows up as that with whom I am in an inevitable conflict. To this end, I seek to reduce the Other to a (nonfree) objectivity, so as to then steal his or hers power to alienate me from a certain foundation of my being. For similar reasons and motivations, the Other's aim is toward objectifying me. So we have it that, so long as I have for myself a project of being self-caused, every possible relationship I develop with others is ultimately a dynamic of "transcend or be transcended." At all costs, consciousness must avoid being given a foundation that lies outside of itself (in the Other). But this is something worth avoiding only insofar as I consider it worthwhile to flee from my contingency. Said otherwise, there is value in transcending the Other only if there is value in the God-project. Hence, relations of intersubjectivity are of the order of an ontological conflict precisely because "being self-caused" is regarded by consciousness as that which is of utmost value.[87]

By the end of *Being and Nothingness*, Sartre insinuates toward conditions on which relations with others could be less conflictual and more positive. Hence, despite his use of a language that presents such conflict as original to the structures of intersubjectivity, he does open up the possibility that this might be otherwise. "What will become of freedom if it turns its back upon this value [of being self-caused]? . . . In particular, is it possible for freedom to take itself for a value as the source of all value, or must it necessarily be defined in relation to a transcendent value which haunts it?"[88] By such questions, Sartre seems to undermine the assumption that consciousness's desire to be its own foundation is structurally inevitable, and can instead be regarded as one of two possible fundamental projects. He defers the pursuit of such questions to a more overtly ethical analysis, and this is precisely what the sketch in his *Notebooks* represents. Nevertheless, *Being and Nothingness* sufficiently indicates that he had already formulated the possibility of authenticity as that which would replace a mode of existence that desired the being of God, with "[a] new '*authentic*,' way of being oneself and for oneself, which transcends the dialectic of sincerity [spirit of seriousness] and bad faith . . . A thematic grasping of freedom, of gratuity, of un-justifiability."[89]

With this choice of authenticity, consciousness moves beyond the alienation that results from a conflict-ridden, inauthentic encounter with others. This is because it chooses freedom (in its "'gratuity' and 'un-justifiability'") to be the sole and most absolute source of value, and in so doing, understands the futility of a project that desires an "in itself" kind of reification for a "for itself" being. This means that, upon this "conversion," I take on a radically different attitude toward the Other. When I come to understand my freedom as the only unconditional (the only source of value), I must also then apprehend all freedom, including the freedom of others, as unconditionally valuable as well. This means that I no longer encounter the Other as a *look* that steals from me my freedom, but rather as another freedom in pursuit of projects that will be realized alongside my own.[90] In this regard, instead of transcending the Other's transcendence, I regard that transcendence, along with my own, as a unique and unconditional source of creativity. Thomas Anderson writes, "[By] choosing to help others' freedom I thereby will that Being be disclosed and given meaning from multiple perspectives. Because each freedom is in its own unique way a creative source of the world, to aid others' freedom is in effect to will the maximum creation of meaning."[91] To be sure, this already implies that this conversion pertains to a modification of the *social*. In other words, Sartre's account of authenticity presupposes that we are already in what he calls the "city of ends," where all individuals have replaced their "bad faith" desire to be God with an authentic recognition of freedom as the only source of justification.[92] Hence, authenticity becomes a viable option for me if and only if it is equally viable for everyone.[93]

A main criticism that Sartre lays against the idea of realizing ends based on obligation is that, in so doing, consciousness does not yet regard freedom as absolutely unconditional. As we have seen, those ends founded on duty have their justification independently of the concrete, lived experience of consciousness. My duty precisely signifies as "absolute, unchanging and a-temporal,"[94] and as such, comes to my concrete and contingent situation *from* the outside. Insofar as the freedom of consciousness is always situated, and is meaningful only in the project of "doing" or praxis, an authentic valuing of freedom requires that consciousness remain "in the concrete," and avoid what Sartre refers to as "a quest for

Being." It is in this sense that freedom is grasped in its full "gratuity and unjustifiability." "Authenticity reveals that the only meaningful project is that of *doing* (not that of being) and that the project to do something cannot itself be universal without falling into what is abstract. . . . The only meaningful project is that of acting on a concrete situation and modifying it in some way. . . . So, originally, authenticity consists in refusing any quest for being, because I am always *nothing*."[95] In authenticity, my ends are justified solely in terms of the concrete, since it is solely in terms of the concrete that my freedom exists. As such, the Other is apprehended as another unconditionally valuable freedom that signifies in his or her concrete "doing" (or work). To regard the Other in this way is to acknowledge that I am called to facilitate the modifications in being, which his or her projects seek to bring about.[96] In that facilitation, I also support the freedom of the person in (or behind) that work. In this vein, Sartre declares that "freedom, in respect of concrete circumstances, can have no other end and aim but itself; and when once a man has seen that values depend upon himself, in that state of forsakenness he can will only one thing, and that is freedom as the foundation of all values . . . the actions of men of good faith have, as their ultimate significance, the quest of freedom itself as such."[97]

All this would mean that, instead of realizing a world founded on duty (or demand), my world would be the realization of spontaneous and concrete choices that not only embrace the contingencies of my situation, but also allow for other consciousnesses to do the same. In such a world, I am neither the recipient nor giver of duty-grounded demands. This means that I do not find myself *obligated* to bring about the freedom of Others, at least not in a way whereby I no longer find myself in such an end. However, in choosing authenticity, I do encounter a certain modulation of a demand.[98] In formulating his ethics, Sartre recognizes that insofar as "no one is free unless all are free," the freedom of others is given to consciousness as a value to be realized. But because this is facilitated by and in authenticity, it will be the case that consciousness is not alienated by this end. Said otherwise, I *will* recognize myself in the future of the Other, which means that I find myself in the end or goal of "bringing about his freedom." It is not at the *expense* of my freedom that my concrete praxis will bring about this end. Rather, as a member of Sartre's city of ends, my freedom would already include the freedom of the Other, a value that is simultaneous to the value of my own spontaneity.

As Anderson writes, "[According to Sartre], men who choose to value their freedom in place of God . . . choose to increase concretely this freedom in the world . . ."[99] Such men are no longer motivated by obligation, but by freedom itself. So even though Sartre writes, in *Existentialism is a Humanism*, that "I am obliged to will the freedom of others at the same time as mine,"[100] it is very much the case that my own freedom is valued most supremely. In this regard, the work of this sense of "obligation" is already doing something differently from what we see in Levinas, where my obligation toward the Other rests on a fundamental *asymmetry* between my being and the Face of the Other.[101] This indicates an important difference between Sartre's and Levinas's conceptions of "the ethical." Both seem equally as committed to articulating a compelling account of our responsibilities toward each other, which would apply when we find ourselves navigating a social space in which our choices create a world that *everyone* must inhabit. Nevertheless, their respective approaches to this question are unique and should be read on their own terms.

For Levinas, ethics, or rather, the meaning of the ethical, lies in the undoing of identity in its proximal relation to "the metaphysical." Very often, he describes this "metaphysical" in terms of the Face, but, as I have argued, it should be understood more generally as that moment when identity is "without identity," radically compromised by the proximity of alterity. I discuss this shortly, in the following section. But at present, it is worthwhile to note that Levinas identifies the ethical moment in a radical asymmetry between "self" and "Other." The Other is "infinitely other," which means that he or she is not simply "another freedom," as is the case in Sartre's account. Her proximal approach is from a height (the height constitutive of the metaphysical), which is to say that alterity is located on a plane that is other than the plane of (coexisting) freedoms. Sartre's *Notebooks*, somewhat differently, understands the ethical in terms of conditions that facilitate this kind of (symmetrical) existence among freedoms. In this vein, Sartre determines ethics to be founded on the fundamental value of freedom, and concretized through intersubjective relationships of a mutual recognition (or willing) of freedom. In other words, for Sartre, the ethical relation is a symmetrical relation, or a relation that acknowledges the radical *equality* between myself and the Other. To this end, Thomas Anderson's reading of *Anti-Semite and Jew* is correct when he represents the impetus of Sartre's analysis of the Jewish question as follows: "What is implicit [in the analysis] is a belief in human equality. . . . Since all intrinsic or objective values have vanished in Sartre's ontology, no man can claim any ontological superiority over another. . . ."[102] So even though, upon the conversion to authenticity, my fundamental project includes supporting the freedom of others, their freedom does not *supersede* my own. The Other's ends become a value for me, without being venerated at the expense of my own ends. According to Sartre, in the absence of the "passionately useless" pursuit of being self-caused, consciousness creates a world, the social dimensions of which are shaped by conditions of love and generosity instead of duty and alienation. This is because, I encounter the Other as equally free, despite his or her radical difference.[103]

In this vein, Sartre does not articulate a *duty* to promote the freedom of others, nor does he suggest that the freedom of others should take precedence over mine. However, he does advocate for acting on behalf of others in the midst of my own pursuits. Again, from *Anti-Semite and Jew*: "If we are conscious of these dangers [of anti-Semitic hatred] . . . we shall begin to understand that we must fight for the Jew, no more and no less than for ourselves."[104] The freedom of others, or conversely, the lack thereof, is very much my concern as I authentically realize my own ends. In my concrete situation, I cannot, with consistency, act as though the Other's oppression or disenfranchisement is that about which I can be apathetic. More strongly, I cannot, with consistency, realize my own concrete freedom *alongside* the oppression of the Other, since Sartre's insinuation seems to be that as long as freedom is threatened "somewhere," it is threatened "everywhere," absolutely and without limitation. This means that, in authenticity (the only conditions to which these positive interpersonal relations apply), consciousness acts not only on *its* behalf, but also on the behalf of others as well, so that freedom prevails as the sole unconditional value.

To reiterate, in Sartre's city of ends, the Other also acts on behalf of me, and values my ends no less than his or her own. This kind of symmetry is significant as we turn more fully toward Levinas's conception of substitution. It is also important to be clear on the ramifications of what can be regarded as a Sartrean notion of ethical responsibility, particularly in light of his explicit disdain for those conceptions of ethical duty and obligation. In the account of *Being and Nothingness*, where the condition captured was that of a "not yet social" consciousness whose existence was inauthentic, Sartre already identified a very radical account of individual responsibility. As a consciousness, my freedom is absolute, which is, again, to say that "there is no compulsion that can get a hold of freedom."[105] Everything about my existence, including the world in which I exist, is what I have directly chosen, and for which I am also absolutely responsible. Despite my own lack of foundation, I am the foundation of the world insofar as I have freely chosen it.[106] In this regard, Sartre claims that "[we] have the responsibility that we deserve."[107] In the more social conditions of authentic existence, I chose a world in which all people are free. This would mean that, as the foundation of this world, I find myself with the responsibility to realize the freedom of others. Concretely, this would mean taking explicit action against forms of oppression and hatred that would undermine the free existence of other men and women.

Hence, it seems to be the case that, included in Sartre's account of authenticity, is a level of ethical responsibility for the Other, which must be met by the subject. As we will see shortly (and for reasons to which I have already eluded), this does not give us the kind of responsibility found in Levinas's account of substitution. However, it does present Sartre as someone who recognizes the ways in which my individual freedom is already called into question as I navigate a concrete social space in which I, along with others, bring about a city of ends. In my everyday choices, I am responsible for supporting the Other's freedom, which means that my actions are limited to those that genuinely pursue authentic ends that regard the Other as free. In this sense, in a moment of realizing an end, I might find reason to pause or "double back" as I determine how this end affects the Other in the pursuit of his or her own ends. To reiterate, this is all in the spirit of a radical *equality* between myself and the Other. In Levinas's account of substitution, to which we now turn, this equality is replaced with a radical asymmetry on which he grounds the meaning of the ethical.

IV. Levinas's Substitution: Freedom Is Not Primary

In *Totality and Infinity*, Levinas writes, "The Other imposes himself as an exigency that dominates [my] freedom. . . . Thus, in the presence of the Other is contained the ethical impossibility of killing him resulting in the end of my powers. . . . The presence of the Other, a privileged heteronomy does not clash with freedom, but invests it."[108] In this description of the instant of being substituted for the Other, it is clear that Levinas's understanding of alterity is shaped by a conception of human identity that is radically different from Sartre's. To recall from my analysis in chapter 2, Levinas understands the subject to be a diachronous unity of the *moi* and the *soi*, already dispossessed and vulnerable in its "position" as a subject. As such, his notion of ethics rests on the signification of this disruption that is primary to identity. Hence, his conception of substitution is geared toward the question of how this "identity in disruption" might inform the meaning of the ethical. Insofar as Levinas's analysis is guided by these fundamentally metaphysical concerns, substitution is not geared toward establishing the possibility of the kind of action that might be a response to one's radical ethical responsibility. To be sure, Levinas's account of responsibility comes out of his understanding of identity as a depositioned locus of vulnerability. As such, he reads, in an encounter with the Other, the subject's substitution *for* the Other. However, this call to substitution is *obsessive*, anarchic, and absolute. Indeed, the subject is called to a kind of self-sacrifice, insofar as his or her place in being is primordially delegitimized (or rather, *never* legitimate), given the Other's suffering. As such, it is notoriously difficult to determine, out of this account, the possibility of ethically responsible action in the sphere of the political.[109] Given the singularity of the Other, and my absolute vulnerability under the weight of the Other's being, any "negotiations" of my responsibility for *several* "Others" would be to undermine the severity of my obsession.[110] This should not be read as a short-coming in Levinas, since it was never his intention to articulate an account of the political, or to establish what it means to take action on being called to substitution. Nonetheless, the question of a possible transfer of Levinas's radical responsibility into the political is one worthy of pursuit. In this vein, I use the resonance between his notion of substitution and Sartre's account of an ethics of authenticity to ground my claim that Sartre's account of committed political action can be used to take a Levinasian conception of responsibility into the political with minimal betrayal.

In Levinas's formal account of substitution, one "[passes] from the outrage undergone [by alterity] to the responsibility for the persecutor."[111] In other words, my substitution is so severe that, in a condition of being oppressed, I am even called to support the being of my oppressor. However, it is this very severity in which my freedom is dethroned that, for Levinas, saves me from a slave-like condition of being alienated from my freedom, the way one might expect me to be, on encountering the master's Look.[112] Very clearly, Levinas states that "[substitution] is . . . not an alienation, because the other in the same is *my* substitution for the other through responsibility."[113] For Sartre, alienation presupposes a theft, or an illegitimate pillaging *by* the Other of what is rightfully mine (namely, my freedom). In the case of Levinas's account of substitution, the subject is always already "for the Other," in the sense that the very structure of this subject *is* dispossession. My substitution for the Other does not imply that the Other steals what is rightfully mine. On the contrary, as primordially elected and thus unique through my responsibility, there is no place in being for which I can claim this kind of primordial propriety.

Hence, for Levinas, the trauma of an encounter with alterity is beyond the negativity of a failed self-determination, and as such, beyond the offense of alienation.[114]

We return, again, to Levinas's structure of identity, in order to fully understand how substitution captures the subject's encounter with alterity in a way that does not result in a Sartre-like alienation. Levinas uncovers an existent that is not reducible to the "leaving and returning to self" of consciousness, but rather must be understood in terms of recurrence.[115] Of the relationship between the ego (or *moi*) and itself (or *soi*), Levinas writes, "The ego is in itself like a sound that would resound in its own echo."[116] The imagery is one of an undeniable yet discordant union, such that the identity of the subject is the impossibility of being completely free from itself, *as well as* the impossibility of being completely one with itself. In this sense, though the subject is tethered to a corporeal existence, its incarnation is not that of Sartre's "in-itself" being. The latter possesses an identity of equivalence, as in the objectivity of a stone. The recurrence of the subject to itself means that "[the] oneself takes refuge or is exiled in its own fullness."[117] In order to understand this from a Sartrean point of reference, one would have to situate recurrence in some third mode of being that is neither the "for-itself" nor the "in-itself." In other words, what one finds in the notion of recurrence (as a nonmapping of the subject onto its "self") already bypasses the alternatives of "materiality's nonfreedom" and "freedom's nonmateriality." Instead, an identity in recurrence gestures toward what Levinas describes as "the ultimate secret of the incarnation of [a] subject," who, as a result of incarnation, is passive in a way that exceeds substantiality.[118]

Recurrence means that the "I" is backed up into itself, to the point of the very breakup of identity. But instead of allowing for an ecstatic surpassing of self, the breaking-up of identity sustains the hostage-like condition of the subject, trapped in itself as "in its own skin." "Recurrence," Levinas tells us, "is the contracting of an ego, going to the hither side of identity, gnawing away at this very identity." Insofar as this impossibility of identity takes me behind the safe haven that would have substantialized me *in* being, recurrence takes me *out of* being, and into proximity with the Other. His being becomes my fundamental concern, replacing the *conatus essendi* that governed a subject in being, and who is only concerned with her being.[120] In other words, the structure of recurrence is the very inversion of identity that ends in my being substituted *for* the Other.

According to Levinas's analysis, the vulnerability with which I am overcome in the proximal approach of the Other is already present in the structure of recurrence.[121] It is *as* a discordant identity, or as *without* identity, that the subject is already radically "dispossessed." Such a dispossession is not an annihilation of the subject, so even though this demarcates a limitation of the powers, it is not a limitation that tends toward the subject's nonbeing.[122] On the contrary, the dispossession that pertains to the structures of recurrence signifies a *fullness* of being, or "a negativity caught up in the impossibility of evading."[123] Death's eradication (what *would* take the subject over into nonbeing) might give the incarnate subject an avenue from which to escape the wounding brought about by alterity. But it is precisely this escape that is impossible. It is in the fullness of embodiment that the subject's being is replaced by a responsibility for the Other, such that identity is an openness onto alterity. In this vein, Levinas finds, in corporeality, the signification of the weight of this radical responsibility, and the possibility of giving and sacrifice. "In [recurrence] the body . . . makes giving possible [and] makes one *other* without alienating."[124]

Even more severe than discovering myself to be an object for the Other (the discovery that prevails throughout Sartre's account of alienation) is what I discover as a consequence of substitution. There, I find myself *in the Other's place*. In front of the Other (as a face, and *not* as a look), I *am* only insofar as I am already *for him*. This "for" is of a different order from the "for" in Sartre's "being for others," which describes an encounter between two consciousnesses in terms of one becoming an *object* for the other.[125] The "for" in substitution rests on an embodiment that, as we have said, is more passive than objectification. "Prime matter," Levinas tells us, retains the power of "resistance and impenetrability."[126] As such, it is not yet the "absolute passivity" of substitution. The call to substitute myself for the Other constitutes the passivity of a persecution precisely because of the impossibility *not* to respond. There is no resisting the trauma undergone by alterity's proximity, since the freedom to resist "comes too late."[127] The subject's absolute debt originates on the "hither" side of freedom, prior to the formation of any will that could either accept or deny it. It is in this sense that alterity passes by as a trace, clothed in an unassumability, never in the present and as such, unrepresentable. "The neighbor concerns me before all assumption, all commitment consented or refused."[128]

Quite aporetically, in these structures of substitution, Levinas finds the possibility of the radical escape included in excendence. "In this most passive passivity, the self liberates itself from every other *and from itself* [emphasis added]. Its responsibility for the other, the proximity of the neighbor ... means an openness in which being's essence is surpassed in inspiration."[129] Substitution means that the subject has always already been transported beyond the modalities of being, insofar as it just *is* the gutting-out or rupturing of being. "[The subject] is a being divesting itself, emptying itself of its being."[130] Interestingly enough, Sartre also employs notions of an emptiness of being to account of the structure of consciousness. Furthermore, it is *as* empty of being that Sartre locates in consciousness the meaning of transcendence. However, the sense in which Levinas identifies the subject's transcendence as an "emptying of itself" is quite different from the sense we read in Sartre. Insofar as an identity in recurrence is equivalent to a *non*identity, Levinas identifies the subject as "the fact of 'otherwise than being.'"[131] Hence, subjectivity's divesting of itself signifies as a rivetedness to an obsessive responsibility for the Other. For Sartre, consciousness, which is also without identity insofar as it is without an "in-itself" identity, is the fact of being's negation. Consciousness is a *nothingness* of being. This difference between an "otherwise than being" and a "nothingness of being" is much more than stylistic. It captures the difference between what Levinas describes as a density of being, which then conditions a vulnerability, and what Sartre describes as the emptiness of being that conditions a spontaneity. The Levinasian subject signifies an "otherwise than being" since it persists in so radical a *disruption* that its "beginning to be" is troubled.[132] It pulses in a demented ambiguity between being and nonbeing, insofar as this beginning is undergone and never assumed. Though a Sartrean consciousness exists as a persistent rupturing of definition, this rupture is completely spontaneous. This means that consciousness's nothingness is ultimately assumed *by* consciousness, and acts as the ground for *acts* of consciousness. For Sartre, nonidentity is a consequence of freedom, and safeguards freedom. In Levinas, it is an indication of the absolute passivity of incarnation and, ultimately, substitution.

Hence, as Levinas celebrates substitution as that which ultimately opens up the possibility of transcendence, it is not to undermine the severe wounding on which this possibility rests. Situating this transcendence-in-substitution against Sartre's transcendence-in-intentionality makes this quite clear. To transcend in substituting oneself for the Other, or to divest oneself of one's being, is to respond to a call for absolute sacrifice. The burden of the weight of one's existence is transcended, but it is precisely in exchange for the immemorial and unassumable weight of the obligation to support all. In this regard, implied in a Levinasian transcendence is a forsakenness, to which the monstrosity of death pales in comparison.

To be sure, Levinas will establish that, in replacing the "useless suffering" of my own death with the suffering of the Other, "a beyond appears in the form of the inter-human. [My] own experience of [senseless] suffering . . . can take on a meaning, the only one of which suffering is capable, in becoming a suffering for the suffering (inexorable though it may be) of someone else."[133] The implication is that the absurdity of death loses its evil character when it becomes a dying for the sake of the Other. But this is not to suggest that the "Here I am" of substitution is any less absurd or insidious than it actually is. Responsible to the point of being responsible for my persecutor, my being substituted for the Other is a clear "defiance of all logic." "For the order of contemplation it is something simply demented."[134] The very rupturing of the texts in which Levinas articulates the meaning of substitution indicates the nonsense, or anachronism of being accused of all fault, for nothing.[135]

In this sense, it is imperative to maintain the essential "difficulty" in Levinas's way of transcendence. The proximal approach of radical alterity does not result in an alienation, but there is nevertheless an essential difficulty in the "for nothing" of this sacrificial transcendence, or this transcending in a sacrifice that is never quite sufficient to counter the immemorial debt of one's responsibility. This is evident in Levinas's emphasis on the unassumability of alterity's passing. The subject must *undergo* this approach insofar as the latter remains without reason or meaning. The futility of one's own death might be in its failure to bring about a genuine transcendence, but one's substitution for the Other is also "useless" in its own right. I am divested of being in substituting myself, which means that taking up this burden does not service (the good of) my being in the least. It is genuinely *for nothing*. As such, the goodness of absolute responsibility bears the very absurdity and delirium found in the *il y a*, where Levinas already locates the alterity that the subject is called to support in substitution.

V. Limitations and Values

In "Being Jewish," that essay in which Levinas discusses Sartre's analysis of the alienation of the Jew under the anti-Semitic gaze, we find further elaboration on the intricacies of substitution. There are many criticisms of *Anti-Semite and Jew*, the most common being that Sartre too hastily reduces the identity of the Jew to a borrowed identity that emerges solely as a response to anti-Semitism. Such criticism holds that not only does this further rob the Jew of autonomy as a Jew, but it also seems to come from a dismissal, on Sartre's part, of that Judaic religious history informing the identity of the Jew, and which stands independently from forms of anti-Semitic hatred. In "Being Jewish," Levinas's criticism comes from a markedly different place insofar as it calls into question the very assumption that Sartrean authenticity is a sufficiently universal structure that can apply to the singularity of the Jewish experience. Levinas presents Judaism's unique relation to Being as that which is resistant to these Sartrean dichotomies of "inauthentic" and "authentic" modes of existence.[136] Responding to Sartre's call for an authentic Jewishness, Levinas writes, "Jewish existence cannot be fit into the set of distinctions by which Sartre, for example, attempts to grasp it."[137] Levinas proposes that, instead, Jewish facticity, or the positioned existence of the Jew, should be understood in terms "other than the 'facticity' of a world that understands itself starting from the present."[138]

The presentation of Jewish facticity as distinct from "facticity in general" underscores what I have thus far demonstrated as the structural difference between the (Levinasian) recurrence of an identity in substitution, and (the Sartrean account of) consciousness's impenetrable objectification in the experience of being alienated. Levinas's claim is that a Jewish "facticity" is only approximately so. As a rootedness in being, the Jewish condition carries an affectivity that is beyond the parameters of Sartre's conception of facticity insofar as this latter structure presupposes a temporality that is simply absent, on Levinas's account, in a Judaic sensibility. A Sartrean consciousness "understands itself starting from the present,"[139] and presupposes access to an interior life, even amid the experience of facticity, or the experience of having its freedom compromised in a moment of alienation before the Other. For this reason, Sartre can identify self-determination as a possible response to forms of oppression, and applies this to the Jewish condition as well: "The authentic Jew . . . wills himself into history as a historic and damned creature . . . and it is as such that he asserts his being."[140] Despite the theft of this alienated subject's world, "the authentic Jew" can *freely* choose a meaning for his or her situation, which ultimately robs the Other of that signification as "oppressor."

Sartre's advocating for a reappropriation of freedom in those experiences of alienation is consistent with a project such as his. But without the commitments and presuppositions of this project, the vulnerability undergone in an encounter with alterity bears its own signification. From a Levinasian vantage point, it is not yet something to be overcome by an assertion of freedom. Rather, this moment of vulnerability on encountering alterity references the imploded identity of the subject-in-substitution. To be sure, this reading is conditioned by Levinas's conceptions of identity, embodiment, and positionality. Given Sartre's formal account of consciousness as a radical escape from being, embodiment could never signify more passively than "prime matter," or objectivity. In this regard, the subject's nonfreedom on encountering the Other would be, on Sartre's account, *against* the Other's will (and not, as is the case in Levinas, *prior* to there being a will). A fair assessment of Sartre's notion of alienation alongside Levinas's conception of unremitting responsibility would be one that recognizes these important differences. In the end, my claim is not that we reject either of these two accounts of alterity in favor of the other. Instead, I aim to establish the limitations that a Sartrean conception of authenticity encounters if one rejects, as Levinas does, Sartre's presuppositions concerning the structures of identity.

Conversely, we also recognize those limitations in the Levinasian project. Alongside his criticism of Sartre's analysis of the Jew, Levinas inadvertently identifies what might be uniquely valuable to Sartre's conception of authenticity. Describing the kind of (non-Jewish) facticity that would be more relevant to Sartre's analysis, Levinas writes, "[its] relation with being in everyday life is *action* [emphasis added]."[141] Unlike the "passivity of election" that marks Judaism's fundamental relation with being, there are those other facticities that are grounded in the priority of activity. Sartre's account of authenticity is useful insofar as it is built on this fundamental value of action, or praxis on behalf of the Other. This positions Sartre to negotiate questions concerning political action in ways that Levinas's analysis is less equipped to engage. This is because Sartre's account of an authentic response to alienation includes responding to the Other's appeal by acting on behalf of his or her freedom. Robert Bernasconi describes the conception of responsibility coming out of this Sartrean account as "hyperbolic," whereby the free subject is responsible not only for acts that can be traced back to his or her agency, but also for the entirety of the subject's situation, past and future.[142] "Sartre's philosophy of freedom does not lead to resignation, or stoic indifference to one's circumstances, but to taking responsibility. There are no excuses, whatever the conditions."[143] This is clearly Sartre's intentions when he describes the responsibility of all of France, regardless of political affiliation, for the marginalization of the Jews: "In this situation there is not one of us who is not totally guilty and even criminal; the Jewish blood that the Nazis shed falls on all our heads."[144]

Even though this position is not identical to the radical responsibility found in Levinas, it certainly resonates with it.[145] Indeed, Levinas's exposition of a notion like substitution might be read as the *condition that accounts* for the possibility of taking such action on behalf of the Other, even when such action means that we are less concerned for our own death than we are for the death of the Other.[146] But it is in Sartre that we find an overt emphasis on concrete action as a response to one's obligations to bring about the freedom of others. In his account of Sartre's ethical position, Thomas Anderson refers to those interviews that Sartre gave between the late 1960s and early 1970s, in which his position on what he called a "living morality" (one that placed the importance of concrete praxis above abstract moral principles) is clear. "[According to Sartre], no longer can the intellectual serve the oppressed masses simply from his office or study. He must join with them bodily in demonstrations, hunger strikes, counterviolence against police violence. . . . The intellectual must . . . put himself *directly* at the service of the oppressed."[147]

In the end, even though Sartre's account of authenticity does not support the severe notion of passivity found in Levinasian substitution, both, on their own terms, provide a robust conception of responsibility. For Levinas, this responsibility comes from a conception of the subject whose very structure is interruption, trauma, and dispossession. Though the ontology from *Being and Nothingness* does not identify this level of affectivity in consciousness, I have shown that the phenomenology of the text does lend itself to a Levinasian understanding of an identity-in-disruption, gesturing toward an account of freedom that is called into question. This is not to interpret Sartre as saying that, in that moment of authenticity, I prioritize the Other's freedom at the expense of my own. Nevertheless, that other freedom does present a living (and not abstract) consideration against which I gauge the justification of my actions. This would mean that these actions, and by extension, my freedom, are not in a position to justify themselves, as is the case in Levinas's critique of the priority of freedom. Instead, it is only insofar as I regard and support the Other that I am justified.

Concluding Remarks

My hope is to have demonstrated the convergence between the concrete phenomenologies of Jean-Paul Sartre and Emmanuel Levinas. Such convergence requires both Sartrean and Levinasian scholars alike to open anew the question of transcendence, and how it figures into the formal level of the work of these thinkers. Sartre gives us a conception of consciousness as spontaneous, always in the process of creating a world that is reflective of a freely taken-up fundamental project. Hence, his is an account of transcendence-as-intentionality that completely exhausts the structure of consciousness. Levinas augments this account of the subject-as-intentionality with a layer of vulnerability that, he holds, conditions the possibility of that creative freedom. In this sense, a Levinasian conception of transcendence-as-excedence does not oppose transcendence-as-intentionality, but, rather, determines the latter as an incomplete depiction of the totality of the human condition. As such, Levinas reads intentionality as that which conceptualizes a *constituting* encounter with Being, and presents a cohesive phenomenology on which he identifies another kind of encounter with Being, which precisely falls outside of this constituting relationship. His conception of transcendence-as-excedence rests on the claim that Being is also given over in its radical alterity, in the form of the *il y a*. In this regard, he determines the need for a notion of identity that can account for this encounter, which manifests as a *disruption* of constitutive powers. Identity, as a dissonant unity between the *moi* and *soi*, responds to this need, and ultimately shapes Levinas's account of transcendence-as-excedence, as well as his more overtly ethical conceptions of alterity.

There are illusions to this modality of being in Sartre's analysis of the experience of nausea, and some commentaries on *Nausea* read, in the novel, a portrayal of a kind of "brute existence." Michael Brogan's piece, "Nausea and the Experience of the '*Il y a*': Sartre and Levinas on Brute

Existence," is one such example.¹ Adrian van der Hoven's exposition of the emphasis on the biological in *Nausea* also alludes (though not explicitly) to the presence of a nonconstitutive encounter with Being. Nevertheless, these authors do not read this encounter as one that goes behind an intentional (and ultimately constituting) structure of consciousness. Similar to Christina Howells's commentary on the novel, they portray Roquentin's nausea as an outcome of his anguish before the radical nature of his freedom (to constitute both himself and the world).² As such, among Sartrean scholarship, *Nausea* remains a work that describes the experience of "the natural attitude" falling away, as consciousness comes to terms with the radical nature of its freedom. Howells does mention that, throughout the novel, Roquentin finds himself no longer to be a self-sufficient and autonomous subject (namely, the kind of subjectivity of which Levinas is suspicious). However, her analysis goes on to say that, although Roquentin appears unstable, this instability is due to the "experience of unselfhood."³ We know that, from as early on as *The Transcendence of the Ego*, this lack of a "self" within consciousness only serves to reinforce Sartre's formal account of radical freedom. A lack of self, for Sartre, means that consciousness is a perpetual surpassing of Being, and as such, is without the kind of positioning that Levinas portrays in his formal structures of identity. So even though *Nausea* has been read as describing a destabilized freedom, it is clear that most understand the work of this destabilization as presenting to the novel's protagonist the "monstrous spontaneity" of consciousness.⁴ To this end, Roquentin's "experience of unselfhood" confirms the human condition as an ecstatic transcendence in Being. My analysis in chapter 3 presents an alternative reading of the work of the radical disruption of Roquentin's subjectivity.

As I have established, one of Sartre's primary motivations for developing his conception of consciousness as an absolute transcendence from Being is to keep uncompromised Husserl's account of intentionality. *The Transcendence of the Ego* argues that, for intentionality to be genuinely the condition for the possibility of experience, it must be the case that the subject is void of and untethered to an in-itself identity. In this sense, intentionality precludes that the subject is nothing other than a lucid reflection of Being. In this regard, my bringing together this Sartrean deployment of Husserl alongside Levinas's work opens up the following question: Does Levinas's account of positionality commit this "crime" against intentionality? Asked otherwise, does that level of the existent represented in the *soi* introduce the kind of opacity of which Sartre is wary, to then render impossible an intentional relation to Being? Like Sartre,

Levinas is a student of Husserl, which means that he would also read into this impossibility of intentionality the positing of a kind of subject for which there is no phenomena. It is clearly the case that this is not Levinas's position. His account of identity establishes an entirely different signification in his notion of the *soi*, and its relation to the *moi*. I return to his reflections on the philosophy of Hitlerism, where he identifies the alternatives in Western liberalism and nationalism to be equally misguided in their respective grappling with the meaning of the human condition. In chapter 2 I discussed Levinas's transcending of these two positions. However, I return to this analysis here to establish that, notwithstanding perfunctory indications to the contrary, the Levinasian conception of positionality does not succumb to Sartre's critique in *The Transcendence of the Ego*. This grounds what I hold to be a significant and fundamental difference between their work. In the "Reflections" essay, Levinas discards the ideology of nationalism in order to argue for a nuanced conception of rootedness that does *not* entrap the subject in the fate of his or her bloodline. In this sense, he seeks to represent, in the *soi*, a primordial anchoring in Being that is not the reification, density, or opacity that fuels Sartre's critique of the transcendental ego. For Levinas, to be free is to be burdened with the responsibility of existing, and so the rootedness to which this responsibility points *allows* for the free transcending movement at the level of the *moi*. In this regard, positionality does not *nullify* our existential freedom, the way a Sartrean "in-itself" identity would. On the contrary, it precisely invests this freedom, since it is only to the subject who is radically set apart (and free) from an ontological destiny that Levinas's sense of responsibility can apply.

To say this otherwise, the nonfreedom implicated in the conception of positionality (in the conception of the *soi*) does not belong to the order of objectification, but rather to the order of responsibility, in which case the freedom of the movement of intentionality remains uncompromised. It is also for this reason that Levinas's more ethical conception of substitution, into which his language of the *moi* and the *soi* translates, does not succumb to Sartre's critique of duty as an alienation of the subject from his or her freedom. My being substituted for the Other limits my freedom in the sense that I am now responsible for the Other's being. But that responsibility does not constitute a theft of my being, the way my objectified being-for-others would, on a Sartrean account. This is because the *soi* has already formalized the sense in which I already am "without identity" for the Other insofar as I am never "for myself." I have argued that Sartre's more concrete descriptions resonate with this imagery of a subject in radical disruption. Nevertheless, his formal account sustains that of a consciousness that is radically "for itself" in its transcendence toward Being.

I have shown that, despite this formal account, Sartre's more political writings develop an account of authenticity that captures an ethical responsibility very similar to what we find to be supported by Levinas's account of positionality. Unlike the experience of alienation, whereby the subject feels his or her freedom stolen by the will of the Other, a more authentic intersubjectivity does not regard this invasion as a "theft," but rather as an interjection of an obligation to promote the freedom of all. It must be noted that this Sartrean account, according to which I advocate the Other's freedom so as to guarantee the possibility of my own, differs from Levinas insofar as it presupposes a fundamental equality between "self" and "other." All the same, both analyses clearly recognize that, by virtue of being a subject, I am unable to remain ambivalent toward the Other's existential condition. In this regard, the Other is particularly privileged by both thinkers, when it comes to understanding how alterity performs as a disruption of subjective freedom. For both Sartre and Levinas, it is the Other as persecuted and oppressed that most significantly halts the trajectory of my fundamental project, calling into question the priority of my freedom over my obligation to end the Other's suffering.

In the end, I have shown that the account that presents intentionality as the conditions for the possibility of experience can be sustained while adopting a Levinasian account of transcendence-as-excendence, which is founded on a conception of identity as radically disrupted. To be sure, this "without-identity" would render intentionality as an *incomplete* depiction of the human condition, but accurate nonetheless. Sartre and Levinas part ways at this formal level, where transcendence-as-intentionality stands over and against transcendence-as-excendence. Nonetheless, the concrete levels of both analyses are characterized by a pervasive presence of a phenomenology that gestures toward a subject whose freedom is called into question, and who is radically interrupted by that which is radically otherwise. To this end, Sartre and Levinas do meet across a theme of disruption that determines the subject to be more primordially vulnerable than free.

Notes

Introduction

1. Jean-Paul Sartre, "Intentionality: A Fundamental Idea of Husserl's Phenomenology," trans. Joseph P. Fell, *Situations, I* (Paris: Librairie Gallimard, 1947), 5. Hereafter cited as "Intentionality."

2. I identify Levinas's *Existence and Existents* as a text in which the endeavor is akin to that of *Being and Nothingness*, insofar as it establishes our most fundamental encounter with being. See Emmanuel, *Existence and Existents,* trans. Alphonso Lingis (Pittsburgh, Pa.: Duquesne, 2001). Hereafter cited as *EE.*

3. Sartre, "La Transcendence de L'Ego, Esquisse d'une description phénoménologique," *Rechercheers Philosophiques* VI (1936–67): 86–123, trans. Forrest Williams and Robert Kirkpatrick under the title *The Transcendence of the Ego, An Existentialist Theory of Consciousness* (New York: Noon Day Press, 1972). Hereafter cited as *TE.*

4. Sartre, *L'être et Le Neant, Essat d' ontologie phenomenology* (Paris: Librairie Gallimard, 1943), trans. Hazel E. Barnes under the title *Being and Nothingness: An Essay on Phenomenological Ontology* (New York: Philosophical Library, 1956). Hereafter cited as *BN.*

5. François Raffoul reads, in Sartre, an underlying indebtedness to Cartesianism, in his conception of "willful subjectivity and the motif of authorship [present in his work]." See *The Origins of Responsibility* (Bloomington, Indiana University Press, 2010), 122.

6. I discuss this in detail in chapter 4, alongside other modes of affectivity in Sartre, which escapes his formal account of transcendence.

7. Levinas, *De l'évasion* (Montpellier, France: Fata Morgana, 1982), trans. Bettina Bergo under the title *On Escape* (Palo Alto: Stanford University Press, 2003). Hereafter cited as *OE.*

8. Levinas, *Totalité et Infini, Essai Sur L'Extériorité* The Hague: Martinus Nijhoff, 1961), trans. Alphonso Lingis under the title *Totality and Infinity, An Essay on Exteriority* (Pittsburgh, Pa.: Duquesne University Press, 1969). Hereafter cited as *TI.*

9. See Christian Howells's "Sartre and Levinas," in *The Provocation of Levinas, Rethinking the Other*, ed. R. Bernasconi (London: Routledge, 1998), 91–99); Joanne M. Pier's "Sartre/Levinas, An Is/Ought Gap of Ethics?" *Dialogue* (April 1989): 52–57; Arne Vetlesen's "Relations with Others in Sartre and Levinas: Assessing Some Implications for an Ethics of Proximity," *Constellations* 1, no. 3 (1995): 358–382; and Dan Zahavi's "Beyond Empathy, Phenomenological Approaches to Intersubjectivity," *Journal of Consciousness Studies* 8, nos. 5–7 (2001): 151–167.

10. Sartre, *La Nausée* (Paris: Librairie Gallimard, 1938), trans. Lloyd Carruth under the title *Nausea* (New York: New Directions, 1964).

11. Sartre's novel was first published some nine years prior to the first publication of *Existence and Existents*; one wonders how much (if any) of *Nausea* influenced Levinas in 1947. Both publications follow Levinas's *On Escape* (1935–36). Even at these early stages of Levinas's thought, one finds precursors to the ideas developed in *Existence and Existents*. The main theme of *On Escape* is our rivetedness to being, and ultimately, the encounter with being as burdensome. I show that all three texts explicitly illustrate experiences in which we are riveted to our position in being, positions from which there is no avenue for escape. Considering the chronology of these somewhat similar texts, the possibility of Levinas's exposure to Sartre, and Sartre's to Levinas, are worth pursuing. I do not take this up at this stage, as it is out of the range of my more explicit concerns.

Chapter 1: The Role of Being in Sartre's Model of Transcendence-as-Intentionality

1. Stephen Priest, *The Subject in Question: Sartre's critique of Husserl in The Transcendence of the Ego* (London and New York: Routledge, 2000), 148.

2. Sartre's views on the *epoché* can be found in *Imagination*, trans. Forrest Williams (Ann Arbor: University of Michigan Press, 1972). "How do I distinguish after reduction between the centaur I imagine and the blossoming tree I perceive? The 'imagined centaur' is also the noema of a fulfilled noetic consciousness. . . . But before reduction we were able to find in that very unreality a way to distinguish a fiction from a perception, for the blossoming tree existed somewhere outside us. We could touch it, clutch it, turn away from it, then, retracing our steps, come upon it again in the same spot. The centaur, on the contrary, was nowhere, neither in me nor outside me. Bracketed now, the tree-*thing* is now known only as the noema of our actual" perception, and thus as an irreality (*unirreel*), just like the centaur," (139–140).

3. In his tracing of Sartre's critique of Husserl, Stephen Priest aptly gestures toward the possibility that Sartre hastily interprets Husserl as ignoring the significance of a 'trans-phenomenal" being. "[It] would be a crude and naïve misunderstanding of Husserl to think that the phenomenological reduction or epoché entailed the non-existence of the external world. Manifestly and importantly

the epoché entails no denial of a world existing outside consciousness. On the contrary, the existence of the world is neither affirmed nor denied in the epoché" (Priest, 147). In *How to Read Sartre*, Robert Bernasconi also notes that Sartre's dominant rendition of Husserlian phenomenology is, for many, not "real Husserl" (London: Granta Books, 2006), 20.

4. Françoise Dastur discusses the influence of both Husserl and Heidegger on Sartre, and indeed, how Sartre was partly responsible for introducing both German works into French philosophical thought. See "The Reception and Nonreception of Heidegger in France," *French Interpretations of Heidegger*, ed. David Pettigrew and Francois Raffoul (Albany: State University of New York Press, 2008), 286–271.

5. Of the work in *Being and Nothingness*, Nik Farrell Fox writes, "... his narrow individualist perspective effectively debars any form of collective solidarity or positive social existence by placing conflict at the heart of our being-with-others." To be certain, his account is one that situates the trajectory of Sartre's work in light of his (undulating) relationship to Marxism. But it is certainly the case that, of all possible periods, the one represented by *Being and Nothingness* is the most politically ambivalent of Sartre's career. See Nik Farrell Fox, *The New Sartre, Explorations in Postmodernism* (New York: Continuum Literary Studies, 2003), 114–115.

6. Priest, *The Subject in Question*, 148.

7. Sartre, *TE*, 105.

8. T. Storm Heter references this distinction between ontological and practical freedom in his article, "Authenticity and Others: Sartre's Ethics of Recognition," *Sartre Studies International* 12, no. 2 (2006): 17. He credits the work of David Detmer for this distinction, and finds it helpful to understand how the exposition of freedom in *Being and Nothingness* relates to the more practical (political) notions in Sartre's later works.

9. David Detmer, *Freedom as a Value* (La Salle, Ill.: Open Court, 1986), 64.

10. "In *Being and Nothingness* Sartre insists that all situations are equally transcendable by the individual; however much they impact upon us, we are always free, by dissolving their significance, to sidestep or 'nihilate' the force of this impact." See Nik Farrell Fox, *The New Sartre, Explorations in Postmodernism* (New York: Continuum Literary Studies, 2003), 11.

11. Thomas Martin's work in *Oppression and the Human Condition: An Introduction to Sartrean Existentialism* will be important for the overall claims of my book. Martin explicitly states that his work understands Sartre "[in] opposition to readings ... that maintain that his account of human reality presents 'man' as unbridled transcendence" (1). I fully develop my relation to this claim in later chapters, but for the moment, suffice it to say that I am in agreement with Martin's position, but only from the distinction with which I work, between Sartre's "formal" and "concrete" analyses. See Thomas Martin, *Oppression and the Human Condition; An Introduction to Sartrean Existentialism* (New York: Rowman & Littlefield, 2003).

12. Reisman, 31

13. David Detmer traces Sartre's appropriation of Husserl in order to establish his own position as a transcending of both idealist and realist conceptions of the relation between "subject" and "world." "[The] realism that [Sartre] criticizes . . . is representational realism, as opposed to the direct realism he endorses. . . . In short, while Sartre interprets phenomenology as a kind of realism, he embraces it in part precisely because it represents a viable alternative to the two dominant traditions in early twentieth French philosophy, idealism and (nonphenomenological) realism, both of which he finds indefensible." See *Sartre Explained: From Bad Faith to Authenticity* (Chicago: Open Court, 2008), 34. A similar discussion can also be found in David Reisman's *Sartre's Phenomenology*, where he discusses Sartre's rejection of a consciousness that houses "representations of objects and sense data" (New York: Continuum International Publishing Group, 2007), 27.

14. Sartre, "Intentionality," 4

15. It is important to note that Sartre wrote *The Transcendence of the Ego* in 1937, the same year Levinas published his essay, *Of Escape* ("Evasion"). Like Sartre's text, *Of Escape* outlines a model of transcendence that attempts to capture our concrete human condition. As such, it is no insignificant matter that both texts are written in the same year, and indeed, published in the same journal, *Les Recherches philosophiques*.

16. "[It] is far from clear that Sartre interprets Husserl correctly here. Husserl's thought, while sufficiently complex as to permit of a range of interpretations, is often understood to be closer to idealism (the doctrine that the essential nature of reality lies in consciousness)" (Detmer, 34).

17. Sartre, "Intentionality," 5.

18. Detmer, 31.

19. Detmer, 64.

20. "In its very being [consciousness] is oriented toward the in-itself. It pursues the in-itself, structuring it into a world . . . ." (Detmer, 104).

21. Aron Gurwitsch, "A Non-Egological Conception of Consciousness," *Philosophy and Phenomenological Research* 1 (1940–1941): 326.

22. Sartre's framing of the ontological question should be understood as one that pursues "the way or manner in which something exists" (Detmer, 64). Hence, the question of being is ultimately the question of object X's manner of *appearing*.

23. "It is true that consciousness, does, in some respects, rely on its object. If all consciousness is consciousness of something, there clearly must be something in order for there to be consciousness" (Martin, 2). On this account, though the *way of being* of the phenomenon is dependent on the *way of being* of consciousness, it is important to note what, for Sartre, must be the relation of dependence between consciousness and world. The *being* of the object of experience cannot be dependent on the *being* of consciousness, and he reads Husserl's account of the hyletic material of experience as one that precisely makes this error. "As Sartre sees it, in making the being of the object depend upon the being of consciousness, Husserl has made the object into a sort of nothingness," which would mean that being belongs to

consciousness. "Sartre thinks that Husserl got things backwards: he based the being of things on the being of consciousness" (Reisman, 31–33). Instead, Sartre's claim is that the being of consciousness, as exhaustively a reflection of objects in the world, depends on being of the object (of which it is a reflection).

24. Michael Sukale, *Comparative Studies in Phenomenology* (The Hague: Martinus Nijhoff, 1976), 81.

25. Objects appear to consciousness positionally (or thetically), while consciousness appears to itself nonpositionally. This distinction is discussed in detail shortly, as it plays a significant role in Sartre's quarrel with Husserl.

26. Jean-Paul Sartre, *TE*, 40.

27. Sartre, *TE*, 41.

28. Phyllis Berdt Kenevan, "Self Consciousness and the Ego," *The Philosophy of Jean Paul Sartre*, ed. Paul Arthur Schilpp (Carbondale: Southern Illinois University Press, 1981), 199.

29. Kenevan ultimately argues for the claim that nonpositional self-consciousness does not capture the meaning of pure reflection. She proposes "a modification in the structure of intentionality" to rectify this: "[The] suggestion here is that the for-itself can be known to itself in special instances whereby the intentional mode of knowing is modified by a self-attention which does not *replace* normal intentionality, but accompanies it" (Kenevan, 206).

30. In the chapter 4 of his book on Sartre, Peter Caws describes another possible Sartrean misreading of Husserl's (this time explicitly pertaining to formulation of the transcendental ego). "Sartre appears to attribute to Husserl a view of the substantiality of the Ego . . . as a substantial *inhabitant* of the conscious world, which inverts Husserl's position, placing the Ego in the world rather than the world in the Ego" (Caws, *Sartre*, 52). I reiterate that my project's claims take into account the very real possibility that Sartre's Husserl is "not real Husserl." That Sartre arrives at his own nonegological conception of consciousness through this (possibly inaccurate) reading of Husserl is what concerns us here. More importantly is Sartre's application of the theory of intentionality to this claim (that the ego is transcendent rather than transcendental).

31. Phyllis Morris Sutton, "Sartre on the Transcendence of the Ego," *Philosophy and Phenomenological Research* XLVI, no. 2 (December 1985): 180.

32. Gurwitsch, 326. Again, this conception is found in the *Ideas*, a work through which Husserl wears his idealist "hat."

33. Ronald Breeur traces the implications of Sartre's conception of consciousness as impersonal, or as being the source of an ego or subject that stands "as an internal limit within a spontaneity" (418). He uncovers two notions of freedom that come out of Sartre—an "egological or subjective" freedom, and an absolute freedom to which the former "owes its life" ("Consciousness and the Self," *International Journal of Philosophical Studies* 11, no. 4, (2003): 415–436.

34. "Sartre's postulation of non-positional self-awareness is intended to escape the problem of an infinite regress. While positional consciousness must be

conscious (of) itself, non-positional self-consciousness is of a different nature than the positional. There is no requirement for consciousness of or (of) non-positional consciousness" (Martin, 8).

35. Thomas Martin, 6–7.

36. Sartre, *TE*, 41.

37. Breeur, 417.

38. To recall, my focus lies in establishing the influence of intentionality on the model of transcendence that Sartre adopts in *Being and Nothingness*. Subsequently, I claim that contrary to this model, some of Sartre's concrete descriptions point to a *non*intentional relationship between being and consciousness. In other words, these phenomenological descriptions call into question the model of transcendence that Sartre shapes from his reading of Husserl's account of intentionality.

39. Sartre, *TE*, 41.

40. "[Consciousness] is a being that appears immediately to itself, so it needs nothing outside itself in order to appear to itself as an intentional relation" (Breeur, 420). For Sartre, positing a transcendental ego explicitly undoes this "immediate self-appearing."

41. Sartre, *TE*, 42.

42. That there exists a level of subjectivity not constituted by a movement of intentionality is an important element of the overarching thesis of this project. In my discussion of Levinas's account of transcendence, it will be seen he posits such a level in his conception of identity. This Levinasian positionality would not be subject to the kind of criticism that Sartre reserves for Husserl's transcendental ego (at least, on *his* reading of the transcendental ego). This will become clear in later chapters, but for the moment, one should note that Levinas's account of positionality does not substantialize (or reify) the subject, as is the case with a Sartrean "in-itself" identity.

43. "[Reflective] consciousness is a positional consciousness that takes consciousness as its object" (Martin, 9). But given that such positional acts can only grasp an object that is "not consciousness," it is necessarily the case that the "I," or ego, of which there is positional consciousness, is not the consciousness for which it is an object.

44. Sartre, *TE*, 45.

45. Sartre, *TE*, 51.

46. Sartre, *TE*, 81.

47. This pre- or im-personal reading of consciousness is the source of much of the critique against Sartre's take on Husserl's transcendental ego. In addition to Breeur's "Consciousness and the Self," see also Peter Caws's work in *Sartre*. Caws addresses a similar problem, concerning the nature of self-consciousness if, indeed, it is not an unreflective awareness of a "self." "[We] might wish to maintain that even if, at first this unreflective consciousness is not the consciousness of self, it might subsequently become so." See Caws, *Sartre*, ed. Ted Honderich (London, Boston: Routledge & Keegan Paul, 1984), 55. In *The Power of Consciousness and the Force of Circumstance in Sartre's Philosophy*, Thomas Busch identifies the

"ideal distance" that characterizes consciousness's presence-to-self as that which prevents Sartre's nonegological conception of consciousness from being a series of nonpersonal *events*. "There could be no awareness of what is other than self were there no contrasting apprehension of self, nor any awareness of an object as distinct from subject were there no self-apprehension on the part of the subject" (Busch, *The Power of Consciousness and the Force of Circumstance in Sartre's Philosophy* [Bloomington & Indianapolis: Indiana University Press, 1990], 21).

48. Breeur, "Consciousness, in its essence, is not yet subjective: it is characterized by a self-presence that is so radical that it threatens every form of self-knowledge and [thetic] self-consciousness" (418–419).

49. Sartre, *TE*, 99. This can be read as a precursor to the experience of anguish, as described in *Being and Nothingness*. In anguish, we come face to face with our freedom, insofar as we feel ourselves unjustified by nothing other than ourselves (our own free choice). Sartre's descriptions of vertigo are depictions of the experience of anguish (*EN*, 66; *BN*, 29, and *TE*, 99). In later chapters of this present work, I will contrast the role of the consciousness's noncoincidence with itself, with Emmanuel Levinas's conception of identity. In this conception, Levinas also identifies a necessary noncoincidence between the subject and its "self." For the moment, suffice it to say that this will be used by Levinas to ground a fundamental vulnerability (or exposure) at the heart of the existent. This is in contrast to the radical freedom that Sartre reads out of the noncoincidence between consciousness and its "ego" construction.

50. "[It] is consciousness that splits apart being, transforming it into a world of discrete things" (Martin, 13).

51. Sartre understands intentionality to mean that consciousness must "posit a transcendent object," which furthermore means that consciousness "reaches an object that is only outside of it" (Reisman, 30–31). To the degree that transcendence can be understood in opposition to immanence, I read, in Sartre, a collapsing of the notions of "intentionality" and "transcendence."

52. Detmer, 34.

53. Martin, 19.

54. Ibid.

55. Thomas Anderson, *Sartre's Two Ethics: From Authenticity to Integral Humanity* (Peru, Ill.: Open Court, 1993), 22.

56. Martin, 19.

57. Anderson, 22. David Detmer employs two possible ways of understanding freedom in an attempt to minimize the above differences. If, by freedom, we mean a "freedom from . . . ," then Sartre's "absolute" rendition of freedom comes to the foreground. Detmer coins this understanding of freedom as an "ontological freedom." If, on the other hand, we mean "freedom to do . . . ," then we would need his "limited" rendition of freedom, or what Detmer names "practical freedom" (Detmer, *Freedom as a Value* [Ill.: Open Court, 58–64). From this distinction, he argues that Sartre's work can be read, without contradiction, to be saying that consciousness is both limited and without limit. This seems to be the impetus

behind what we also find in Anderson's analysis, when he writes that the "[absolute and total] freedom is at most a freedom of consciousness, not the concrete freedom of a situated human being" (64). The latter sense of freedom (one would imagine) would quite easily map onto Detmer's conception of practical freedom.

58. Jean Wahl, *A Short History of Existentialism*, trans. Forrest Williams and Stanley Maron (Westport, Conn.:, 1949), 28. (Hereafter cited as *SHE*.)

59. Sartre, *PI*, 233.

60. Sartre begins his ontological proof with this claim: "Being has not been given its due" (*EN*, 27; *BN*, lx).

61. Thomas Busch, "La Nauseé': A Lover's Quarrel with Husserl," *Research in Phenomenology* XI (1981): 5.

62. "Being-in-itself is best understood as a mode of being (that is, a manner of existing) in which a being is identical with itself" (Martin, 12). It is precisely this "principle of identity" that does not apply to consciousness, or being-*for*-itself.

63. This is another point of significance in the Sartre-Levinas dialogue. In chapter 2, I show that Levinas also identifies a certain "non-identity" in the human condition. However, the implications of this will develop quite differently under a Levinasian analysis.

64. The reader should anticipate this to be a significant point of dialogue between Sartre and Levinas. There are similarities between what Levinas refers to as a field of impersonal existence, and what I introduce here as a Sartrean transphenomenal being. In particular, both thinkers use these structures as the ground on which there can be experiences of embodiment and other such moments of vulnerability. Nevertheless, within the Sartrean framework of consciousness as a transcending movement of intentionality, transphenomenal being seems to already prioritize freedom and spontaneity in ways not found in Levinas.

65. Sartre, *EN*, 27; *BN*, lx.

66. Sartre, *EN*, 29; *BN*, lxii.

67. Sartre, *EN*, 12; *BN*, xlvi. According to Kant, noumenal realities stood behind what are, properly speaking, appearances for us.

68. This is evident in Sartre's account of facticity, which I discuss shortly.

69. We will see more on the relation between the transcendence and facticity of consciousness in section 3, where I draw the full implications of the negative relation between being and consciousness.

70. As Peter Caws states, "The appearance that I confront, the phenomenon, has a being *of its own* [emphasis added]" (Caws, *Sartre*, 63).

71. Anderson, *Sartre's Two Ethics*, 24.

72. Indeed, Sartre's "ontological proof" rests on the freedom of consciousness. It is through consciousness's absolute existence that we can be assured of the actual existence of phenomena. But because we now see that these phenomena are appearances of *Being*, we also have it that the absolute existence of consciousness "proves" the existence of an actual world. To recall, "Consciousness is born *supported by* a being which is not itself. This is what we call the ontological proof" (*EN*, 27; *BN*, lx).

73. Sartre, *EN*, 31; *BN*, lxiii.

74. David Reisman adequately sets Sartre's analysis in opposition to the dualism of the Cartesian "mind-body" problem. (Reisman, *Sartre's Phenomenology*, 98).

75. Martin, 15.

76. Hazel Barnes outlines the difference between (1) consciousness's relation to a transphenomenal being, and (2) its relation to being-in-itself. "Although consciousness reveals being, the fundamental opposition on which [Sartre] builds his ontologies is not that between consciousness and being but the distinction between two regions of being... These are being-in-itself and being-for-itself" (Hazel E. Barnes, "Sartre's Ontology: The Revealing and Making of Being" *The Cambridge Companion Guide to Sartre*, ed. Christina Howells {Cambridge, U.K.: Cambridge University Press, 1992), 13–18).

77. Sartre, *EN*, 38–39; *BN*- 4–5.

78. Sartre, *EN*, 60; *BN*, 23.

79. Indeed, as Sartre points out in "Intentionality," "Consciousness and the world are given at one stroke: essentially external to consciousness, the world is nevertheless essentially relative to consciousness" ("Intentionality," 4).

80. Caws, *Sartre*, 68.

81. "[In] being conscious of X, X is not just not consciousness, it is also *not* any other thing. Importantly, for Sartre, negations do not exist in the world independently of consciousness. Consciousness brings nothingness into the world" (Martin, 4).

82. Sartre, *TE*, 98.

83. For a discussion of Sartre's three ekstases, see Reisman's *Sartre's Phenomenology* (59–60).

84. Kenevan, 199.

85. This is a vital point for the dialogue between Sartre and Levinas. In later chapters, I show that Levinas recognizes instances of density in the phenomenology of human identity. In addition to the "present" experienced by subjectivity, there are always those moments when the subject experiences being "with herself" in a way that could not be explained by Sartre's account of "ekstasis."

86. From Sartre's distinction between "being" and "existing," it is clear that existing, unlike "being" (in the verbal sense) requires a creative freedom, or activity. Existing is insofar as one creates oneself, or rather, creates what one must be. In this sense, existence pertains to consciousness (and not to that mode of being-in-itself). "Consciousness never attains the sort of being that worldly objects have. They are exactly what they are at every moment. Consciousness, by contrast, is 'perpetually ahead of itself'' (Sartre, *Being and Nothingness*, p. 270)" (Reisman, 39).

87. Caws, *Sartre*, 70.

88. Here, I refer to my earlier discussion of Thomas Anderson's and David Detmer's analysis of Sartrean freedom (section II).

89. Martin, 4.

90. Sartre, *EN*, 230; *BN*, 181.

91. For Levinas, transcendence performs a radical *exit* from Being, which must open up the "otherwise than being" or the "beyond being."

92. To be certain, Sartre recognizes certain experiences in which consciousness "feels" itself unable to generate the distance required for an intentional relation to being. Nevertheless, it is the case that, even in these moments, *meaning* remains accessible to consciousness.

93. Sartre, *EN*, 230; *BN*, 181.

94. The central thesis of the work is that, though this might be Sartre's explicit aim, he betrays it in undermining several of those descriptions that suggest a "less free" (or more vulnerable) subject. Before presenting evidence for this (in chapters that follow), I use this chapter to present the overall structure of Sartre's model of transcendence.

95. Sartre, *EN*, 99–100, *BN*, 59–60.

96. Detmer, *Sartre Explained, from Bad Faith to Authenticity*, 79.

97. Detmer notes that if the waiter outright denied his facticity (of occupying this social role of "waiter"), he would also continue to be in bad faith. "One can lie to oneself by denying one's transcendence . . . or by denying one's facticity" (78). This is insofar as consciousness is this "slippery ambiguity of facticity and transcendence, and the relationship between them."

98. Bernasconi, *How to Read Sartre*, 38.

99. In his article, Ron Santoni argues that bad faith is an ontological (originary) structure of consciousness. This means that every fundamental project of consciousness is already shaped by its flight from freedom. This, he argues, happens prior to an encounter with the Other. (Ron Santoni, "Is Bad Faith Necessarily Social?" *Sartre Studies International*, 14, no. 2 (2008): 23–39.

100. Sartre, *EN*, 101; *BN*, 61.

101. Sartre, *EN*, 102; *BN*, 62. David Reisman understands Sartre's examination of bad faith as "his exploration of the nature of human reality as '*non-being*' [emphasis added]" (Reisman, *Sartre's Phenomenology*, 116–117.

102. Sartre, *TE*, 98–99. In section 4, I devote more analysis to Sartre's notion of facticity.

103. Sartre, *TE*, 99.

104. In Mishka Jambor's paper ("Sartre on Anguish"), she argues against the following: "An absence of anguish in experience indicates for Sartre the veiling operation of bad faith" (112). This finds resonance in David Reisman's identification of "three roles" of bad faith, one of which is to "explain why anguish is a relatively rare phenomenon even though the freedom of which it is the revelation is a fundamental characteristic of being-for-itself" (Reisman, *Sartre's Phenomenology*, 116). Jambor says that "the necessity of such a link" (between anguish and freedom) "is far from obvious." One might read her paper as an indirect exposition on what Sartre might have been referring to in the idea of authenticity (introduced very briefly at the end of *Being and Nothingness*). Authentic consciousness no longer strives to be God (being-in-itself-for-itself); this also means that it can encounter its freedom without an experience of anguish. Jambor suggests that, without this ideal

(of desiring the being of God), there is no reason for an individual to be anguished over the absence of objective value, nor is there reason for an individual to flee from this in bad faith. In other words, she claims that it is only for a consciousness that seeks a "being-in-itself-for-itself" that bad faith acts to veil to onslaught of anguish.

105. Sartre describes this decision as a "spontaneous determination of our being," and as such, it is impossible to identify the moment in which we explicitly chose to deceive ourselves as such (*EN*, 109; *BN*, 68). In contrast to this choice of self-deceit, he conceives of the choice of authenticity, whereby the subject recognizes freedom as the source of all value. I discuss this at length in chapter 5, where I analyze Sartre's more ethical position.

106. Mishka Jambor, "Sartre on Anguish," *Philosophy Today* (Summer 1990): 111.

107. Ibid.

108. Sartre, *TE*, 101.

109. Chris Falzon describes Sartre's sense of freedom as an "imprisonment" in his paper, "Sartre, Freedom as Imprisonment" (*Philosophy Today* [Summer 2003]: 126–137). "Everything we encounter is reduced to a function of [the freedom of consciousness].... what imprisons us is an all-embracing conception of freedom (135–136). Falzon emphasizes what I wish to bring out here. Sartre's sense of freedom means that all is a constitution for consciousness and by consciousness, and there is nothing outside of this constitutive activity to which one might appeal.

110. See note 5.

111. Refer to Detmer's descriptions of this "slippery and ambiguous" interrelation between transcendence and facticity in *Sartre Explained* (75–89).

112. Sartre, *EN*, 561; *BN*, 482. Later in Sartre's career, in the *Critique of Dialectical Reason, Volume I*, he gives a fuller account of experience as historical and socialized. In this sense, the work in *Being and Nothingness* reads as more individualistic and subjective when compared to the *Critique*.

113. Sartre, *EN*, 562; *BN*, 482. In *Sartre Alive*, Thomas Anderson underscores this relationship between freedom and facticity in the early Sartre: "Though the Sartre of *Being and Nothingness* admitted that human freedom was immersed in facticity, he tended to minimize the power of facticity to restrict and curtail freedom" (188). (See Anderson's "Sartre's Early Ethics and the Ontology of *Being and Nothingness*," in *Sartre Alive*, ed. Ronald Aronson and Adrian van der Hoven [Detroit: Wayne State University Press, 1991], 183–201).

114. Martin, *Oppression and the Human Condition: An Introduction to Sartrean Existentialism*, 22.

115. Sartre, *EN*, 563; *BN*, 483.

116. Sartre, *EN*, 99; *BN*, 59.

117. Sartre, *EN*, 100; *BN*, 60.

118. Bernasconi, *How to Read Sartre*, 39.

119. Sartre, *EN*, 563; *BN*, 483.

120. Sartre, *EN*, 565; *BN*, 486.

121. Sartre, *EN*, 568; *BN*, 487.

122. Sartre, *EN*, 569; *BN*, 489.

123. Defining "situation" in Sartre, Detmer writes, "an ambiguous synthesis of the factual givens of our life (facticity) and our ways of living them by surpassing them (transcendence—which involves selectively focusing on some features and not others, interpreting those in a certain way, forming projects with reference to them, and so forth" (*Sartre Explained*, 78).

Chapter 2: Positionality in Levinas's Transcendence-as-Excendence

1. Bettina Bergo makes an invaluable contribution to how one understands the development of Levinas's conception of transcendence. Throughout this chapter, I frequently refer to the work in her essay, "Ontology, Transcendence, and Immanence in Emmanuel Levinas' Philosophy" (*Research in Phenomenology* 35 [2005]: 141–177).

2. As Robert Bernasconi points out, "Levinas . . . rejects the [traditional] notion of transcendence and [does] so in part from his concerns for identity" (Bernasconi, "No Exit: Levinas' Aporetic Views on Transcendence," *Research in Phenomenology* 35 [2005]: 102).

3. In her tracing of Levinas's early analyses of transcendence, Diane Perpich cites Dominique Janicaud's critique of Levinas's relationship to phenomenology. Of this relationship, Janicaud writes that "[Levinas] reintroduces phenomenology after having challenged the phenomenological method." In so doing, he reads Levinas's corpus as one without phenomenological justification, but rather "metaphysico-theological" justification only (Perpich, *The Ethics of Emmanuel Levinas* [Palo Alto: Stanford University Press, 2008], 20–21). Alongside François Raffoul's countercritique to this kind of criticism (in *The Origins of Responsibility* [Bloomington: Indiana University Press, 2010], 185–186), Peter Gratton also presents a more sympathetic account of Levinas's relationship to the phenomenological method. "Phenomenology, Levinas argues, can help us to understand the phenomena of the face, the glimmer of it that points us to the ethical relation. . . . Nevertheless, phenomenology can only get us as far as that 'glimmer,' without providing access to the . . . face-to-face encounter" ("Heidegger and Levinas on the Question of Temporality," *Journal of Philosophical Research* 30 [2005]: 167).

4. Diane Perpich documents Levinas's indebtedness to Jean Wahl's framing of the question of transcendence (*The Ethics of Emmanuel Levinas*, 28–39).

5. Diane Perpich, *The Ethics of Emmanuel Levinas*, 33.

6. My analysis in chapter 3 is positioned to establish that Sartre's work suggests a Levinasian understanding of identity, whereby the subject is positioned in Being.

7. Emmanuel Levinas, "Reflections on the Philosophy of Hitlerism," trans. Sean Hand, *Critical Inquiry* 17 (Autumn 1990): 62–71. (Hereafter cited as "Reflections.")

8. François Raffoul discusses Levinas's relation to Heidegger in chapter 5 of *The Origins of Responsibility*. "For Levinas, the access to ethics ... and *to responsibility* took place in a break with ontology, that is, in a break with Heidegger." In that regard, for Levinas, it cannot be conceptualized as "one moment in being, as one existential in the analytic of Dasein" (Raffoul, *The Origins of Responsibility*, 166). For a discussion of this relationship between Levinas and Heidegger, see Françoise Dastur's "The Reception and Nonreception of Heidegger in France" (*French Interpretations of Heidegger*, 271–275).

9. Levinas, ibid., 68.

10. Bergo often refers to Levinas's work on transcendence (insofar as it, in so many ways, is a response/critique to Heidegger) as a "counter-ontology." As such, it is difficult to ignore, "despite its emphasis on facticity," the formalization of these circumstances that Levinas presents (Bergo, 154).

11. In his foreword to *Existence and Existents*, Robert Bernasconi writes that the text is "from first to last dominated by Levinas' ambiguous relation to the thought of Martin Heidegger, an ambiguity summarized by his stated aim to leave 'the climate' of Heidegger's philosophy for a philosophy that would not be pre-Heideggarian" (*EE*, viii).

12. Lars Iyer, "Levinas on Existence," *Journal of the British Society for Phenomenology* 33, no. 3 (January 2002): 40.

13. In this regard, the influence of Jean Wahl is quite apparent. "... Levinas' formulation of the problem of transcendence as a problem about how the two terms in the transcendence relation can be *in relation* without thereby being assimilated on to the other finds an earlier expression in Wahl's thought" (Perpich, *The Ethics of Emmanuel Levinas*, 30). See also Levinas, "How can a being enter into relation with the other without allowing its very self to be crushed by the other?" (*Totality and Infinity*, 77).

14. Levinas, *Ethics and Infinity, Conversations with Philippe Nemo*, trans. Richard Cohen (Pittsburgh, Pa.: Duquesne University Press, 1985), 52. (Hereafter cited as *EI*.)

15. Judith Butler traces the performance of this aperture (or rupture) in Being in her essay, "Precarious Life," and utilizes the notion of precariousness to underscore this ambiguity. "To respond to the face, to understand its meaning, means to be awake to ... the precariousness of life itself," 7 (Butler, "Precarious Life," in *Radicalizing Levinas*, ed. Peter Atterton and Matthew Calarco (Albany: State University of New York Press, 2010), 3–19).

16. Robert Bernasconi, in his essay, "No Exit: Levinas' Aporetic Account of Transcendence," presents Levinas as a philosopher of transcendence fundamentally, and subsequently, a philosopher of ethics. He reminds us that this is on the request of Levinas himself (*Research in Phenomenology* 35 [2005]: 100–117).

17. Adriaan Peperzak, "Freedom," *International Philosophical Quarterly* 3 (Summer 1971): 341–361.

18. Levinas, "Reflections on the Philosophy of Hitlerism," 66.

19. For Levinas, the philosophy of the West presumes that "ego and world are opposed to one another and the ego is understood and valorized principally in

terms of its quest for self-unity and self-determination in opposition to the world which would determine or disperse it" (Perpich, *The Ethics of Emmanuel Levinas*, 31).

20. "To become conscious of one's social situation is, even for Marx, to free oneself of the fatalism entailed by that situation" (Levinas, "Reflections," 67).

21. Though this project as a whole does not address the relationship between Levinas's Jewishness and his account of transcendence-as-excendence, this relationship is of utmost importance. Bettina Bergo discusses this in her paper, pointing out that Levinas's claim that we are "permanently riveted" to our bodies resounds in his Talmudic writings, where he describes Judaism as "desert Judaism, despite the politics of assimilation" (Bergo, 174).

22. The final section of this chapter will discuss these ideas of death and suffering as, paradoxically, the way in which the individual ultimately begins to exit materiality. However, much more needs to be said in preparation for discussing that stage in Levinas's thought.

23. Levinas, "Reflections," 68.

24. Levinas, *Time and the Other*, trans. Richard Cohen (Pittsburgh, Pa.: Duquesne University Press, 1987), 69. (Hereafter cited as *TO*.)

25. Certainly, there have been (and will be) instances where individuals, for their own reasons, freely decide to orchestrate physically painful circumstances for themselves. However, the idea behind Levinas's analysis is that the individual always encounters that pain (at the heart of suffering) in avid refusal. For reasons similar to this, Levinas also claims that suicide—as the *willful* abnegation of one's life—is impossible. Like all cases of approaching death, the suicide victim clings to life at the very end.

26. In his conception of "rivetedness," Levinas is also against Heidegger's formulations of throwness and facticity. To the degree that Sartre's work in *Being and Nothingness* borrows from this Heideggarian framework, Levinas's conception can also be understood in opposition to Sartrean facticity. "Though Heidegger [like Sartre] is . . . attuned to the facticity of human existence and to our throwness into a world of meanings not of our own making, he nonetheless emphasizes the possibility of taking up our thrown being explicitly in an authentic self-understanding and thus confirming the primacy of freedom once again" (Perpich, *The Ethics of Emmanuel Levinas*, 31).

27. Sections of chapter 5 are devoted to the question of identity in Sartre, and the implications of engaging his concrete descriptions through the lens of Levinas's conception of this duality. However, for the moment, suffice it to say that there is no equivalent, in Sartre's conception of passivity, for what Levinas develops as the relationship between the level at which the existent rebels, and the level at which the existent is riveted.

28. Levinas, "Reflections," 68.

29. To reiterate, this spontaneous escape is already accomplished insofar as the subject can apprehend, as meaningful, his or her encounters with being. For the reason, I read Sartre's account of facticity as sustaining of this escape. In

the experience of facticity, consciousness continues to encounter being through networks of meaning (of phenomena).

30. In *Otherwise than Being, Or Beyond Essence*, Levinas brings out the full meaning of identity (given in concrete phenomena like suffering, embodiment, and sensibility). At this stage of his thought, the role of the Other cannot be avoided (*Otherwise than Being* is essentially a work on responsibility). I ask that the reader bear in mind that, though much of Levinas's thoughts on identity are located on the pages of this text (in particular, without those that delineate the concept of substitution), my treatment of *Otherwise than Being* in this chapter is sparse. This is because one of my overall aims is to present Levinas's understanding of transcendence independently of his account of ethical responsibility.

31. Diane Perpich, *The Ethics of Emmanuel Levinas*, 32.

32. Sartre's notion of embodiment follows, in chapter 3.

33. To reiterate, I ask that the reader anticipate a similar structure *implied* in Sartre at the level of his concrete descriptions.

34. Levinas, *OE*, 49.

35. Levinas understands Heidegger's formulation of transcendence to rest on this movement (from being toward the Being of beings). "The great interest of Heideggarian philosophy lies in showing at the basis of man's *ontic* adventure something more than a relation of 'being' to 'being': the understanding of Being, ontology ... Heidegger [gives] fundamental transcendence as accomplished not in the passage from one 'being' to another but from 'being' toward Being" (Levinas, "Letter Concerning Jean Wahl," *Unforeseen History*, trans. Nidra Poller [Urbana and Chicago: University of Illinois Press, 1994] 66). See also François Raffoul's analysis of Levinas's reading and critique of Heidegger in *The Origins of Responsibility* (170–175).

36. Perpich, *The Ethics of Emmanuel Levinas*, 31.

37. Levinas, *OE*, 55.

38. "Levinas maintains that certain philosophically neglected experiences, such as insomnia, fatigue and suffering, are ... uniquely disclosive [of] the 'elementary truth' that being *is* and that there is no escaping it" (Perpich, *The Ethics of Emmanuel Levinas*, 33).

39. Levinas, *Of Escape*, 63.

40. I discuss the similarities and differences between Sartre's and Levinas's accounts of shame in chapter 4.

41. Levinas attempts to find, in shame, a meaning more fundamental than a typically social reading of shame. Shame is not essentially shame before the Other, and as such, what we wish to hide is not solely from other people. "Shame's whole intensity ... consists precisely in our inability not to identify with this being who is already foreign to us and whose motives for acting we can no longer comprehend" (*Of Escape*, 63). This inability, though problematized in the other's presence, is a source of distress even before others come onto the scene. (This is another important difference between Levinasian and Sartrean shame, as we will see in chapter 4. Bettina Bergo seems to forget this important peculiarity to Levinas's

understanding of shame when she says that "one must care about those from whom one wants to hide one's nakedness..." (153). She presents this as evidence of some alignment between Levinas and Heideggarian attunement of "care." I am not sure that one can say that Levinas "presupposes" care anymore than he "presupposes" intentionality—they are both approaches to being that he acknowledges, but as *derived* and not fundamental.

42. Levinas, *Of Escape*, 64.

43. François Raffoul, *The Origins of Responsibility*, 168.

44. Perpich, 31.

45. This resonates with Sartre's analysis as well, an analysis that also determines nausea to be primarily an experience of being mobilized against one's will.

46. If one follows Levinas's analysis of shame to its completion, one finds the ethical implications of our desire to escape our position in being. Our presence to ourselves prompts the feeling of nausea (or of a refusal to remain in place) precisely because we find ourselves unjustified (or in "bad conscience"). It is only later, in Levinas's piece on "Substitution" (1968) that we understand that his radical responsibility for the Other underlies our fundamental encounter with existence (with our existence). In other words, substitution completed the formulation of duality within identity, showing that it is the disturbance of the Other that makes it impossible for us to rest comfortably in our "selves." The sentiments of shame (which reveal that the "I" is uncomfortable in its "self") culminate in the "identity of substitution," whereby the identity of the "I" just *is* its being-for-the-Other. Diane Perpich's analysis is pertinent in this regard, when she points out that "the alterity of the other gains currency [in Levinas's work] primarily because of the role it plays in opening this path [of escape from being]" (*The Ethics of Emmanuel Levinas*, 36).

47. Bergo, 153

48. Levinas, *Of Escape*, 66. This will be significant in the chapters that follow, where I bring Sartre and Levinas together in more overt ways. The quote from Levinas can easily be construed as coming from Sartre. The current analysis of this chapter shows that, for Levinas, this impossibility grounds a structural *interruption* of identity, which ultimately points to a primordial passivity (vulnerability, or subjection) of the human condition. Quite the contrary, for Sartre, consciousness is an unavoidable movement of spontaneous transcendence. It is in *this* sense that I cannot be who I am. In other words, Sartre understands this noncoincidence as the condition for our radical freedom.

49. Levinas locates the meaning of transcendence "in a relation in which the ego is affected in its mode of being, but in which this being affected remains outside of models of domination or subordination" (Perpich, 36). This will be an important distinction to consider in chapter 5, when I bring Levinas into conversation with Sartre, around their phenomenologies of the "intersubjective." I establish that what Levinas develops as a "substitution for the Other" is entirely different from Sartre's formal analysis of the Look as a fundamental violence and source of alienation. This important distinction is echoed in what François Raffoul

establishes as the difference between "weakness" and "vulnerability." He points out that "for Levinas . . . heteronomy, subjection, and obligation are not synonyms of submissiveness, slaver or bondage" (*The Origins of Responsibility*, 188).

50. It is arguable that Levinas's critique of the liberal subject, discussed thus for, led to a model of transcendence much like the one we find in Sartre. Both liberalism and Sartre's account of consciousness conceptualize a subject that is essentially free not only to surpass his- or herself, but to be engaged in being across a perpetual detachment. We have already discussed Sartre's model of transcendence in chapter 1, where it was shown to have been built on intentionality. Barring the important differences between Sartre's account of intentional consciousness and the liberal notion of autonomy (and by no means reducing the two), both seem to neglect the level of positionality, and the severity of the rivetedness to being that Levinas's *soi* (or rather, its relation with the *moi*) reveals.

51. Perpich, 30.

52. Raffoul, 169.

53. Levinas, *On Escape*, 52.

54. Such "woes" could easily find a place in Sartre's account of consciousness as a nothingness of being (see chapter1).

55. This can be read as a critique of Heidegger's notion of *Dasein*'s anguish before its own death. In *Being and Time*, one understands anguish as the revelation of *Dasein*'s nearest possibility—of its impossibility. Levinas opposes this anxiety over no longer being, with a more primordial anxiety over having to "always be." "[Anxiety] as being-for-death is also the hope to reach the deep of non-being. The possibility of deliverance [from Being] arises in death anxiety" (*OB*, footnote 10, 194).

56. "This sense of being riveted within being and to one's own being shapes Levinas's early descriptions of the self as a "solitude" and an "enchainment within being" (Perpich, 33). I trace the relationship between solitude and Levinas's notion of excendence in chapter 4. Perpich's point is noteworthy, particularly in light of critical readings of Levinas's formulation of the ethical, which determine that he compromises the truth of the solitariness of the human condition in his analyses of alterity and the Face.

57. Levinas, "From the One to the Other: Time and Transcendence," 142. See also *Time and the Other*, trans. Richard Cohen (Pittsburgh, Pa.: Duquesne University Press, 1990) 45. Levinas makes sure to point out that his separation of existence and personal existents would be "absurd" to Heidegger (*Time and the Other*, 45). Again, this is because, for Heidegger, we access Being only insofar as it is already "possessed" by a particular being. Furthermore, the *throwness* of Dasein is ultimately a comportment toward Being, and thus does not yet call into question the primacy of Being.

58. Levinas, *EI*, 49.

59. The sense in which an existent is there, ambiguously relating to the impersonal field of the *il y a*, must be differentiated from Heidegger's "*Da*." The "*Da*" of *Dasein* signifies an attunement with being, such that *Dasein* has access to

the meaning of being and is at home in being. At the level of the *il y a*, an existent is there, but as precisely horrified in face of a radical meaninglessness. There no feeling of being at home for the existent who is positioned in the *il y a*. Rather, it is as a radical alterity that the *il y a* signifies.

60. I deploy the term "expression" with the intention of pursing the interplay between the Face and the *il y a* in Levinas. I develop this further in chapters 3 and 4, but I note here that is it imperative to take seriously Levinas's own admission, in his later interviews, that the Other (the face of the Other) is already present in the *il y a*.

61. Levinas, *EE*, xi.

62. Iyer, 43.

63. Levinas, *OE*, 52.

64. Levinas, *EE*, xi.

65. Jean Wahl, *A Short History of Existentialism*, trans. Forrest Williams and Stanley Maron (Westport, Conn.: Greenwood Press, 1971), 11.

66. Jean Wahl, 14.

67. For a clear account of Levinas's relationship to Heidegger's account of death as our ownmost possibility, see François Raffoul, *The Origins of Responsibility*, 173–174.

68. Levinas, *TO*, 8.

69. Levinas, *TO*, 46.

70. This is also the case in Sartre's phenomenological descriptions of an experience of nausea. In chapter 3, I present this in fuller detail, with the intention of establishing resonance with Levinas's conception of the *il y a*, and ultimately with his account of identity.

71. Levinas, *EE*, 3.

72. John Sallis, "Levinas and the Elemental," *Research in Phenomenology* 28 (1998): 152.

73. This would seem to betray the absolute otherness (undefinablity) of the "there is." It would seem as though, for the thought experiment that ultimately gets us to existence in general, we are required to let go of all concepts that might continue to render it meaningful ("nature" being one of them).

74. Iyer, 43.

75. Sallis, 154.

76. Levinas, *EE*, 61.

77. Raffoul, *The Origins of Responsibility*, 214.

78. Levinas, *EE*, 62.

79. In his exposition of the phenomenology of insomnia, Levinas establishes the groundwork for his later and more explicit position on the reversal of subjectivity that underscores his conceptions of responsibility and substitution. I discuss these fully in chapter5. However, for the moment, I reference aspects of François Raffoul's critique of Levinas's relationship to philosophy's egological tradition, whereby he gestures toward the possibility that Levinas fails to go beyond the Cartesian *cogito* in his conception of "hyperbolic responsibility." Though noteworthy, Raffoul's

criticism of Levinas does not significantly alter the thesis of my work, which postulates that the Levinasian conception of identity more successfully captures certain phenomenologies of affection, which both he and Sartre capture, than does a Sartrean account of consciousness.

80. Raffoul, 214.

81. Bergo describes the work of *Existence and Existents* as a trajectory that spans from "the unconscious" to "consciousness," meaning that the analysis exposes us to the events that take place prior to the consciousness of subjectivity. She makes sure to point out that this sense of the unconscious is *not* that utilized by psychoanalysis—"psychoanalysis *missed* the *ontological* function of the unconscious [according to Levinas], which is to be the ground for transcendence" (157–158). Hence, unconsciousness, probably better understood in Levinas's schema as *pre*consciousness, concerns the event on which consciousness stands.

82. Levinas, *EE*, 61.

83. "[Hypostasis] describes the specific manner of an existent's relation to *il y a*, where *il y a* is posited neither as the essence of the existent, nor as the condition of possibility of the existent" (Elizabeth Louise Thomas, *Emmanuel Levinas: Ethics, Justice and the Human Beyond Being* [New York: Routledge, 2004], 36).

84. "The problem of transcendence [and, to be sure, the *realization* of transcendence], then, is experienced, as this desire and its seemingly inevitable frustration" (Diane Perpich, *The Ethics of Emmanuel Levinas*, 33).

85. *EE*, 11.

86. Levinas, *EE*, 16.

87. Levinas, *EE*, 12. For a thorough analysis of Levinas's phenomenologies of refusal and hesitation, see Elisabeth Louise Thomas, *Emmanuel Levinas: Ethics, Justice and the Human Beyond Being* (New York: Routledge, 2004), 19–23).

88. I reiterate that, for Levinas, being is encountered as a refusal of being before it is encountered as "dwelling" (in the Heideggarian sense). "The thought of a beyond to this relation of existence and the existent is approached as a relation to another who interrupts this ontological attachment and introduces a notion of 'world' distinctly different from the Heideggarian notion" (Elisabeth Louise Thomas, 25).

89. Levinas, *TO*, 67.

90. We see this in Sartre's ontology. As Levinas points out in *Existence and Existents*, it is in this sense that intentionality is "negative" (85); the being of consciousness remains forever empty, as it is perpetually *not* that which appears (for it). This "not" grounds the sense in which the ego (of course, this is "ego" in a Levinasian sense, and not in the sense critiqued by Sartre in *The Transcendence of the Ego*) remains always detached from the world with which it engages across intentionality.

91. This also founds Levinas's analysis of the experience of shame. I discuss this in chapter 4.

92. Levinas, *EE*, 85.

93. Levinas, *EE*, 84.

94. I develop a fuller account of Levinas's conception of beginning in chapter 3.

95. Levinas, *On Escape*. Of Levinas's relationship to the Heideggarian model of transcendence, Elisabeth Thomas writes, "In other words, the tragic finitude of an *ecstasis* toward the end masks the tragic necessity of being oneself—of being inescapably attached to one's singular and finite being" (*Emmanuel Levinas: Ethics, Justice and the Human Beyond Being*, 36).

96. Levinas, *EI*, 52.

97. "'Living from' is sensibility proper, insofar as, in this case, sensibility is understood as the subject's being subjected to the elemental . . ." (John E. Drabinski, *Sensibility and Singularity: The Problem of Phenomenology in Levinas* [Albany: State University of New York Press, 2001]).

98. "The way in which in art the sensible qualities which constitute an object do not lead to an object and are in themselves is the very event of sensation qua sensation, the esthetic event" (*EE*, 47). Aesthetics, in this sense, prepares us for a reality that is essentially "wordless"—void of the categories of immanent subjectivity and external objectivity. It prepares us to think existence without existents.

99. Elisabeth Louise Thomas, 36.

100. Levinas, *OB*, 15.

101. Levinas, *TO*, 55.

102. Levinas, *EE*, 40.

103. Levinas, "Useless Suffering," *Entre Nous*, trans. Michael B. Smith and Barbara Harshav (New York: Columbia University Press, 1998), 92.

104. Levinas, *TI*, 187.

105. Drabinski, 115.

106. Richard Cohen describes the life of sensibility (or the happy life) as an "originary emergence" ("Emmanuel Levinas: Happiness Is a Sensational Time," *Philosophy Today* 23, no. 3 (1981): 197.

107. "Since Heidegger we are in the habit of considering the world as an ensemble of tools. Existing in the world is acting, but acting in such a way that in the final account action has our own existence for its object. Tools refer to one another to finally refer to our care for existing" (*TO*, 62).

108. John Drabinski writes, "The structure of sensibility, then, institutes the general structure of relationality; this relation is pure, and so does not rest upon the work of constitution or representation" (*Sensibility and Singularity*, 110). The "pureness" of this relationality captures the immediacy (or unmediated nature) of the (enjoying) subject's immersion in being.

109. In the essay "Intentionality and Metaphysics," Levinas identifies a similar thematic in what Husserl identifies as the transcendental function of sensibility. Levinas understands this move as an attempt to uncover a more fundamental access to being than that captured by the noema-noesis relationship. "[The] sensible, the hyletic *datum*, is an absolute datum. Intentions animate it, to be sure, to make it an experience of an object, but the sensible is given immediately, before being sought.

Before thinking or perceiving objects, the subject is steeped in it [emphasis mine]" (*Discovering Existence with Husserl*, trans. Richard Cohen and Michael Smith [Evanston, Ill.: Northwestern University Press, 1998], 124). The essay ultimately critiques Husserl for betraying this attempt. Levinas determines that he makes all intentionality representational (even the "incarnate intentionality" of sensibility).

110. Levinas, *TI*, 129.

111. Levinas, *TI*, 132.

112. John Drabinski writes that "sensibility provides the structural item necessary for access to the relation of/to transcendence [insofar as] the logic of sense-bestowal [is] from the outside" (108). For Levinas, transcendence happens as (or in) this radical rupture (of being, totality, or interiority) through which exteriority signifies.

113. Levinas, *OE*, 60.

114. Levinas, *OE*, 61.

115. Ibid.

116. Elisabeth Louise Thomas, 77.

117. Levinas, *TO*, 67.

118. Again, despite this reduction in distance, these objects do retain some semblance of otherness, as there is always a distinction between the subject who enjoys, and the enjoyed element.

119. Drabinski, 207.

120. An important aspect of Levinas's model of transcendence is that the journey takes us, indeed to that which is wholly otherwise. In other words, the "I" must not only take leave of itself, but there should be a journeying toward that which is radically other than "I." The transcendence attempted in enjoyment (what Levinas calls the "transcendence of need") fulfills this criterion, insofar as the subject does not *loose* itself in the object that gives it enjoyment. "The subject is absorbed in the object it absorbs, and nevertheless keeps a distance with regard to the object" (*TO*, 67). The object of need is, in this sense, essentially exterior to me, even in the moment of enjoyment and satisfaction.

121. Levinas, "Without Identity," *Collected Philosophical Papers*, trans. Alphonso Lingis (Pittsburgh, Pa.: Duquesne University Press, 1970) 149.

122. Levinas, "Without Identity," 148.

123. In chapter 3, I argue for a distinction between solitude and isolation, to show that the former represents the condition of the Levinasian existent, who is always already ruptured by the radical alterity of the Other. In this regard, I use "isolation" to convey a certain obliviousness to alterity as such.

124. "[Knowing] is essentially a way of relating to events while still being able not to be caught up in them" (*EE*, 42).

125. Richard Cohen establishes that Levinas calls the movement of sensations happiness precisely because "at the level of sensibility the subject is entirely self-satisfied, self-complacent, content, sufficient.... Sensible self-reference makes the subject happy because it is an independence within bodily dependency" (Cohen, 201).

126. Levinas, *TO*, 64.

127. "The materiality of the body in proximity to the face of the Other is described as the exposure of the body.... Incarnated and passive makes the *ethical* subject susceptible to trauma, pain, and persecution prior to the will [emphasis added]" (Drabinski, 207).

128. Levinas understands the possibility of suicide to rest on those structural conditions of identity, which then places the "I" in relation to radical alterity (to the Other). In this regard, the "taking leave of oneself" for which, in suffering, the subject yearns, happens only in *selfless* concern (disinterestedness toward) the Other. "[Suicide] is the possibility of an existence already metaphysical; only a being already capable of sacrifice is capable of suicide" (Levinas, *Totality and Infinity*, 149).

129. "Levinas... explains that Heideggarian being-toward-death is radically opposed to the Platonic conception of death [which is] the condition of theoretical thought and of the access to the absolute" (Dastur, "The Reception and Nonreception of Heidegger in France," 274).

130. Levinas, *TI*, 234.
131. Levinas, *TI*, 233.
132. Levinas, "Useless Suffering," 93.
133. Levinas, *TI*, 232. In "Useless Suffering," Levinas tells us that death is rendered meaningful in the transformation from the fear of *my* death to a fear *for* the other's. "[The] constitutional or congenital uselessness can take on a meaning, the only one of which suffering is capable, in becoming a suffering for the suffering (inexorable though it may be) of someone else" (94). In *The Origins of Responsibility*, François Raffoul offers a clear exposition of this movement from a fear of my own death to a concern for the death of the Other (193–196). I treat this more fully in chapter 4.

134. Dennis King Keenan aptly describes this moment using the words of Springsteen, "Nowhere to run ain't got nowhere to go" (*Death and Responsibility*, 68).

135. Levinas, *Ethics and Infinity*, 100–101.
136. Levinas, *TI*, 274.
137. Levinas, *TO*, 42.
138. Levinas, *TI*, 233.
139. Levinas, *TI*, 56.
140. This would reinforce my claim that, for Levinas, transcendence points back to the primary disruption of subjectivity, and only subsequently involves the more overtly ethical account of the Face of the Other.

Chapter 3: Levinasian Positionality in Sartre's Account of Nausea

1. I reiterate, here, that in my reading of Levinas, I prioritize the structures of positionality and solitude in his conception of transcendence, insofar as I prioritize the notion of disruption in that conception of transcendence. Elsewhere,

I discuss the implications of replacing the priority of the Face in this way, when it comes Levinas's sense of ethics ("The Primacy of Disruption in Levinas's Account of Transcendence," *Research in Phenomenology* 40, no. 3 (2010).

2. To recall, I understand the account of consciousness, in *Being and Nothingness*, to be one of radical freedom. This is despite and alongside Sartre's analyses of "being in situation," facticity and engagement. In this regard, I align my work with scholars like Thomas Anderson, David Detmer, and Nik Farrell Fox. (See chapter 1 for full analysis.)

3. Rudi Visker argues that, unlike Sartre, Levinas ignores the fundamentally solitary nature of human existence by insisting on the face of the Other as the primary source of alterity (Visker, "The Stranger Within Me," *Ethical Perspectives* 12, no. 4 (December 2005): 425–441). I show, elsewhere, that this critique should really be laid against a particular reading of Levinas, which too quickly reduces his account of alterity. For Levinas, alterity signifies as that which is "never there," either because it is yet to arrive or has already gone-by. Ultimately, this leaves the subject alone and open onto a perpetual absence. Levinas uses the Face to capture the performance of this absence, but we should not read in these references some primordial intersubjective space. It is in solitude, and not before the Other, that Levinas locates the conditions for the concretization of transcendence. The Other is an absence, signifying precisely as that which leaves us *alone*. The agony of the [alterity's] disruption means that I find no one, or no way, to bring justification or wholeness to bear on my existence.

4. Chapter 1 alluded to the difference between "being" and "existence," where Sartre's radical sense of the freedom of consciousness was presented. On Sartre's account, "being" refers to that which simply is (absolute fullness, or plenitude), without cause. By "existence," he refers to that *relationship* between consciousness and this plenitude. Levinas's use of existence (or the "there is") somewhat maps onto Sartre's conception of being as an undifferentiated plenitude. Hence, I liken the "pure being" that is encountered in an experience of nausea to what Levinas conceptualizes as the brute fact of existence.

5. Even though I use "position" to describe what is more correctly a Sartrean account of identity, it is important to note that Levinas's conception of positionality renders something entirely different. From my exposition in chapter2, "positionality" in Levinas underscores the *lack* of position (home, base, or ground) in identity. At least at the formal levels of his analysis, we cannot say the same for Sartre.

6. As David Reisman explains, "[nausea] is how one's superfluity manifests itself" (*Sartre's Phenomenology*, 39). For Sartre, it is on the ground of this (somewhat absurd) meaninglessness that the for-itself creates a complex of instrumentalities that is a meaningful world.

7. This is clear when Sartre writes *Being and Nothingness*, "I am responsible for everything ... abandoned in the world, not in the sense that I might remain abandoned and passive in a hostile universe ... but rather in the sense that I find myself suddenly alone and without help" (555).

8. Levinas, *EE*, 8. This description can easily find its place in those of Sartre's accounts of the experience of nausea, which will be discussed in this chapter.

9. Levinas, *EE*, 89.

10. Rudi Visker, "Is Ethics Fundamental: Questioning Levinas on Irresponsibility," *Continental Philosophy Review* 36, no. 3 (July 2003): 271.

11. Levinas, *OB*, 55.

12. From his "Reflections" essay, it is clear that Levinas does not subscribe to the biologism of Nazism. Hence, the "inevitability" of the existent's contract with existence does not mean, for Levinas, that her life is predetermined in a way that is immune to her free choice. As was discussed in the last chapter, Levinas identifies a "third way," between the perils of both biologism and liberalism. In my analysis of Sartre's and Levinas's treatments of alterity (chapter 5), I show how this "third way" informs Levinas's conception of passivity, and determines how Sartre and Levinas ultimately part ways in their conceptions of what it means to encounter the Other. Elsewhere, I also pursue the implications of Levinas's understanding of passivity (in terms other than those that lead to an essentialization of the self) for the more political notions of community and solidarity. (See, "Levinas, Sartre, and the Question of Solidarity," in *Levinas Studies*, special issue on "Levinas and Race," ed. John Drabinski, 2012).

13. "This loosing of one's base [in the event of hypostasis] is a modality of transcendence that, while the subject remains an item in the relation, is an extension of the subject outside itself" (Drabinski 62).

14. Levinas, *EE*, 9.

15. Levinas, *EE*, 10.

16. As John Drabinski points out, "[the] notion of the instant provokes Levinas to rethink subjectivity, against the ecstatic stretch of care, in terms of hypostasis" (Drabinski, 61).

17. Robin Durie succinctly traces the Bergsonian influence on Levinas's critique of Heideggarian temporality, and the sense in which his conception of diachrony is ultimately indebted to Bergson's work (Durie, "Wandering among Shadows: The Discordance of Time in Levinas and Bergson," *The Southern Journal of Philosophy* 48, no. 4 (2010): 371–392).

18. Levinas, *OE*, 66.

19. Dennis King Keenan's definition of "dead time" seems appropriate here, as "a colloquial French phrase [*le temps mort*] that refers to time wasted, an idle period [in, or 'before' intentionality's effective movements], an interruption" (Keenan, *Death and Responsibility, The "Work" of Emmanuel Levinas* [Albany: State University of New York Press, 1999] 22). In one sense, we might situate this moment of "dead time" as that which is always anterior to the time of intentionality (time as past, present, future). But there is also Levinas's focus on the duration (of time), or what "flows *within* time," as that which founds the passivity of patience and, ultimately, death. In this sense, the interruption of time is both anterior and interior to time. (See Peter Gratton's exposition of Levinas reworking of Heidegger's

notion of time in "Heidegger and Levinas on the Question of Time," *Journal of Philosophical Research* 30 [2005]).

20. Basil Vassilicos juxtaposes Levinas's and Sartre's conceptions of temporality in terms of their respective notions of the image. He traces Levinas's analysis in the essay, "Reality and Its Shadow" to establish the sense in which the "time of the image" is founded on the material passivity (the passivity of sensation) of consciousness. In contrast, he shows that, in *The Psychology of the Imagination*, Sartre determines "every image [to be] the product of a free act [through which] an intentional relationship is established with the object . . ." ("The Time of Images and the Images of Time: Levinas and Sartre," *Journal of the British Society for Phenomenology* 34, no. 2 [May 2003], 170).

21. The term "obsession" is used by Levinas to portray the sense in which we are required to be that which we can never wholly be. At this point of our analysis, this immemorial origin is obsession's source. However, I later present Levinas's language of alterity as that which concretizes this obsession, emphasizing that it is precisely insofar as alterity *cannot* be reduced to the Face that it retains its ability to concretize this obsession.

22. In Levinas, one finds a tension between identity being disrupted by its welcoming of the Other, or identity being disrupted as it is invaded, or taken hostage by the Other. François Raffoul's commentary on Levinas's conception of hospitality is helpful here. "Hospitality is not an act performed by a sovereign subject at home in its domain. Hospitality names the pre-originary openness to the other that the subject is" (Raffoul, 179).

23. In the first chapter of *Death and Responsibility*, Dennis Keenan offers a clear analysis of the relation between interiority and exteriority in Levinas. The chapter traces his deployment of Descartes's *Meditations on First Philosophy*, and describes how, for Levinas, "[the] infinite is *in* me as it *interrupts* a 'me' that would comprehend or include it . . . I have received an idea, I have it in me, before there is an I that is capable of receiving it" (Keenan, *Death and Responsibility*, 13).

24. I liken an interpretation of Levinas's position, as one which does not account for the truth of metaphysical solitude, to one that identifies the Face as that aperture in Being that formalizes the fundamental signification of alterity. Such a reading determines that insofar as my subjectivity is (un-)constituted in an ethical responsibility for the Other, this Other's trace compromises the possibility of a solitary existence.

25. This diachronous time founds Levinas's sense of the ethical, whereby "the subject [is] late to itself and its obligations" (Drabinski, 11).

26. Drabinski, 131.

27. I use "unanchored" to capture that sense in Sartre's account of consciousness, whereby a relation to being is exhausted by an appearing of being (in terms of a meaningful world) for intentionality. There is nothing beyond this active organization of being into what can signify, or appear as signifying. As I have already show in chapter 1, this is also the case for Sartre's notion of facticity.

28. "The world and light are solitude. These given objects, these clothed beings are something other than myself, but they are mine" (Levinas, *EE*, 85). Under my analysis, "solitude," here, would refer to what I name a "first order" solitude.

29. This Levinasian sense of disruption and impossibility of closure should not be read in terms of violence (which more properly belongs to Sartre's formal account of my being-for-others). Levinas makes this clear in the essay "Phenomenon and Enigma," where he describes the trace as that which "disturbs order without troubling it seriously" (*Collected Philosophical Papers*, 66). This is underscored in Diane Perpich's description of the trace in terms of "diplomatic language or sexual innuendo, in that its proposals are made in terms such that 'if one likes, nothing has been said' [quoting again from 'Phenomenon and Enigma, 66]" (Perpich, *The Ethics of Emmanuel Levinas*, 114).

30. Levinas, *EE*, 84.

31. Levinas, *EE*, 66.

32. Levinas, *EE*, 64.

33. Levinas's analyses of death and suffering are poignant for this reason.

34. Elisabeth Louise Thomas, *Emmanuel Levinas: Ethics, Justice and the Human Beyond Being*, 132.

35. Rudi Visker, "Is Ethics Fundamental? Questioning Levinas on Irresponsibility," *Continental Philosophy Review* 36, no. 3 (July 2003): 263.

36. A closer look at Visker's argument reveals that it pays insufficient attention to the structural implications of positionality insofar as they precisely include the fact of solitude. Levinas's articulation of positionality is significant mostly for its unique portrayal of the relationship between interiority and exteriority. To recall, the event of hypostasis signals the birth of a personal existent that is set apart from the anonymous field of the *il y a*. Hence, another way of reading hypostasis would be to read it as the birth of interiority. "Existence in personal form" captures the triumph through which the inner life of an existent becomes distinguished from an exterior field of existence. But in this account of positionality, Levinas precisely troubles the dichotomy of interiority and exteriority by showing that the position out of which the existent stands is also a perforated position, incessantly interrupted by the threat of exteriority in the form of the *il y a*. I identify similar insinuations in Sartre's analysis of the experience of nausea, in which intentional directionality of consciousness is stunted by the meaninglessness of an anonymous field of existence. Although Sartre's formal analysis of this event is that, when subsumed in moments of nausea, consciousness faces its radical freedom (to constitute a world *for* itself), I hold that this engulfing by brute existence reveals a positioning of the subject similar to what Levinas identifies. Positionality signals a separation of genuine interiority, but this separation takes place *as an openness* onto exteriority. For this reason, Levinas's sense of positionality is more of a "depositioning," or debasing, of the self. Visker's argument seems to hold on to a relationship between interiority and exteriority that Levinas explicitly rejects in his account of positionality. Of the condition of the subject, as portrayed by Levinas, Visker writes: "Something has already managed to slip inside us and no degree of interiority will ever rid us of

the intruder. The reason is that, by definition, interiority presupposes a capacity to close oneself off. It presupposes privacy *in an ontological sense* [emphasis added]" (273). The underlying suggestion here is that solitude precludes the possibility of interiority, or the possibility of "that capacity to close oneself off" (273). Implied in this formulation is a subject who is nonsupportive of alterity, and who subsequently exists in solitude. For Visker's reading, insofar as Levinas describes identity as the very *impossibility* of interiority, Visker understands him to be opening up the subject to the Other, and thus undermining the significance of this metaphysical solitude.

37. Levinas, *OB*, 104.

38. Elisabeth Louise Thomas, 132. I pursue this more exhaustively in chapter 5, where I introduce Levinas's conception of substitution alongside Sartre's account of consciousness's relation to the Other.

39. Levinas, *EE*, 56. In this account, Levinas seems dismissive of the possibility that nausea might capture the kind of depositioning constitutive of an encounter with existence. However, he also states that "[in] nausea . . . we are . . . riveted to ourselves . . . We are there, and there is nothing more to be done, or anything to add to this fact that we have been entirely delivered up, that everything is consumed: *this is the very experience of pure being . . .*" (*OE*, 66–67).

40. I read David Detmer's analysis as one that echoes my proposed reading of Sartre's novel. "What happens to Roquentin in the novel is that his ability . . . to elevate parts of his perceptual field to the foreground . . . begins, inexplicably and against his will, to break down . . . In this way he achieves a direct awareness of reality—an awareness of existence itself. This awareness is, of necessity, nonconceptual" (Detmer, *Sartre Explained*, 54).

41. "It is probably for this reason that Sartre chose the medium of fiction to convey this point [that the moment of nausea precisely stands for the moment in which conceptual tools of description and/or conveying meaning fail]" (Detmer. 54).

42. Sartre, *Nausea*, 7.

43. Sartre, *Nausea*, 17.

44. Sartre, *Nausea*, 18.

45. Jager, "Sartre's Anthropology: A Philosophical Reflection on *La Nausée*," *The Philosophy of Jean-Paul Sartre*," ed. Paul Arthur Schilpp (La Salle, Ill.: Open Court, 1981), 482.

46. Levinas, *On Escape*, 66.

47. Ibid.

48. Ibid.

49. Of Levinas's account of nausea as a form of malaise, Elisabeth Thomas writes, "[Nausea] is the experience of an internal antagonism and an evasion that is *imposed* [against and/or not of the order of freedom]" (Thomas, *Emmanuel Levinas: Ethics, Justice and the Human Beyond Being*, 28).

50. *Nausea*, 10.

51. Detmer, 53–64.

52. Sartre, *Nausea*, 10.

53. Sartre, *Nausea*, 25.

54. Consciousness as inevitably embodied plays a significant role in my analysis in chapter 4.

55. It is for this reason that Sartre, in *The Transcendence of the Ego*, points out the gratuity of Husserl's transcendental ego when it comes to unifying consciousness—unification (like nonthetic self-awareness) is to be found *in* the transcendent object.

56. Sartre, *BN*, 338.

57. Sartre, *Nausea*, 127.

58. This is also evident in Levinas's analysis of shame, in *On Escape*. I treat this account of shame in chapter 4.

59. In his treatment of the role of nausea in Sartre's work, François Raffoul writes, "At the moment of the givenness of existence [at the moment of nausea], there is a radical senselessness.... Consequently the meaning *of* existence (as a subjective genitive) is opened as a possibility [for consciousness] by the factical givenness of existence" (Raffoul, *The Origins of Responsibility*, 125). Raffoul goes on the use his reading of nausea as a gateway through which to understand what he cites as a "hyperbolic responsibility" in Sartre. So though his exposition is similar to others that identify a radically free consciousness throughout Sartre's phenomenology of nausea, I also read Raffoul's work to be unique in his underscoring of Sartre's (somewhat radical) conception of responsibility. This is relevant to my analysis in chapter 5, where I trace the relation between Sartrean and Levinasian conceptions of responsibility.

60. Thomas Busch, "'La Nausée': A Lover's Quarrel with Husserl," *Research in Phenomenology* XI (1981): 12. This echoes David Detmer's analysis, which states that "we generally look at things under the color of our interests and projects [and] remain oblivious to, precisely because they are irrelevant to our present concerns, the infinite excess of meanings and information they contain" (*Sartre Explained*, 53). He equates this excess with the "whatness" of objects, or what Busch here understands as existence itself.

61. Busch, 12.

62. Sartre, *BN*, 486.

63. Busch, 12.

64. Sartre, *Nausea*, 133.

65. Brogan, Michael "Nausea and the Experience of the *Il y a*, Sartre and Levinas on Brute Existence," *Philosophy Today* 45, no. 2 (Summer 2001): 144–153.

66. Thomas Busch, in *The Power of Consciousness and the Force of Circumstances in Sartre's Philosophy*, discusses the possible inconsistencies that the (positive) fullness of being-in-itself might introduce into the structure of *Being and Nothingness*. Brogan follows up on one of these: "For if the being which transcends consciousness must be affirmed, in order to avoid idealism, as the common ground of the phenomenon (i.e., of both consciousness and its object), and consciousness in turn is held to be the origin of all differentiation, then it follows that pure being,

being prior to, or in abstraction from, its relationship to the for-itself, must be characterized as sheer undifferentiated positivity" (Brogan, 145).

67. Levinas, *TO*, 47.

68. It appears as though Brogan undermines this important difference when he says that "To be sure, their shared belief in the [irremissibility] precludes either of them from positing a means of simply getting out of the difficulty altogether—there are 'no exits.'" (Brogan, 148). I stand in disagreement with him on this point.

69. It is because this formal structure of consciousness (as absolute negativity) remains uninterrupted throughout Sartre's descriptions of nausea that we find, at the end of the novel, Roquentin's ultimate desire "to be" as that which holds the "cure" from his nausea. The horror of the experience rests on consciousness's essential *lack* of being, and as such, the possibility of an escape from that horror lies in the possibility "to be."

70. Brogan, 149.

71. For this reason, our rivetedness is felt most intimately as incarnation (in our actually "taking up a place" in being).

72. Chapter 4 pursues this difference in a comparison of Levinasian and Sartrean shame.

73. Busch, 7.

74. Bernd Jager, 482.

75. Needless to say, this does not reduce the phenomenological method to an idealism; rather, the rose *is* as it appears. It only means that, without this intentional act, there is no longer an appearance of a "pleasant rose." By performing the phenomenological reduction, an individual realizes this, and recognizes the absolute existence of consciousness—the world appears as it is precisely because consciousness allows it show up as such.

76. *Nausea*, 98.

77. Busch, 15–16.

78. In a paper that brings Sartre and Heidegger into dialogue, Thomas Anderson points out that Roquentin's experience uncovers the contingency of human existence (Thomas Anderson, "The Rationalism of Absurdity: Sartre and Heidegger," *Philosophy Today* 21 [1997]: 263–272). Nothing truly explains why things are the way they are (or why they even *are*) precisely because nothing, including Roquentin himself, has a reason for being. In this sense, nausea exposes the fact that consciousness exists without needing to be. Anderson uses this to explain Roquentin's solace in the blues melody sung by the Negress. Unlike his existence, which is without reason, the song *is*, definitely and firmly, succumbing to no threats of being something other than what it positively *is*. "Each note," Anderson writes, "has a reason for being. Each is *necessary* to the overall melody ... each *must* be and just be where it is. Thus everything [in the song] has its place, nothing is superfluous" (268). Hence, the song does not simply bear an existence, but rather, that it possesses being, and Roquentin, as well, wanted to be (*Nausea*, 175). However, not only is it the case that Roquentin exists without having

to, but more importantly, he exists without *being* anything at all. According to Anderson's reading, Roquentin's nausea points to the contingency of his existence insofar as he is "an insufficiency of being." I argue that the "contingency" reading of Sartrean nausea rests on the very assumption that my (Levinasian) approach calls into question, which is that consciousness is absolutely free. To exist contingently is to also perpetually transcend toward being. Such transcending means that consciousness can never *be*, to then possess the necessity that a contingent existence lacks. In this vein, this "contingency" reading of Sartre would sustain his formal ontology *against* the impetus of his concrete descriptions.

79. In chapter 5, I discuss Sartre's sense of responsibility as one that is radical enough to stand for a politicized instantiation of Levinasian substitution. Nonetheless, Sartre's responsibility ultimately rests on the primacy of freedom in a way that Levinas's does not.

Chapter 4. Levinasian Positionality Implicit in Sartre's Affective Experiences

1. In my discussion of Sartre's treatment of alterity in chapter 5, I show that his conception of "being in situation" already includes an alienation by the existence of the Other. Though this forces him into a language of disruption, he nevertheless maintains the primacy of freedom in his account of "situation."

2. Levinas, *OE*, 63.

3. This will ground his radical conception of responsibility, whereby the subject is responsible for her entire world. (See, Sartre, *BN*, 553–556.)

4. In chapter 1, I trace Thomas Martin's analysis of this relationship in Sartre, between facticity and freedom (*Oppression and the Human Condition*, 19–25), as well as Thomas Anderson's (*Sartre's Two Ethics*, 14–26).

5. Sartre, *BN*, 307.

6. Sartre, *BN*, 308.

7. Sartre, *BN*, 309.

8. Sartre, *BN*, 325. David Reisman recognizes that Sartre understands this conception of the body as the "body-*for-itself*" (emphasis added), thus, capturing the sense in which the body is in terms of a spontaneous activity of organizing and arranging objects in the world (*Sartre's Phenomenology*, 78–80).

9. Anderson, *Sartre's Two Ethics*, 17–18.

10. Sartre, *BN*, 329.

11. Ibid.

12. In Sartre's work, the distinction between "positional" and "nonpositional" awareness is an epistemological one. It describes the different levels awareness that is possible for consciousness. Positional awareness can be likened to a theoretical surveying, across the distance of scientific detachment. Nonpositional awareness would refer to that of which I am conscious, without being able to explicitly give

account. The concept of positionality in Levinas as far removed as it can be from these Sartrean terms.

13. Sartre, *BN*, 330.
14. Ibid.
15. Hence, in reference to my earlier examples of grief and joy, Sartre would hold that I have already surpassed myself, in the immediacy of those moments, in order to then spontaneously create an ego object that represents a "self as grief-stricken/joyful."
16. Sartre, *BN*, 333.
17. Sartre, *BN*, 332.
18. Sartre, *BN*, 333.
19. Sartre, *TE*, 40–42.
20. This will become important for my analysis in chapter 5. There, I establish the difference between the Sartrean and Levinasian interpretations of a subject undergoing objectification. While Levinas is able to understand this "being for the other" in terms other than the inertness of matter, Sartre is obligated to resort to a reading of my being for the other in terms of in-itself reification.
21. Sartre, *BN*, 332–333.
22. Sartre, *BN*, 333.
23. Levinas, *OE*, 52–53.

I develop this elsewhere, in a treatment of Sartrean and Levinasian conceptions of solidarity ("Levinas, Sartre and the Question of Solidarity," *Levinas Studies, an Annual Review* 7 [September 2012], ed. John E. Drabinski)

24. Forthcoming volume on "Levinas and Race," ed. John Drabinski.
25. Sartre, *BN*, 333.
26. Sartre, *BN*, 333.
27. In his discussion of shame, Sartre also uses this imagery of a fissure, to describe to "nothingness" that separates consciousness from its seen-being.
28. Here I am preparing for a reading of Sartre's descriptions of affectivity, for which his distinction between "positional" and "nonpositional" consciousness cannot account. I fully bring this to bear in a subsequent section devoted to Sartre's account of shame.
29. "Retaining the name phenomenology and the method of intentionality makes both possible and necessary the fundamental relationality that orients Levinas' method.... Relationality, here, [is] the intentionality uncovered as the structure of ethical subjectivity [that] does not rejoin with its origin.... It is thus not a relation of coincidence and reciprocity, [but rather] a question of nonintentional intentionality" (Drabinski, *Sensibility and Singularity, the Problem of Phenomenology in Levinas*, 172).
30. In his exposition of the role of sensibility in Levinas, Drabinski writes, "To be an ethical subject is to be this double movement. The double movement of ethical subjectivity produces the paradoxical affect of assignation: making the oneself other without alienation..." (215). This captures what I currently emphasize, which is that both Sartre's and Levinas's phenomenologies describe

embodiment as that which the self simultaneously rejects *and* finds itself riveted to. I develop the difference between Sartre's and Levinas's appropriation of the notion of alienation in chapter 5.

31. "[Levinas] questions whether [the silent essencing of being] is a sufficient condition of signification. What is left out of this amphibology is not simply the 'presence of the other' but ... a notion of the sensible [of a mode of relationality] which is not subordinate to theoretical consciousness" (Elisabeth Louise Thomas, *Emmanuel Levinas: Ethics, Justice and the Human Beyond Being*, 140).

32. "I am a slave to the degree that my being is dependent at the center of a freedom which is not mine and which is the very condition of my being" (Sartre, *BN*, 267).

33. Levinas, *OE*, 66.

34. Sartre, *BN*, 261.

35. Christine Andrews, "Jean-Paul Sartre and the Problem of the Other, An Analysis and Reflection," *Dialogue* 27 (October 1984): 25.

36. Vetlesen, 362.

37. Sartre, *TE*, 51–53.

38. Sartre, *BN*, 259.

39. This was discussed in chapter 1's analysis of the relevance of *The Transcendence of the Ego* for Sartre's ontology.

40. Without the "self" of reflection, Sartre points out that there is "nothing ... to which I can refer my acts in order to qualify them" (*BN*, 259). There is nothing (in that prereflective experience) against which I can measure my acts (my motivations or my intentions), to then vindicate them. For instance, I cannot say that I am curious by nature, and so my decision to eavesdrop is vindicated through my desire to be aware of everything around me. Later on, I can reflect on the experience, and *create* this curious "ego-self" in order to answer the question, "Should I have looked through that keyhole?" But in subsequently reflecting, I have already surpassed the experience in question. The curious ego-self that I subsequently create is *not* the same consciousness that looked through the keyhole.

41. "It is only through my awareness of being seen by the Other that the Other becomes a subject for me. I must become an object for the Other in order to 'apprehend the presence of his being-a-subject' (*BN*, 344–345). Furthermore, it is extremely difficult (and perhaps impossible) for me to remain in the mode of prereflective subjectivity when I am aware of "being-seen-by-the-Other..." (David Detmer, *Sartre Explained: From Bad Faith to Authenticity*, 93). In *Sartre's Phenomenology*, David Reisman also discusses that "third dimension" of consciousness, which is brought about by this event of being-seen. In the mode of being-for-itself, consciousness cannot ground any claims to its real or independent existence. In this mode of being, consciousness cannot be sure of an existence that is independent of its own reflective act (of self-consciousness). This guarantee comes from the mode of being-for-others. Through the Look, consciousness comes to understand itself as a physical object, or person, that exists independently of its self-reflective acts (Reisman, 75–82).

42. Sartre, *BN*, 259.

43. "[Before the Look], I obtain a powerful and direct intuition ... of my own embodied objectivity (my consciousness is revealed to be not only a pure point of view on the world, but also an object within it ..." (David Detmer, *Sartre Explained: From Bad Faith to Authenticity*, 92).

44. In chapter 5's comparison of Sartre's and Levinas's treatment of the Other, I discuss Sartre's conception of alienation as that which accounts for the entirety of consciousness's objectification before the Other. Though both experiences of shame and alienation point us in the direction of this encounter, my subsequent focus on alienation will show the sense in which Sartre explicitly resonates with Levinas (namely, the latter's account of substitution). Out of his account of alienation, he generates a notion of responsibility that calls into question an unlimited and arbitrary freedom.

45. Sartre, *BN*, 260.

46. For Levinas, the sense in which the subject is with its "self," or the sense in which the *moi* is riveted to the *soi*, does not reduce identity to a reified substance. This is an important difference between Sartre and Levinas, and plays a substantive role in my comparison of their respective conceptions of alterity in chapter 5. However, for the moment, I note that this "being with oneself" in Sartre can only function like a thinglike objectification.

47. Sartre, *BN*, 268.

48. Sartre, *BN*, 222.

49. In this sense, my objectified seen-being is very much like consciousness in the mode of experiencing physical pain. As we proceed, we will see that another important reason for the failure of consciousness's cognitive powers, in the case of its being-for-others, is that the foundation of this being is precisely in the Other, and not in the consciousness being-seen.

50. In the preceding section on Sartre's account of pain-consciousness, I also employ this language of "fissure" to capture this "non-coincidence without distance."

51. Sartre, *BN*, 269.

52. Sartre, *BN*, lii–liii.

53. "But whence the drama? Why refer to the look of the Other as causing a scandal? In fact we cannot find an answer to this question in Sartre if we stay on a purely ontological level. We must also consider what Sartre says about knowledge. ... [We] would miss the human drama involved here if we were to divorce what takes place on the level of being from what is effected on the level of knowledge; it is not only that the latter must be understood by reference to the former; it is also that what it at stake ontologically can be appreciated *solely* [emphasis mine] by reference to the issue of knowledge" (Vetlesen, 362–363). Thomas Owens also reads Sartre's account to mean that, were it possible for consciousness to overcome the cognitive limits represented by the Other (if it were possible to *know* the Other's interiority the way I know my own), I would be able to coincide with my object-being. "[If] I can somehow lay hold of this agent who effects my reduction to an in-itself, if I can

somehow 'absorb' the other who possesses this power of objectifying me, then I will have reached the goal of becoming an in-itself-for-itself" (Owens, 43).

54. To reiterate, it is this inner fragmentation that verifies for consciousness that it is a real person. "While the reflective modification does not provide an intuition of oneself as another consciousness . . . the modification that occurs with the Look does. This is made possible by an increased 'distance' within consciousness: the reflected-on knows what it is for the reflective, but under the Look the looked-at does not yet know what it is for the Other . . . [This transforms] the apprehension of oneself as merely psychic object into the apprehension of oneself as a full-fledged person" (Reisman, 76).

55. To be sure, this would be the motivation for bad faith, where I reduce myself to an "ego" in order to make my freedom more manageable.

56. In Kalle Pihlainen's paper, she compares the role of embodiment in the philosophies of intersubjectivity of several thinkers, two of them being Sartre and Levinas. She presents an insightful comparison between Sartre's views on intersubjectivity in *What Is Literature* (1978), and his analysis of "being-seen" in *Being and Nothingness*, pointing out that the less immediate, nonembodied relationship between the author and his reader leads to a reciprocal recognition and respect, while the more primary embodied experience of actually encountering a physical Other leads to conflict (130). Pihlainen refers to the experience of "being-seen" (from *Being and Nothingness*) as one that contains certain "embodied *pre-reflective* attitudes," which might lead to a more ethical way of encountering alterity (131). She sets her suggestion against what *does* take place in Sartre's analysis—"a retreat to [a] habitual understanding of [the world]" (131). I think Pihlainen is right to set up her distinction in this way, and if, by "pre-reflective attitudes" she means the attitudes toward my object-being for the Other that do not (yet) attempt to understand/conceptualize it, but rather to "exist" it, then she is also right in situating the promise for a less conflictual picture of the encounter at this level. However, as has already been discussed, Sartre's descriptions of my self-awareness before the Other, though not reflective, is not prereflective in the strictest sense. That it is neither of the two—that consciousness's awareness of its "self" as an object for the Other neither belongs to reflection nor prereflection—*does* suggest an interpretation other than a "retreat to habitual understanding." It suggests an interpretation other than (or beyond) the parameters of the phenomenology of experience. (Kalle Pihlainen, "From Embodiment to Community: Recognition, Alterity and the Existentialist Social Conscience," *Human Affairs* 14 [2004]: 126–134.)

57. Tracing Levinas's descriptions of shame will further strengthen my argument that because of this, shame might fall outside the category of "experience" altogether.

58. Reisman, 76.

59. Here, I disagree with Arne Vetlesen when he warns that "we would miss the human drama involved here [in the encounter between two consciousnesses] if we were to divorce what takes place on the level of being from what it effected

on the level of knowledge" (Vetlesen, 363). Indeed, it may be the case that Sartre intends for his readers to take up his account in this way. But my claim is that nothing in his theory of consciousness explicitly requires such an interpretation.

60. Christina Howells, "Sartre and Levinas," 94.

61. "The acuity of shame lies in the impossibility of *not* identifying with that being . . . that is already strange to us—strange not simply because we do not comprehend the motives for action but also because it is the very revelation of being in incomprehension" (Elisabeth Thomas, 27).

62. Levinas, *OE*, 63.

63. "For Levinas, shame is linked to a moment in which a comprehending being confronts the limit of its understanding. [However, this] is not a moment of conscious recognition of the limits of the cognizing subject but is thought in relation to *Dasein*. Shame then points to a limit in *Dasein*'s transcendental trajectory" (Thomas, 27).

64. Levinas, *OE*, 63.

65. Sartre, *BN*, 289.

66. Levinas, *OE*, 64.

67. Levinas, *OE*, 64.

68. "It is therefore our intimacy, that is, our presence to ourselves, that is shameful" (Levinas, *OE*, 65).

Chapter 5: Levinas and Sartre on the Question of the Other

1. Christina Howells's comparative analysis on these two thinkers is of importance here. In her paper titled, "Sartre and Levinas," she defends the thesis that "it is in their *evaluations* rather than their *descriptions* of relations with the Other that Sartre and Levinas come into conflict" (91). I generally agree with her position, and augment her suspicions by presenting the reasons for this departure in Sartre's and Levinas's evaluations (or formalizations) of the phenomenon of being-seen. (See, Howells, "Sartre and Levinas," *The Provocation of Levinas: Re-Thinking the Other*, ed. Robert Bernasconi and David Wood (London and New York: Routledge, 1988.)

2. See chapter 4, section II.

3. In his book, *The Subject in Question*, Stephen Priest points out that Sartre's commitment to the political and the ethical informed the trajectory of the development of his theory of consciousness. In that theory, Sartre made sure to avoid certain constructions of subjectivity that would ground the "escapist doctrines," which isolated man from the "real problems" of the world (Priest, 148–146).

4. Drew Dalton's work in *Longing for the Other: Levinas and Metaphysical Desire* establishes the centrality of Levinas's reworking of the metaphysical (Pittsburgh, Pa.: Duquesne University Press, 2009).

5. In an article published in the collection, *Difficulties of Ethical Freedom* (ed. Shannon Sullivan and Dennis J. Schmidt, 2008), Robert Bernasconi argues for bringing Sartre and Levinas together across this issue of ethical responsibility. I owe a great deal to his exposition.

6. In an essay that discusses the "Sartre-Levinas" dialogue on the Jewish question, Peter Gordon defends the position that "Levinas' philosophy would appear to offer a welcome corrective to Sartre's politically fraught choice between abjection and self-assertion," insofar as "Levinas *invalidates* the drama of Jewish authenticity" (Gordon, "Out of *Huis Clos*: Sartre, Levinas and the Debate over Jewish Authenticity," *Journal of Romance Studies* 6, no 1–2 (2006): 155). I, also, read Levinas as "invalidating" authenticity as a viable option for the Jew, given the singularity of his facticity. However, there is little in Levinas's critique of Sartre's *Anti-Semite and Jew*, or in the broader spectrum of his texts, which suggests that Levinas might be a corrective to a Sartrean politics. I argue for a reading of Sartrean alienation (and authenticity) as a political position that allows one to simultaneously subscribe to Levinas's conception of substitution. Said otherwise, my position is that we find, in Sartre, a viable means by which we can use substitution to ground political action.

7. Levinas, *OB*, 193, note 35.

8. For an exposition of Levinas's relationship to the phenomenological method, see Bettina Bergo's "What Is Levinas Doing? Phenomenology and the Rhetoric of an Ethical Un-Conscious" (*Philosophy and Rhetoric* 31, no. 2 [2005]: 122–144).

9. Bergo, 123.

10. Dennis King Keenan, *The Question of Sacrifice* (Bloomington, Indiana University Press 2005): 75–83.

11. Thomas J. Owens, "Absolute Aloneness as Man's Existential Structure: A Study of Sartrean Ontology," *New Scholasticism* 40 (July 1966): 347.

12. P. J. Crittenden, "Sartrean Transcendence: Winning and Losing," *Australian Journal of Philosophy* 63, no. 4 (December 1985): 446.

13. This is discussed in chapter 1.

14. Sartre, *BN*, 488.

15. "When I regard [the Other] merely as an object, I understand him in terms of the same categories I use to comprehend the objects standing near him.... Because I apprehend him solely as an object, I do not perceive any subject-object relationship between him and the other objects present" (David Detmer, *Sartre Explained: From Bad Faith to Authenticity*, 93).

16. "It is only through my awareness of being seen by the Other that the Other becomes a subject...." (Detmer, 93). In other words, for Sartre, there is a prereflective (noncognitive) awareness of the Other only insofar as I become an object *for him*.

17. Sartre, *BN*, 235.

18. Sartre, *BN*, 232.

19. Robert R. Williams, "Sartre's Strange Appropriation of Hegel," *The Owl of Minerva* 23, no. 1 (Fall 1991) 6.

20. Sartre, *BN*, 203.

21. On this, Levinas and Sartre are in agreement. Levinas writes, in 1972, "And Sartre, though stopping short of a full analysis, makes the striking observation that the Other is a pure hold in the world. The Other proceeds from the *absolutely Absent*" (Levinas, *Humanism of the Other*, trans. Nidra Poller (Urbana: University of Illinois Press, 2003), 39).

22. For an analysis of Sartre's critique of Heidegger's *Mitsein*, see Zahavi's "Beyond Empathy, Phenomenological Approaches to Intersubjectivity," *Journal of Consciousness Studies* 8, nos. 5–7 [2001]: 157).

23. Vetlesen, 362. Vetlesen explains that it is this which Sartre wishes to convey when he says that "being-for-others is not an ontological structure of the for-itself" (*BN*, 376).

24. Sartre, *BN*, 230.

25. Zahavi, "Just like Sartre, Levinas also takes the problem of intersubjectivity to be first and foremost a problem of radical otherness, and he explicitly denies that any form of intentionality . . . will ever permit us to understand this encounter" (159).

26. "This mode of negating while taking refuge in what one negates delineates the same or the I [and, therefore, does not constitute that rupture of totality, which transcendence signifies]" (Levinas, *Totality and Infinity*, 41).

27. See Bettina Bergo's article, "What Is Levinas Doing? Phenomenology and the Rhetoric of an Ethical Un-Conscious," for its elucidation of the role of phenomenology in Levinas.

28. As François Raffoul writes, "Far from being included as one moment in being, as one existential in the analytic of Dasein for instance (being-with), and far from being inscribed within the element and horizon of being, ethics [an encounter with radical alterity] is situated in the relationship to the other person . . . a relation which for Levinas takes place, as he puts it, "beyond being." (*The Origins of Responsibility*, 166.) It is also important to note that one should not expect from Levinas an ethical theory (or an ethical principle). Rather, his work represents that which every ethical theory presupposes, which is the meaning of the ethical *as* the absolute alterity of the other. In one of the interviews compiled in *Unforeseen History*, Levinas discusses the difference between what he tries to accomplish and "moralism": "In fact morality had a bad reputation. It was confused with moralism. That which is essential in ethics is often lost in this moralism reduced to a set of particular obligations." ("On the Utility of Insomnia," *Unforeseen History*, trans. Nidra Poller [Urbana and Chicago: University of Illinois Press, 2004], 128.)

29. In *Totality and Infinity*, Levinas writes, "The encounter with the Other in Sartre threatens my freedom, and is equivalent to the fall of my freedom under the gaze of another freedom. Here perhaps is manifested most forcefully being's [or ontology's] incompatibility with what remains veritably exterior." (*TI*, 303.)

30. "Levinas found the sources of his critique of totality first in Franz Rosenzweig's critique of Hegel (but also in moments in the history of philosophy

such as Plato's Good beyond being, or Descartes' Third Meditation with its idea of God as infinite . . ."). (Raffoul, 169.)

31. Levinas, *TI*, 50.

32. "[The idea] has been *put* into us . . ." (Levinas, "Philosophy and the Idea of Infinity," *Collected Philosophical Papers*, trans. Alphonso Lingis [Pittsburgh, Pa.: Duquesne University Press, 1998], 54).

33. Diane Perpich, *The Ethics of Emmanuel Levinas*, 64.

34. Levinas, *TI*, 54.

35. Perpich, 64. Here, she cites Levinas's essay, "The Ruin of Representation" (1959) as the place in which he articulates the relation of his work on exteriority to the Husserlian theory of intentionality.

36. I have established, in chapter 4 (note 1) that my working through Levinas's conception of transcendence has resulted in my regarding the notion of disruption to be more fundamental than the signification of the Face. Because the focus of this current chapter is on the relation between Sartre's and Levinas's conceptions of the Other, the role of the Face, in Levinas, comes to the forefront of my analysis. Nevertheless, I regard Levinas to be employing the face of the Other to capture a disruption that already "constitutes" an existent in solitude, and positioned in the *il y a* through hypostasis. For this reason, Levinas's phenomenology of embodiment should be read as preparing the way for his account of the expression (and nonmanifestation) of the Face. In this regard, to Diane Perpich's question, "Can the face call me into question if the ground for such a call is not prepared in the body?" I would respond in the negative (the grounds for which I establish in chapters 3 and 4). (Perpich, 64.)

37. Levinas, *TI*, 50.

38. Sartre, *BN*, 251.

39. Sartre, *BN*, 529.

40. "If, for Levinas, my freedom, in what is fundamental to it, begins with my obligation to the Other, coming before being requested, before being called for, for Sartre it seems to end with it" (Michael de Saint Cheron, *Conversations with Emmanuel Levinas, 1983–1994*, trans. Gary D. Mole (Pittsburgh, Pa.: Duquesne University Press, 2010), 57).

41. To reiterate, my reading of Sartre does not sanction the critique that Sartre presents a version of Descartes's dualism. In the early pages of *Being and Nothingness*, this is clearly demonstrated: "[Although] the concept of being has this peculiarity of being divided into two regions without communication, we must nevertheless explain how these two regions can be placed under to the same heading" (lxiii). For Sartre, the nothingness of being is but a mode of being-in-itself; consciousness and being are inseparable, precisely because the former is that which allows for the manifestation of the latter.

42. Joanna Pier, "Sartre/Levinas, An Is/Ought Gap of Ethics," *Dialogue*, April 1989, 53.

43. Sartre, *BN*, 223–232.

44. Sartre, *BN*, 524.

45. Sartre, *Critique of Dialectical Reason, Volume I, Theory of Practical Ensembles*, trans. Alan Sheridan-Smith, ed. Jonathan Rée Paris: Editions Gallimard), 1976 (hereafter cited as *Critique*).

46. I have shown that this is the case for Sartre's conception of facticity in general. To encounter those factical aspect of my world is to already find them with meaning, and thus to have already surpassed them.

47. This language of a "new dimension" was discussed at length in chapter 4's analysis of shame.

48. Sartre, *BN*, 524.

49. Sartre, *BN*, 524.

50. Sartre, *BN*, 488.

51. Sartre, *BN*, 526.

52. Ibid.

53. Busch, 153.

54. Sartre, *BN*, 526.

55. In his tracing of Sartre's conception of freedom across the trajectory of his work, Thomas Anderson emphasizes Sartre's criticism of the position that gives to history a deterministic role. "One of [Sartre's] early aphorisms summarizes his position: 'Existentialism Against History Through the Affirmation of the Irreducible Individuality of the Person' (*Notebooks for an Ethics*, 25). Still, in his discussions Sartre demonstrates his awareness that economic, political, scientific, and technological factors form the concrete milieu of situated human freedom. Though he repeatedly rejects a simple determinism, he admits that the technological and economic components of society do prescribe limits outside of which free historical action . . . is impossible." (Anderson, *Sartre's Two Ethics: From Authenticity to Integral Humanity*, 48–49.)

56. Sartre, *Critique*, 184.

57. He describes materiality as that which is always in the act of "vaporizing human actions" (*Critique*, 184).

58. Sartre, *BN*, 526.

59. Sartre ends *Being and Nothingness* with such an account of radical responsibility, demonstrating that the weight of the entire world rests on the shoulders of consciousness, despite the fact that this weight is "unassumable." "[Whatever] may be the situation in which he finds himself, the for-itself wholly [assumes] this situation with its particular coefficient of adversity, even though it be insupportable" (*BN*, 553–554). The for-itself is the "incontestable author" of every event and every signification that belongs to its world, even in light of the inversion of its *praxis* by an alienating materiality.

60. "[Sartre's] sense of authorship differs from the traditional accountability for one's actions . . . since we are dealing here with an authorship with respect to my being, and to the whole world as a way of being. . . . [Sartre's] hyperbolic inflation of responsibility as accountability will in fact lead to the exceeding of [the classical

definition of responsibility], opening onto other senses, if one understands that [he] extends the scope of authorship so far that he ends up deconstructing it" (Raffoul, *The Origins of Responsibility*, 122–123).

61. Saint Cheron, *Conversations with Emmanuel Levinas, 1983–1994*, 57.

62. It is worth remembering that even though Levinas might use this language of obligation, it means something significantly different from how Sartre employs the word in his critique in his *Notebooks for an Ethics*. What Sartre refers to as obligation indicates a "submission to the other's will," which is something entirely different from Levinas's understanding of my being substituted for the Other. I demonstrate this more fully in the next section.

63. This claim drives much of the analysis in Sartre's *Critique of Dialectical Reason*, and can also be found in *Anti-Semite and Jew: An Exploration of the Etiology of Hate*.

64. This distinction is drawn by Thomas Anderson in is analysis of Sartre's ethical position. I am indebted to the insight of his work (Anderson, *The Foundation and Structure of Sartrean Ethics* 78).

65. Jean-Paul Sartre, *Notebooks for an Ethics*, trans. David Pellauer (Chicago: The University of Chicago Press, 1992).

66. Thomas Anderson, *The Foundation and Structure of Sartrean Ethics* (Lawrence, Kansas: The Regents Press of Kansas, 1979), 5.

67. In his assessment of Sartre's response to Dostoyevsky's claim, François Raffoul writes, "Will [the death of God] imply some impossibility of ethics as such, and of responsibility, since there is no longer a way to rely on *a priori* values in our decisions? Not so for Sartre, for he does not claim that there are no values . . . but rather that there are no *transcendent, given, a priori, objective* values" (Raffoul, *The Origins of Responsibility*, 123).

68. "In *Notebooks*, Sartre even undertakes a fairly concrete study of the nature of feudalism in the Middle Ages in order to illustrate how economic factors set limits to but do not determine human freedom. . . . He stresses the point that, if human beings are to relate to each other and to themselves as free individuals, the present socioeconomic structures . . . that steal the workers' products from them and reduce them to anonymous forces of production whose destiny is beyond their control, must be radically changed." (Anderson, *Sartre's Two Ethics: From Authenticity to Integral Humanity*, 49.)

69. Sartre, *BN*, 554–555.

70. Sartre, *Notebooks*, 60.

71. Thomas Anderson gives an insightful analysis of the role of recognition (of freedom) in Sartre's later ethics in *Notebooks*, and identifies several potential inconsistencies of this claim (*Sartre's Two Ethics*, 68–77). I treat Sartre's conception of recognition in more detail as this chapter progresses.

72. Sartre, *Notebooks*, 60.

73. Sartre, *Notebooks*, 60.

74. François Raffoul, *The Origins of Responsibility*, 124.

75. Sartre, *Notebooks*, 257.
76. Sartre, *Notebooks*, 254.
77. Sartre, *Notebooks*, 251.
78. Sartre, *Notebooks*, 253.
79. Sartre, *Notebooks*, 257.
80. Sartre, *Notebooks*, 254.
81. Sartre, *Notebooks*, 259.

82. T. Heter Storm gestures toward an implied distinction in Sartre's work, between the Other in terms of her Look, and the Other in terms of her goals. It is on the latter that Sartre builds his notion of authenticity and the city of ends in *Notebooks*. (Storm, "Authenticity and Others: Sartre's Ethics of Recognition," *Sartre Studies International* 12, no. 2 [2006], 20). I use this insight to affirm my claim that the Look, in Sartre, performs a very specific function, to which the entire signification of the Other is not reducible.

83. Under such conditions, the Other does not *steal* from me what I *give*, in (loving) generosity. In his reading of *Notebooks*, David Detmer writes, "In Sartre's classification, the highest values, in ascending order, are passion, pleasure, criticism and the demand for evidence, responsibility, creation, and, at the very top, generosity" (Detmer, *Sartre Explained*, 141). Upon arriving at authenticity, intersubjectivity is built on this highest value of generosity, which is to say we recognize that "all of our actions and all of the objects we create, including the object we ourselves are for others, are inevitably *given* to others to freely respond to [emphasis added]" (Anderson, *Sartre's Two Ethics: From Authenticity to Integral Humanity*), 66).

84. Anderson, *The Foundation and Structure of Sartrean Ethics*, 17.

85. Sartre, *BN*, 364.

86. This was discussed at some length in my analysis of Sartre's conception of shame. I reiterate it here for the purpose of understanding the implications of his conception of authenticity.

87. "[If] both the Other and I . . . reject the God-project, and choose our mutual freedoms as our goal, our objectification of each other is not oppressive nor a source of conflict . . ." (Anderson, *Sartre's Two Ethics: From Authenticity to Integral Humanity*, 66).

88. Sartre, *BN*, 627.

89. Sartre, *Notebooks*, 474.

90. In *Sartre's Two Ethics: From Authenticity to Integral Humanity*, Thomas Anderson questions the source of my obligations to regard the Other's freedom to be of equal value as my own. "By preferring my freedom to that of others, I need not imply that it possesses some objective value that theirs lacks. . . . Furthermore, to choose to value one thing that possesses no intrinsic value over other things that also lack intrinsic value does not involve any inconsistency, as far as I can see" (68). Ultimately, Anderson identifies Sartre's appeal to a pseudo-Kantian universalism as what most convincingly grounds his claims pertaining to authenticity.

91. Anderson, "Authenticity, Conversion, and the City of ends in Sartre's *Notebooks for an Ethics*," *Writing the Politics of Difference*, ed. Hugh J. Silverman (Albany: State University of New York Press, 1991), 108–109.

92. In this society, "my freedom asks other people to make themselves freedom by recognizing my own freedom as freedom" (Sartre, *Notebooks*, 208).

93. "Personal salvation is impossible. . . . for no individual can solely by his own efforts achieve a fully free existence." (Anderson, *The Foundation and Structure of Sartrean Ethics*, 68.)

94. Sartre, *Notebooks*, 262.

95. Sartre, *Notebooks*, 475.

96. "When another person appeals to me, I simultaneously recognize that she has purposes that she freely pursues and recognize that I have purposes that I freely pursue" (T. Heter Storm, "Authenticity and Others: Sartre's Ethics of Recognition," 20).

97. Sartre, *Existentialism and Humanism*, trans. P. Mairet (London: Eyre Methuen), 51.

98. T. Heter Storm references Sartre's use of "appeal," and it is helpful insofar as it better aligns Sartre's work on authenticity with Levinas's conception of the demand of the Face. We might say that the Other *appeals* to an authentic consciousness, so as to then obligate that consciousness in the Levinasian, and not the Sartrean sense. ("Authenticity and Others: Sartre's Ethics of Recognition," 20.)

99. Anderson, *The Foundation and Structure of Sartrean Ethics*, 77.

100. Sartre, *Existentialism Is a Humanism*, 29.

101. My claim here is not that Sartre's position on authenticity conceives of the individual to be motivated solely by self-interest. Rather, I argue that his position continues to prioritize the value of freedom, and to ultimately understand responsibility for the Other only in terms of that freedom. "At first glance Sartre's argument appears to be . . . based on self-interest (for it seems to advise me to value and promote others' freedom so that they will value and promote mine [across a mutual recognition among freedoms]. . . . We should, however, take seriously his phrase 'the city of ends,' for it indicates that Sartre is not advocating that we turn others into mere means for our personal justification." (Anderson, *Sartre's Two Ethics: From Authenticity to Integral Humanity*, 77.)

102. Anderson, 85–86.

103. According to Simone de Beauvoir's interpretation of Sartre's position, this acknowledgment of the symmetry between "self" and "other" facilitates the mutual recognition we all need for our lives to have real meaning. I desire, more than anything else, justification for my otherwise contingent existence. This can either come from me, or it can come from other men. Given that my own freedom is without justification, it does little to give *myself* justification, since this justification would be coming from an ultimately unnecessary origin. This leaves others, on whom I must then depend for my justification. But to derive meaningful justification from other, I must also, in the name of consistency, choose to value, pursue and promote

the other as a freedom of equal value to my own. As de Beauvoir says, "Man can find justification of his own existence only in the existence of other men" (Simone de Beauvoir, *The Ethics of Ambiguity*, trans. Bernard Frechtman [New York: Citadel Press, 1967], 72). But these other men must be my "peers." "The man to whom I do violence is not my peer and I need men to be my peers" (Ibid., 116). We might be inclined to read in this a form of egoism that implies that I am using other freedoms as means to promote my own end (the end of my maximal justification). However, not only would this conflict with Sartre's conception of the city of ends, it would also be self-defeating to my own project. In other words, precisely because I *must* find justification in another *freedom*, I am obligated to apprehend this freedom *as such*, and not as a nonfree means/instrument.

104. Sartre, *Anti-Semite and Jew*, 151.

105. Sartre, *BN*, 554–555.

106. "I am thus responsible for myself and for all men, and I am creating a certain image of man as I would have him be. In fashioning myself I fashion man" (*Existentialism is a Humanism*, 29).

107. Sartre, *BN*, 555.

108. Levinas, *TI*, 87.

109. For such a exposition, see Howard Caygill's *Levinas and the Political* (London and New York: Routledge, 2002).

110. So when Levinas writes that we should "take the bread out of our own mouths" in order to feed the Other, this, in no way, should be read as a feasible prescription for engaging in political action on behalf of the Other. It is precisely insofar as such gestures are *never* responsible enough that they fail as viable courses for political action.

111. Levinas, *OB*, 111.

112. "Levinas reinvents with [positive] value precisely those elements of the existential world-view which seem to Sartre most negative [one of which is his account of alienation before the Other]" (Howells, 94).

113. Levinas, *OB*, 114 (emphasis added). As Robert Gibbs points out, "the self allows for this substitution to be [its own] . . . preserving the self from complete dissolution into the other, from becoming the tool or slave for the other" (Gibbs, "Substitution: Marcel and Levinas," *Philosophy and Theology* 4 [Winter 1989] 172).

114. Here, Levinas's analysis is similar to how Sartre's conception of generosity functions to undermine the possibility of alienation. In the city of ends, I relate to the Other across love and generosity. This means that I give to the Other my being and my actions, to which he then freely responds. (Anderson, *Sartre's Two Ethics*, 66.) This means that the Other cannot *steal* what is already *given* in this sense.

115. "Subjectivity cannot be reduced to consciousness" (Levinas, *OB*, 100).

116. Levinas, *OB*, 103.

117. Levinas, *OB*, 104.

118. Levinas, *OB*, 111.

119. Levinas, *OB*, 114.

120. Judith Butler describes the Other's proximity to signify as follows, "[I am frightened for my own life, but anxious that I might have to kill]" ("Precarious Life," *Radicalizing Levinas*, ed. Peter Atterton and Matthew Calarco [SUNY Press, 2010], 9). The Other can be my oppressor, but even in such cases, my substitution for him means that "murdering in the name of self-preservation is [never] justified" (Butler, 8).

121. "Persecution is not something added to the subjectivity of the subject and his vulnerability; it is the very movement of recurrence" (Levinas, *OB*, 111).

122. "This 'passing over' which is not death, not not-being..." (Philip Maloney, "Levinas, Substitution and Transcendental Subjectivity," *Man and World* 30 [1997], 51).

123. Levinas, *OB*, 109.

124. Levinas, *OB*, 109.

125. To be sure, this would pertain to preconversion, while the consciousnesses in question remain in a "bad faith" pursuit of the God-project.

126. Levinas, *OB*, 110.

127. This is not to imply that the subject *always* takes up this call to sacrifice. Rather, we should read Levinas's account as one that explains how this kind of sacrifice is possible (when it does occur).

128. Levinas, *OB*, 87.

129. Levinas, *OB*, 115.

130. Levinas, *OB*, 117.

131. Ibid.

132. See my account in chapter 3.

133. Levinas, "Useless Suffering," *On Thinking of the Other: Entre Nous*, trans. Michael B. Smith and Barbara Harshav (New York: Columbia University Press, New York), 93–94.

134. Levinas, *OB*, 113.

135. Levinas, *OB*.

136. Alongside the criticisms in the essay, we also find, in "Existentialism and Anti-Semitism," an appraisal of Sartre's treatment of the situation of the Jew. "The overall philosophy of Sartre is simply an attempt to think man, encompassing his social, economic, and historical situation within his spirituality, without making him a simple object of thought. It recognizes commitments for the mind that are not knowledge. Commitments that are not thoughts—that's existentialism!... Until then [referring to Sartre's exposition in *Anti-Semite and Jew*] the persecuted vainly sought protection in Descartes and Spinoza... hanging on for dear life to those truths proclaimed as the very essence of humanism." (Levinas, "Existentialism and Anti-Semitism, *Unforeseen History*, trans. Nidra Poller, University of Illinois Press, Urbana and Chicago, 2004, 74–75.)

137. Levinas, "Being Jewish," trans. Mary Beth Mader, *Continental Philosophy Review* 40 (2007): 208.

138. Ibid.

139. Levinas, "Being Jewish," 207.

140. Sartre, *Anti-Semite and Jew, An Exploration of the Etiology of Hate*, trans. George J. Becker (New York: Schocken Books, 1948), 136–137.

141. Levinas, "Being Jewish," 207.

142. François Raffoul also employs this language in his description of Sartre's notion of responsibility as hyperbolic. He identifies it as "the absolute responsibility of an essenceless existence for itself and for all that is . . ." (*The Origins of Responsibility*, 124).

143. Bernasconi, "Before Whom and for What? Accountability and the Invention of Ministerial, Hyperbolic, and Infinite Responsibility," 140.

144. Sartre, *Anti-Semite and Jew*, 136.

145. Another important difference, which I hope is clear from my comparing Levinas's and Sartre's accounts of identity, is that Sartrean responsibility is without limit insofar as *freedom* is without limit. "Responsibility with Sartre would become boundless, as it arises out of the groundlessness of existences [a groundlessness that is the very signification of absolute freedom]." (Raffoul, *The Origins of Responsibility*, 126). This is not the case for Levinas who, on the contrary, identifies a boundless responsibility that *exceeds* my (free) capacities.

146. "Freedom here can be thought as the possibility of doing what no one can do in my place. . . ." (Levinas, *God, Death and Time*, trans. Bettina Bergo [Palo Alto: Stanford University Press, 2000], 181).

147. Anderson, 8.

Concluding Remarks

1. Brogan, "Nausea and the Experience of the '*Il y a*': Sartre and Levinas on Brute Existence," *Philosophy Today* (Summer 2001): 144–153.

2. Christina Howells, "The Novels," *Sartre: The Necessity of Freedom* (Cambridge U.K.: Cambridge University Press, 1988), 46–69.

3. Howells, 53.

4. Sartre, *TE*, 99.

Bibliography

Alford, C. Fred. *Levinas, The Frankfurt School and Psychoanalysis.* Middletown, Conn.: Wesleyan University Press, 2002.

Anderson, Thomas. "Sartre's Early Ethics and the Ontology of Being Nothingness." In *Sartre Alive*. Edited by Ronal Aronson and Adrian van den Hoven. Detroit: Wayne State University Press, 1991, 183–199.

———. *Sartre's Two Ethics: From Authenticity to Integral Humanity.* Peru, Ill.: Open Court, 1993.

Barnes, Hazel E. "Sartre's Ontology: The Revealing and Making of Being." *Cambridge Companion Guide to Sartre.* Edited by Christina Howells. Cambridge, U.K.: Cambridge University Press, 1992, 13–38.

Berdt Kenevan, Phyllis. "Self-Consciousness and the Ego." *The Philosophy of Jean Paul Sartre.* Edited by Paul Arthur Schilpp. Carbondale: Southern Illinois University Press, 1981, 197–210.

Bernasconi, Robert. "Levinas: Philosophy and Beyond." *Philosophy and Non-Philosophy Since Merleau-Ponty.* Edited by Hugh Silverman. New York: Routledge, 1988, 232–258.

———. "Skepticism in the Face of Philosophy." *Re-reading Levinas.* Edited by Robert Bernasconi and Simon Critchley. Bloomington: Indians University Press, 1991, 149–161.

Busch, Thomas. *The Power of Consciousness and the Force of Circumstance in Sartre's Philosophy.* Bloomington and Indianapolis: Indiana University Press, 1990.

Caws, Peter. *Sartre.* Edited by Ted Honderich. London, Boston, Melbourne, and Henley: Routledge and Keegan Paul, 1984.

Caygill, Howard. *Levinas and the Political.* London and New York: Routledge, 2002.

Dalton, Drew. *Longing for the Other: Levinas and Metaphysical Desire.* Pittsburgh: Duquesne University Press, 2009.

De Boer, Theodore. "An Ethical Transcendental Philosophy." *Face to Face with Levinas.* Edited by Richard Cohen. Albany: State University of New York Press, 1986, 83–115.

Detmer, David. *Freedom as a Value: A Critique of the Ethical Theory of Jean-Paul Sartre.* Peru, Ill.: Open Court, 1986.
———. *Sartre Explained: From Bad Faith to Authenticity.* Illinois: Open Court, 2008.
Drabinski, John E. *Sensibility and Singularity: The Problem of Phenomenology in Levinas.* Albany: State University of New York Press, 2001.
Fox, Nik Farrell. *The New Sartre: Explorations in Postmodernism.* New York: Continuum, 2003.
Greene, Marjorie. *Sartre.* New York: New Viewpoints, 1973.
Howells, Christina. *Sartre: The Necessity of Freedom.* Cambridge: Cambridge University Press, 1988.
Jager, Bernd. "Sartre's Anthropology: A Philosophical Reflection on *La Nausée.*" *The Philosophy of Jean-Paul Sartre.* Edited by Paul Arthur Schilpp. La Salle, Illinois: Open Court, 1981, 477–493.
Jeanson, Francis. *Sartre and the Problem of Morality.* Translated by Robert V. Stone. Bloomington: Indiana University Press, 1980.
Katz, Claire, "Judaism and the Ethical: Recovering the Other." *Levinas, Judaism and the Feminine: The Silent Footsteps of Rebecca.* Bloomington: Indiana University Press, 2003, 8–21.
Levinas, Emmanuel. "Intentionality and Metaphysics." *Discovering Existence with Husserl.* Translated by Richard Cohen and Michael Smith. Evanston: Northwestern University Press, 1998, 122–129.
———. *Ethics and Infinity, Conversations with Philippe Nemo.* Translated by Richard Cohen. Pittsburgh: Duquesne University Press, 1985.
———. *Existence and Existents.* Translated by Alphonso Lingis. Pittsburgh: Duquesne University Press, 2001.
———. "From One to the Other: Transcendence and Time." *Entre Nous.* Translated by Michael B. Smith and Barbara Harshav. New York: Columbia University Press, 1998, 133–152.
———. "God and Philosophy." *Basic Philosophical Writings.* Edited by Adriaan Peperzak, Simon Critchley, and Robert Bernasconi. Bloomington: Indiana University Press, 1996, 129–148.
———. *God, Death and Time.* Translated by Bettina Bergo. Palo Alto: Stanford University Press, 1993.
———. "Letter Concerning Jean Wahl." *Unforeseen History.* Translated by Nidra Poller. Urbana and Chicago: University of Illinois Press, 1994.
Levinas, Emmanuel. "Meaning and Sense." *Collected Philosophical Papers.* Translated by Alphonso Lingis. Pittsburgh: Duquesne University Press, 1998, 75–107.
———. "No Identity." *Collected Philosophical Papers.* Translated by Alphonso Lingis. Pittsburgh: Duquesne University Press, 1998, 141–151.
———. *On Escape.* Translated by Bettina Bergo. Palo Alto: Stanford University Press, 2003.

———. *Otherwise than Being or Beyond Essence*. Translated by Alphonso Lingis. Pittsburgh: Duquesne University Press, 1998.

———. "Philosophy and the Idea of Infinity." *Collected Philosophical Papers*. Translated by Alphonso Lingis. Pittsburgh: Duquesne University Press, 1998.

———. *The Theory of Intuition in Husserl's Phenomenology*. Evanston, Ill.: Northwestern University Press, 1973.

Martin, Thomas. *Oppression and the Human Condition: An Introduction to Sartrean Existentialism*. New York: Rowman and Littlefield, 2002.

Perpich, Diane. *The Ethics of Emmanuel Levinas*. Palo Alto: Stanford University Press, 2008.

Priest, Stephen. *The Subject in Question: Sartre's Critique of Husserl in* The Transcendence of the Ego. London: Routledge, 2000.

Raffoul, Francois. *The Origins of Responsibility*. Bloomington and Indianapolis: Indiana University Press, 2010.

Reisman, David. *Sartre's Phenomenology*. New York: Continuum International Publishing Group, 2007.

Sartre, Jean-Paul. *The Transcendence of the Ego, An Existentialist Theory of Consciousness*. Translated by Forrest Williams and Robert Kirkpatrick. New York: The Noon Day Press, 1972.

———. *Imagination*. Translated by Forrest Williams. Ann Arbor: University of Michigan Press, 1972.

———. *The Psychology of Imagination*. Translated by B. Frenchtman. New York: Washington Square Press, 1966.

———. *Nausea*. Translated by Lloyd Carruth. New York: New Directions, 1964.

Smith, Michael B. *Toward the Outside: Concepts and Themes in Emmanuel Levinas*. Pittsburgh: Duquesne, 2005.

Sukale, Michael. *Comparative Studies in Phenomenology*. The Hague: Martinus Nijhoff, 1976.

Thomas, Elizabeth Louise. *Emmanuel Levinas: Ethics, Justice and the Human Beyond Being*. Edited by Robert Bernasconi. New York: Routledge, 2004.

Wahl, Jean. *A Short History of Existentialism*. Translated by Forrest Williams & Stanley Maron. Westport, Conn.: Greenwood Press, 1949.

Index

affectivity
  body and, 12
  Levinas's account of Jewish facticity and, 148
  Levinas's account of positionality and, 6, 7, 60, 68
  moments of, in Sartre, 92, 93, 99, 105, 115, 155, 185
  paradox of, in Sartre, 102
  nausea and, 88
  pain in Sartre and, 96, 100, 101, 103
  responsibility in Sartre and Levinas and, 150
  shame in Sartre and, 106
  transcendence in Sartre and, 5
alienation
  being-in-situation and, 128, 184
  duty in Sartre and, 132, 135, 141, 153
  Jew in Sartre and, 147
  nausea and, 91
  Other in Sartre and, 115, 118, 125–129, 138, 145, 148, 154, 187
  responsibility in Sartre and, 129, 130, 149, 187, 197
    substitution and, 118, 143, 144, 147, 149, 170, 185, 190, 197
  vulnerability in Sartre and, 130, 131
alterity, 12, 117, 134, 148, 149, 154, 178, 187, 179
  alienation and, 128, 129, 184

brute existence in Sartre and, 82, 87
Cartesian idea of the infinite and, 124, 125
death in Levinas and, 68, 70, 145
diachronous time and, 78
enjoyment in Levinas and, 68
Face and, 125, 134
freedom in Sartre and, 129, 130
identity in Levinas and, 9, 46, 68, 118, 119, 140, 142, 145, 148, 176
il y a and, 46, 57, 73, 134, 147, 151, 172
Other in Levinas and, 11, 118, 119, 144, 191
transcendence in Levinas and, 7, 46, 117, 120, 124, 140, 147, 170
transcendence in Sartre and, 79
Other in Sartre and, 121, 124, 126, 127, 135, 188
politics in Sartre and, 117
soi and, 69
solitude in Levinas and, 71, 77, 79, 81, 82, 171, 175, 177, 179, 181
substitution and, 143, 144, 145
trace and, 78, 145
Anderson, Thomas, 26, 27, 99, 131, 136, 138–140, 150
Andrews, Christine, 107
anguish, 36
  bad faith and 37, 164
  freedom in Sartre and, 37, 38

Index

anguish *(continued)*
  Heidegger and, 171
  nausea and, 91, 152
  responsibility in Sartre and, 8
  shame in Sartre and, 111
  Transcendence of the Ego and, 161
Anti-Semite and Jew, 140, 141, 147, 190, 194, 198
authenticity
  Being and Nothingness and, 1398
  critique of, in Levinas, 148, 149, 190
  duty and, 139
  ethics of, 118, 142, 161, 193, 194
  freedom in Sartre and, 139, 164, 165, 196
  intersubjectivity in Sartre and, 9, 118, 138, 139, 140, 141, 150, 157, 195
  praxis and, 149
  responsibility and, 9, 10, 12, 13, 118, 142, 150, 154, 196
  substitution and, 119, 120

bad faith, 35, 39, 110, 135, 164
  anguish and, 37, 164
  authenticity and, 138, 158
  duty and, 135
  freedom and, 36, 37, 188
  "God-project" and, 136, 165, 198
  natural attitude and, 37
  spirit of seriousness and, 132, 138
being
  anguish and, 36
  consciousness in Sartre and, 5, 8, 12, 16, 17, 19–22, 25, 31–33, 35, 38
  enjoyment and, 65–68
  excendence from, 6, 7, 43, 45–47, 49, 51, 62, 63, 67–69
  facticity and, 12, 38–40, 88–92
  for itself, 28, 34
  for the Other, 2, 4, 12, 31
  freedom and, 40, 41, 50
  Heidegger's account of, 27, 46, 55, 57, 67
  Husserl's reduction and, 28, 38
  identity in Levinas and, 53, 54, 57, 58, 75–77, 80–82
  il y a and, 46, 53, 56–62, 64, 74
  in itself, 17, 19, 28, 30, 31, 34, 54
  in the world, 51
  looked-at, 12
  nausea and, 83–86
  negation of, 7, 10, 12, 30–33, 35, 36, 41, 54
  riveted to, 7, 8, 10, 43, 44–46, 49–55, 58, 61, 63, 67, 82
  seen *(see* being looked-at), 5
  shame and, 6, 52, 53
  transphenomenal, 16, 19, 25, 26, 28–30, 34, 39, 40
  transcendence in Sartre and, 5, 10, 34, 35, 37, 40, 54, 87, 88
  vulnerability and, 6, 68–70
Being and Nothingness, 2, 5, 9, 10, 132, 135, 150
  authenticity, 118, 138
  being, *see* being
  consciousness, 17, 102, 131, 141
  intentionality, 19, 23–25, 30–32
  nausea, 86, 89
  Other, 125, 126, 129, 131, 135, 136, 137
  pain, 102
  Sartrean transcendence, 15–17, 32–37

Bernasconi, Robert, 35, 56, 57, 149, 157, 166, 167, 189, 190
body, 12, 122, 184
  affectivity and, 101–104, 109
  being-seen and, 108
  enjoyment and, 65, 67
  facticity and, 38, 39, 88, 96–99
  Levinas account of, 45, 49, 53, 64, 145, 176, 192
  non-positional consciousness of, 100, 101
  Reflections on the Philosophy of Hitlerism and, 52
  shame and, 109, 114, 115

Busch, Thomas, 28, 88, 90, 128, 160, 182

Caygill, Howard, 197
Cogito, 122, 124, 125, 172
Critique of Dialectical Reason, 17, 126, 128, 165, 194

de Saint Cheron, Michael, 130
death
  alterity of, 68–70, 147, 178
  excendence and, 70, 145, 146, 168, 198
  Heidegger and, 57, 58, 172
  Levinas' critique of Heidegger's account of, 58, 171, 176
  Other and, 150, 176
Detmer, David, 17, 19, 27, 35, 36, 85, 126, 157, 158, 161, 162, 164, 165, 166, 177, 181, 182, 195
diachrony, 178
  diachronous time, 76
  ethics and, 120
  identity in Levinas and, 54, 76, 79
dialectic, 66, 129, 138
Drabinski, John, 65, 175, 176, 178, 179, 185
duty, 118, 119, 139
  Levinas and, 153
  Sartre's critique of, 130–135, 138, 141

ego, 7, 8, 10, 15, 188
  death and, 69, 70
  excendence and, 70, 81, 170
  Levinas and, 51, 59, 60, 62–64, 67, 69, 144, 173
  Sartre's conception of, 18, 22, 24, 25, 31, 33, 108, 122, 167
  Sartre's critique of Husserl on, 23–25
  transcendent nature of, 36, 109, 110, 161, 185, 186
  transcendental ego, 10, 107, 153, 159, 160, 182

embodiment, 5, 12, 162, 186, 188
  excendence and, 50, 67
  Levinas and (*see* body, Levinas' account of), 43, 45, 49, 50, 63, 105, 169
  pain and, 100, 102
  responsibility and, 145, 149, 192
  Sartre and, 73, 93, 95, 96, 98, 99, 149
  shame and, 52, 106, 108, 114
enjoyment, 64–68
  transcendence and, 175
epoché
  nausea and, 90, 92
  Sartre's critique of, 15, 16, 22, 38, 88, 156, 157
ethical, 150
  alterity and, 151.166, 188
  disruption and, 9, 11, 47.120, 142, 176
  meaning of the, 140, 142, 171, 185, 191
  obligation, 13, 130, 131, 135
  Other and, 115, 118, 119
  political in relation to, 4
  responsibility, 120, 141–143, 154, 169, 179, 190
  substitution and, 9, 153
excendence, 2, 3, 6–8.10, 11
  alterity and, 46, 80, 151
  embodiment and, 50, 67
  identity and, 67, 74, 120, 151, 154
  Of Escape and, 45
  passivity and, 69, 70, 117, 145, 154
  positionality in being and, 43, 44, 47, 49–51, 57, 61, 63, 90, 92, 97
  solitude and, 74, 171
existence, 5, 6, 10, 12, 27, 53, 73
  alterity as, 69–71, 79, 134
  anguish and, 36–38
  beginning and, 75–79
  brute, 12, 64, 74, 83, 87. 89, 114, 121, 127, 151
  consciousness as absolute, 15, 20, 23, 28, 29, 34–37

existence *(continued)*
  existents and, 57–63, 76
  facticity and, 38–40, 88–90
  il y a and, 55–60, 63, 64, 75, 80
  passivity and, 2, 47, 64, 65, 71, 73, 75, 80, 97, 105, 114
  nausea and, 83–87, 91, 92
  riveted to, 55, 58, 62, 66, 67, 75, 90, 114
  solitude and, 80–82, 92
Existence and Existents, 2, 6, 10, 12, 46, 47, 53, 55–57, 59, 89, 90, 134
Existentialism is a Humanism, 140

face, 1, 4, 11, 46, 119
  alterity and, 119, 125, 134, 167, 179
  il y a and, 47, 172
  Look and, 125, 134, 135, 145
  Other and, 140, 145, 196
  solitude and, 82, 171, 177
  transcendence and, 120, 176, 179, 192, 148
facticity *(see also* body and facticity), 12, 16, 17, 164, 168, 177, 179, 190
  freedom and, 39, 40, 115, 165, 184
  positionality and, 44, 95
  nausea and, 88–99, *(see also* nausea and existence)
  transcendence and, 26, 30, 36, 38, 41, 44, 162, 165, 166
fatigue, 6, 11, 57
  affectivity and, 88, 93, 169
  existence and, 60–62, 66, 73, 104

Heidegger
  existential/existential, 44
  death and, 68, 172
  Gerworfenheit, 55
  Levinas' critique of, 46, 57, 58, 65, 167–169, 171, 178
  Mitsein, 122, 123, 191
  Sartre and, 27, 122, 157, 183
history, 38, 48–50, 129, 148

Howells, Christina, 113, 152, 156, 189, 197
Husserl, 5, 15
  intentionality and, 18–21, 25, 30, 152
  Levinas and, 59, 153
  phenomenological reduction and *(see also* epoché), 27, 28, 38, 88, 90–92
  natural attitude and, 37
  Sartre's critique of, 7, 10, 16, 21–24, 31, 46
hypostasis, 61–63, 66, 74, 75, 77, 79–81, 92, 97, 173, 178, 180, 192

identity
  disrupted, 3, 9 53, 54, 56, 59, 60, 64, 74–79, 82, 105, 119, 142, 145, 150, 151, 154
  ethics and, 140, 142, 143
  Levinas' conception of, 2, 8, 40, 41, 45–50, 52, 57, 62, 71, 93, 96, 104, 106, 130, 134
  Other and, 60, 61, 125, 153
  recurrence and, 79, 81, 82, 144, 146
  Sartre and, 28, 29, 35, 44, 89, 90, 92, 93, 130, 146
  shame and, 109–115
  substitution and, 144, 148
  transcendence and, 11, 12, 67, 70, 102, 117
il y a *(see* existence and *il y a)*
immanence, 53, 56, 60, 68, 93, 123, 125, 161
incarnation, 144, 146, 183
infinite, 6, 124, 125.127, 179, 182, 192
insomnia, 6, 11, 56, 59–61, 65, 66, 73, 87, 88, 93, 104, 169, 172, 191
intentionality
  affectivity and, 99, 104, 101, 105, 124
  alterity and, 130
  consciousness and, 22, 24, 26, 98
  disruption of, 11, 78

excendence and,
freedom and, 8, 10, 37, 41, 62, 80, 113
Husserl and, 5, 15, 20, 25, 152
Levinas and, 7, 8, 43, 52, 59, 60, 68, 75–77, 114, 125, 153, 154
nausea and, 85, 89, 91, 93
Sartre and, 3, 17, 18, 20, 21, 34, 71, 86, 95, 101, 129
shame and, 106, 107, 109
solitude and, 74, 78, 79, 81, 87
transcendence and, 2, 4, 6, 9, 19, 23, 29–31, 54, 88, 96, 97, 146, 151
intersubjectivity, 1, 2, 9, 82, 111, 126, 129, 135, 137, 154, 188

Look, 52, 106, 107, 112, 115, 123, 125, 131, 134, 135, 138, 143, 145

Martin, Thomas, 25, 34, 157, 184
materiality, 29, 49, 63–65, 85, 129, 144, 168, 176, 193
moi, 47, 60, 69, 77, 92, 134
freedom and, 54, 61
intentionality and, 50, 80, 153
non-freedom and, 130, 142
positionality and, 55, 62, 63–66, 76, 79, 104, 106, 115, 171, 187
recurrence and (*see also* identity and recurrence), 81, 82, 144
shame and, 52–54
solitude and, 71
transcendence and, 75, 151

Nausea, 2, 11, 28, 82–84, 88–90, 91, 96, 151, 152, 156
nausea, 84
freedom and, 74, 152
il y a and, 2, 71, 82, 93, 151
Levinas and, 83, 85, 86
positionality and, 11, 12, 53, 73, 92
Sartre's account of, 87–91
transcendence and, 5, 79

negation (*see* negation of being)
Nemo, Philippe, 46, 63
non-coincidence
identity and, 8, 11, 25, 54, 103, 111–114, 161, 170
Notebooks for an Ethics, 9, 118, 131, 194
nothingness, 8, 12, 31–34, 36, 38, 54–58, 69, 70, 90, 97, 100, 107, 126, 146

obligation
being with oneself and, 8, 53, 62, 73, 75, 76, 87
ethical, 13, 119, 130, 150, 154, 179, 191
existence and, 10, 36, 43
freedom and, 40, 195
Levinas and, 134, 135, 140, 146, 171, 192
Sartre's critique of (*see* Sartre's critique of duty)
Of Escape, 6, 10
excendence and, 75
identity and, 45, 84, 113, 182
vulnerability and, 85, 156
Other, 46, 71, 115, 122, 137, 148
alienation (*see* alienation and Other in Sartre)
alterity of, 124, 125, 130, 140
disruption of freedom and, 78, 81, 82, 87, 113, 118, 130, 131, 142, 149
ethics and, 135
face of, 119, 120, 140
freedom and, 4, 125, 126, 135, 138–141
negation of, 121, 123, 124
obligation towards (*see also* Sartre's critique of duty), 9, 52, 117, 135, 150
responsibility for, 1, 2, 9, 12, 47, 60, 61, 115, 142, 145, 146
shame and, 5, 106–112, 114, 115
substitution for, 143–145, 147, 153

Otherwise than Being, or Beyond Essence, 9, 64, 169

pain, 49, 64, 66, 68, 69, 81, 96, 99–103, 109, 115, 168, 176, 187
pain-consciousness, 12, 95, 96, 101–108, 187
passivity, 1–3, 7, 8, 12
  death and, 69, 70–73
  excendence and, 67, 68, 124
  identity and, 87, 149, 170
  il y a and, 56, 60, 75, 90, 168
  phenomenology of, 57, 61, 96
  positionality and, 43, 82
  nausea and, 89, 92
  Other and, 115, 130, 134, 145, 146, 150, 178
  shame and, 106, 112, 114
  solitude and, 74, 75
  sensibility and, 63–65, 179
Perpich, Diane, 53, 166, 170, 171, 180, 192
phenomenological reduction, 20, 28, 90, 92, 183
  Husserl and, 15, 22
  Sartre and, *see* Sartre's critique of *epoché*
  Levinas and, 59
political, 4, 12, 16–18, 115, 117, 118
  Levinas and, 143, 178, 197
  National Socialism and, 45, 48, 52
  Sartre and, 119, 120, 130, 149, 154, 157, 189, 190, 193
positionality, 6, 95
  excendence and, 43, 45, 160, 176
  Levinas's account of being and, 44, 54, 64, 76, 77, 97, 149, 152–154, 171, 177, 185
  nausea and (*see* positionality and nausea)
  shame and, 114
  situation and, 40
  solitude and, 75, 82, 180

  vulnerability and, 71
praxis, 119, 120, 129, 138, 139, 149, 150, 193
Priest, Stephen, 156, 189

Raffoul, François, 53, 59, 155, 166, 167, 169, 170, 172, 176, 179, 182, 191, 194, 199
recurrence, 67, 79, 81, 82, 102, 144–148, 198
Reflections on the Philosophy of Hitlerism, 45, 47, 153
Reisman, David, 158, 163, 164, 177, 184, 186
responsibility, 1–3, 8, 9, 12, 131, 167, 172, 190, 193, 194
  authenticity and, 118, 129, 142, 150, 154, 187, 195
  being-for-others and, 110, 111
  freedom and, 74, 91, 93, 182, 196, 199
  hyperbolic, 199, 149
  hypostasis and, 63, 75
  il y a and, 46, 47, 53, 60, 153
  obligation and, 141
  Other and, 115, 119, 130, 145, 146, 169, 170, 179
  praxis and, 120, 143, 184
  solitude and, 77
  transcendence and, 147
rivetedness, 8, 10, 11, 90, 168
  embodiment and, 49, 68, 183
  existence and, 64, 65, 156, 171
  nausea and, 88
  Other and, 146
  transcendence and, 43, 44, 67, 70
  Sartre and, 54, 102, 105, 108
  shame and, 114
  solitude and, 80

sacrifice, 4, 7, 176, 198
  corporeality and, 145
  substitution and, 143, 146

transcendence and, 147
Sallis, John, 58
Santoni, Ron, 164
self-consciousness, 20–23, 33, 107–109, 112, 122, 160, 161, 186
selfhood, 1
   Levinas and, 43, 82
   Sartre and, 152
sincerity, 68, 138
situation, 119, 138, 166
   authenticity and, 139
   being in, 30, 96–98, 177, 184
   facticity and, 44
   freedom and, 26, 40, 41, 92, 121, 128, 129, 133, 148, 157, 168
   Other and, 130, 141
   responsibility and, 149, 193
soi (*see* moi)
solipsism, 120, 121
solitude, 75, 77, 80, 175, 176, 179–181
   alterity and, 71, 73, 78, 81, 82
   first order, 78, 87
   intentionality and, 74, 108
   il y a and, 79, 171, 192
   nausea and, 86, 92
   second order, 79, 87
   transcendence and, 177
spontaneity, 2, 6–9
   being-for-others and, 111
   consciousness and, 23, 25, 27, 29, 32, 33, 35, 99, 117, 146, 159, 162
   disruption of, 60, 64, 86, 95, 126–128
   ego as pseudo-, 24
   embodiment and, 100
   excendence and, 49
   facticity and, 26
   Husserl and, 18
   hypostasis, 80
   nausea and, 152
   Other and, 131, 133, 135, 139
   shame and, 115
Storm, T. Heter, 195, 196

suffering, 9, 16, 93, 169, 176, 180
   excendence and, 47, 69, 70, 147, 168
   identity and, 49, 52, 54, 60, 87, 169
   il y a and, 64, 66, 68
   refusal in, 50
   substitution and,
   Other and, 82, 107, 143, 154
   pain-consciousness and, 102–104
substitution, 9, 12, 119, 120, 141, 142, 169, 172, 184
   alienation and, 115, 118, 145, 148
   authenticity and, 142, 150
   excendence and, 47, 145, 146
   Other and, 134, 135, 144, 147, 149, 153, 170, 181
   praxis and, 143

temporality, 2, 179, 178
   beginning and, 76, 77
   diachrony and, 78
   Sartre and, 96, 148
   solitude and, 71, 79
The Psychology of the Imagination, 179
The Transcendence of the Ego, 5, 7, 10, 153, 158, 173, 186
   bad faith and, 36
   contingency and, 131
   freedom and, 38, 152
   Husserl and, 15, 18, 31, 182
   intentionality and, 21, 33, 35, 109
   phenomenological reduction and, 16
there is (*see* il y a)
Time and the Other, 58, 64, 99, 171
totality, 12, 67, 71, 74, 123, 151, 175, 191
Totality and Infinity, 7, 78, 142, 191
trace, 67, 78, 81, 145, 179, 180

van der Hoven, Adrian, 152, 165
vertigo, 12, 37, 161
Vetlesen, Arne, 107, 188

Visker, Rudi, 75, 81, 177
vulnerability, 3, 5-8, 146, 148, 151, 161, 162, 170, 171, 198
  excendence and, 67, 71, 97
  face and, 135
  identity in Levinas and, 62, 63, 76, 92
  il y a and, 47, 57, 60, 61, 80, 86, 97, 105
  Other and, 118, 119, 130
  recurrence and, 144
  responsibility and, 143
  Sartre and, 44, 73, 93, 97, 130, 131
  sensibility and, 64, 68
  shame and, 113

Wahl, Jean, 27, 57, 166, 167